S0-AUF-189

To six special friends:
  Pete Glyptis
  Jim Hart
  Jeff Herman
  Steve Hoffman
  Jim Pulver
  Peter Schwartz

Acknowledgments

Many people have played important roles in my career and my life. My parents, Norton and Ruth Maloney, offered constant encouragement to me. My wife, Pat, is a constant example of integrity, spiritual strength, and support.

In addition, I'd like to thank the other people who have played positive roles in my life and career. They include: Steve Ankuda; Sue Barrett; Maria Beadle; Dr. Kay Beck; Sue Berniard; William Bowen, editor extraordinaire; Dr. Calvin S. Brown; Priscilla Buckley, Robert J. Buckley, Sr., and his wife Polly; Barbara Callan; Bill Cantor; Ken Childers; Ron Compton; John Cowan; Bill Cox; Elaine Delaney; William C. Douce; Daniel B. Droege, who gave me the chance; Gary Dunton; Dr. Kathy El–Messidi; Robert Fagan; Christine Farley; Tom Fay; Brent Filson; Robert Finney; R. Brooks Garner; Mary Jane Genova; Joan Gentilesco; Deborah Gerlach; Dr. William H. Gilman; Al Gioia; Hal Gordon; Fred Hale, the first friend; Anthony Harrigan; Jeff Harris; John Hawkins; Gail Hoffman; Clay Hooper; Noel Howard; Jan Jones; and Dr. R. J. Kaufmann.

Also, Lorraine Kaulback; Ted Kelly; Dr. Wendy Klein; Dr. Russell Kirk; Edward and Sally Krickel, who taught so well; Elizabeth Krupnick; Gary Kusic; Dr. Albert C. Labriola; Sue Leroux; Tom Latimer; Warren and Patsy Leamon, two very wise friends; James E. Lee; Susan Love; Jim and Lynn Lipchak; Janet Magnussen; George Martin; William F. Martin; Randy Mazur; Jerry McAfee; John McKeough; Dennis and Bonnie McPadden; Bill Maloney; William E. Moffett; Marion H. Montgomery; Steve Morris; Rodger Morrow; Mary Neri, Sisters of Mercy, who confirmed that I was a writer; Ray Noonan; Andy Olanoff; Ann Todd Parker; John Paulus, John Poltino; Tom Power, right from the start; Larry Ragan; Mary Regina, Sisters of Mercy; Charlotte Rush; Mike Salius; Carol Morris Saul; E. J. Searl; Robert Shook; Thomas Sosso; George and Inez Stambrosky; Richard Stone; Dr. Jerry Tarver; Norman Teklinski, Ken Tullar; Bob Tyrrell; Clint Wade; Elaine Wallace; Dr. Robert West; Larry Werner; Bill Wertz; Jan Williams; Larry Wilson; Jim Vergotz; Patricia Ann and Beth Vogel.

There are many more; you know who you are; I thank you all.

Introduction

Speaker's Portable Answer Book is the most comprehensive book ever written about speaking in public. It will be a life raft for beginning speakers fearful of floundering. For experienced speakers, it will provide information, ideas, and inspiration that will help you build on your skills.

It's a book that many of you will want to read straight through. However, its organization and content make it especially useful if you want to "pick 'n choose"—for example, if you're suddenly hit with a request for a business presentation or an introduction of a speaker—or, more exotically, a toast, a "roast," or a eulogy for a deceased friend or associate.

Speaker's Portable Answer Book shows *you* how to: open and close a speech; conduct a meeting; use audiovisuals effectively; inject humor in your remarks; find crucial information for your presentation; handle a media interview; make your "body language" and voice support your message; move an audience to action; make a written speech sound conversational; and deal with every challenge associated with the spoken word.

With the insights you gain from this book, your statements—whether made to an audience of one or one thousand—will become more confident and decisive. You will get advice on how to channel the power of your personality—and your experience—into your statements.

Learning from this book, you will find speaking in public is no longer a source of uncertainty or anxiety. In the process, you will gain greater self-confidence and increased respect from others. That combination should accelerate your career progress.

The information in this book grows out of my 20 years as an adviser to executive speakers at many of America's leading companies: Phillips Petroleum, USX, Gulf, Allegheny International, Rohm & Haas, Aetna, Liberty Mutual, and others. I've derived the advice from communication approaches tried and tested with some of this country's most successful business leaders.

Speaker's Portable Answer Book answers hundreds of specific questions. But it also demonstrates that certain basic principles underlie public speaking. Rely on the principles in this book and you'll succeed every time you go before an audience.

This book uses an easy–to–follow question–and–answer format. The Q & A approach turns the book into a dialogue with you, its readers. The questions are those that many—most—readers have on their minds. The answers are ones you can use in your own business conversations and presentations.

In addition, the book supplements its general points with many real–life examples. Throughout the Q & A sections you'll find tips for strengthening your presentations; cautions and red flags for avoiding pitfalls; and numerous illustrations of successful (and, sometimes, not–so–successful) approaches. In Appendix A you will find three outstanding speeches that exemplify points made in the book. In Appendix B you will find several formats to consider using when you read your speech texts.

I believe that what author R. V. Cassill says is true of writing also holds true for public speaking, that it "is a way of coming to terms with the world and oneself." It accomplishes this, he says, "by giving order, measure, and significance to the flux of experience constantly dinning into our lives." Speaking to others involves going beyond merely stating beliefs and opinions. It also means *defending* your views and *urging* them on others.

The ability to speak well might be the most important skill for modern professionals and managers. True, a U.S. President—one not known for his skill with words—once said: "I define eloquence as action." But it's more accurate to say that *eloquence—speaking convincingly and cogently—is that which encourages and provokes action.*

Communication is the real engine of leadership in a society like ours, an information society. Leaders who act alone soon find they have no followers. *The leader is the individual who can get other people to act.* And the best way to do that is through the skillful use of words.

This book has a larger purpose than just to make you a better speaker. Its goal is give you the verbal tools you need to become more effective, dynamic leader.

Table of Contents

Chapter Twelve: Confronting Special Challenges in Presentations and Language   243

Appendix A: Three Illustrative Speeches   263

Appendix B: Speech Text Formats   279

1

Establishing Yourself as a Confident Speaker

*T*o ask most people "Are you a good public speaker?" is to pose an unfair question. It's like asking: "Are you good at hang gliding? Or polo? Or negotiating labor disputes?" We can't provide definitive answers about our skill in any activity until we engage in it with some regularity.

The first time I played golf I shot 143, not counting the times I missed the ball. Was I a good golfer? I was awful, worse than 95 percent of the people playing the game. But after I had played frequently and practiced faithfully for five years, I was shooting regularly in the seventies—and occasionally in the sixties. That put me in the top 1 to 2 percent of all golfers. As with golf, so with public speaking.

Speaking effectively in public is a *learned activity*—like driving a car or sailing a boat. It's a skill that you can study in books and classes and sharpen through experience. History illustrates many individuals who started out as poor speakers and, through effort and practice, became good ones. Their numbers include Abraham Lincoln, Winston Churchill, and John F. Kennedy.

There are three keys to performing *anything well*. First, approach it with enthusiasm and confidence. Second, learn the correct principles. Third, practice it with determination and intensity. If you do this with public speaking, it will no longer be a source of anxiety and concern, a foreign activity. Instead, it will become familiar, even second nature. At that point, your speaking abilities will become a source of personal pride and of public approval—even acclamation.

1.1 Benefiting from Public speaking

Q: Isn't it possible to get through life without doing much public speaking?

A: Let's look at the phrase "public speaking." For most people, it suggests going up to a lectern and addressing a crowd. Most of us distinguish between that activity and talking to a friend or colleague.

But talking to *someone* doesn't differ profoundly from talking to lots of *"someones."* Speaking in public includes just about every utterance we make other than "talking to ourselves." In this sense, speaking to your spouse—or your boss—is speaking in public. So is offering a comment at a meeting, or even talking over the telephone. So it's not really possible to escape public speaking.

Your question, however, relates to more formal occasions, for example, talking to a civic group or presenting a report in business. A funny thing happens to people who can't "escape" these opportunities, who have to give some talks: They generally become fairly good at speaking in public. That's because the best way to become a good, confident speaker is to go ahead and do it as often as possible. When you have to do something regularly, sooner or later you learn how to do it well.

For anyone who wants to get ahead in business or other organizations, speaking well in public is a vital skill.

Q: Why do you say that?

A: *People who continually avoid opportunities to speak almost never make it to leadership positions.* Why? Because communication is an essential element of leadership. We often hear it said that people lead through their actions, that "actions speak louder than words." Don't believe it.

Do military generals lead by destroying the enemy? No, *they lead through telling—encouraging and motivating—their subordinates to destroy the enemy.* Do Presidents of the United States lead through their actions? Generally, they lead through words. In fact, historians still debate vigorously the actions of a Lincoln or a Roosevelt. But there's no debate about their ability to use words to mobilize public and legislative support for their policies.

In business and the professions, oral communications go hand-in-hand with leadership. Why? Those who remain silent are the followers, the spear-carriers. But the effective speakers are the motivators, the inspirers of others. They're the ones whose ideas and insights don't languish in their heads but are heard by others. They're the ones whose abilities come to the attention both of their peers and their superiors.

Most people who speak in public start out by *enduring* the activity. As they improve their skills and gain confidence, they start to *enjoy* the activity. When they begin to enjoy speaking, they *impress* their audiences, and they *build a strong foundation* for career advancement.

1.2 Overcoming Fear of Speaking

Q: I know some people who are so afraid of speaking in public that they'd rather have boiling oil poured on them. What's the reason for the fear?

A: Many people have tried to answer this question. I once had a very fine psychology teacher who said, "All human fears are related to the ultimate fear, that of dying." I think we fear public speaking—and do so wrongly—for some of the same reasons we fear parachuting out of an airplane or driving a race car at Indianapolis. Fear of speaking is related to what philosophers call "the aloneness of existence."

Think about it. When comedians (or actors) fail to satisfy the audience, what do they say? "I died out there." Any speaker who's given a less-than-satisfactory presentation knows exactly what they mean.

Man is the creature who is born alone, dies alone—and, in a sense, gives speeches alone. Yes, there's an audience, but in speakers' minds, the audience is not *with* us, but there to judge us. That, by the way, is almost never the case.

Making presentations is an unusual activity. In most of our daily lives, we're either alone, by ourselves, or part of a social group. In speaking to an audience, however, we are very much alone in a social setting. That is, we're separated, physically and in terms of function, from the audience. It's a classic case of *us* and *them.*

When *we're* up there speaking, *they're* sitting there, usually in poker-faced silence. As speakers, we are very much aware that we're the focus of the audience's attention. There's great pressure on us to interest our listeners, to keep their attention, and, we hope, to keep from making a fool of ourselves. If we run out of things to say, there's no one to bail us out. That's a situation certain to cause stress.

There's another, very practical reason for "speakers fear." As we grow up, *we don't get a lot of experience speaking in public.* At home and in school, we engage in many conversations. But we spend most of our time listening to others: our parents, our older brothers and sisters, and our teachers. When we enter the work world, we're trainees, people who are seen but not heard. We listen to the more experienced personnel, and follow instructions given by others, our bosses.

Thus, for most of us, public speaking becomes a mysterious, even alien, activity. Unlike the comedians and actors, we resist the spotlight. Like them, we don't want "to die out there."

Q: I've always wondered. Are there types of people who aren't afraid of public speaking?

A: Absolutely. There are many individuals I've met over the years who didn't seem at all afraid to make public presentations. It's important to look at their backgrounds and characteristics. Why? Because their experience suggests ways the average person can overcome fear of public speaking. Confident speakers fit one or more of the following categories:

❏ First, *people with (justifiably) high opinions of themselves, with "good self-esteem."* This group includes people who grew up in supportive, emotionally healthy families. These people not only think well of themselves, but also expect other people to regard them the same way. Because they believe in themselves, they're also confident about what they say, "their message." Their strong sense of self-worth seems to block fear.

❏ Second, *people with a message to which they're devoted.* These are the "true believers." They include people such as religious fundamentalists, environmentalists, supporters and opponents of the right to abortion, crusaders against drugs and drunk driving. In religious terms, these are people "moved by the spirit." Their commitment to a cause gives them the enthusiasm and the conviction that all good speakers need. Their commitment seems to cancel out fear.

❏ Third, *people whose formative experiences included many opportunities to speak in public.* Some schools in the United States—far too few—offer students the chance to make presentations. More often, this group includes members of interest groups or religions that encourage young people to speak, or to "testify," in public. The Latter Day Saints (Mormon) Church is a good example of such an institution. Young people's early experience speaking in front of groups makes them comfortable doing so in later life.

❏ Fourth, *adults who get many opportunities to speak publicly.* Individuals in this group range from business executives and elected officials to members of groups such as Toastmasters to graduates of public speaking courses (in educational institutions and in groups such as Dale Carnegie Courses). Others in this category include members of "recovery groups" (Alcoholics Anonymous, Overeaters Anonymous, Parents Anonymous, and the like) that encourage members to speak about their experiences.

Q: If I'm not an individual in any of those categories, does this mean I'll always be fearful of public speaking?

A: Not if you learn from their experiences. Try the following approaches:

❑ *If your self-esteem is low, build it up by gaining knowledge and experience in making presentations.*

❑ *If your problem is a dull message, seek out interesting subjects about which you feel passionately.*

❑ *If you didn't have opportunities to speak as a child and young adult, make up for it now: take courses; volunteer to speak to business and civic groups.*

In short, make yourself an example of the fourth category: people who gained skill and experience as adult speakers.

Q: Why is it, when I speak in public, I sometimes feel not so much fear as discomfort about being on display?

A: This is what I was talking about earlier: the speaker's feeling of separation from the audience. Most people's "fear of speaking" doesn't really deal with speaking, but with "fear of how I look—or sound."

In other words, the fear relates to their *delivery* of the remarks, not so much to the *content*. In this book, I emphasize the importance of speech content, of substance. If you have a good message, good examples, and a strong "call to action," you have done the best you can do. Just like a football player, if you have the right *preparation*, it leads to good *execution*.

Q: Is "execution" a pun? Doesn't the whole question of fear boil down to a matter of courage, of a willingness to force yourself to face up to a tough situation?

A: You don't hear people talk much today about courage, but it does play a role in this process of overcoming fear. Dale Carnegie discusses "courage" at length in his pathfinding book on public speaking (see section 1.7). I write about the subject from a different perspective in my *Talk Your Way to the Top* (Prentice-Hall, 1992, pages 183–191). The question is: How do you get courage? Maybe some people are born with it. But it seems more likely that *courage, like effective speaking, is something we learn.*

The way to develop courage is to do what the novelist Joseph Conrad urged (in his book *Nostromo*): "immerse yourself in the destructive element." Confront, that is, the very situation you fear. Ride the roller coaster; climb the ladder; ride the horse; give the speech.

Stumble through a presentation or two if you have to, but also commit yourself to getting better. At the end of your initial presentations, you'll discover some interesting facts: You didn't lose the respect of your friends; you didn't lapse into gibberish; you didn't faint; above all, you didn't die.

After we do them once, the things we fear become much less fearful. If you give enough presentations, you will become—sooner than you think—comfortable giving them.

In pushing yourself to overcome fear, remember why it's important to do so. People who speak with confidence in public get ahead. They keep good jobs; they get promotions; they advance to leadership roles, which always require skills in oral communications. Best of all, they use these skills as the foundation for self-confidence and a sense of accomplishment.

Q: I understand the points you're making. But still, what if I get up to speak and my knees tremble...my throat gets dry...and I start feeling dizzy?

A: It's true that, if you "immerse yourself in the destructive element," you might get wet. But at the same time, you can't learn how to swim without going in the water. No matter how difficult your initial speaking experiences are, you'll learn some important lessons.

❑ First, *your listeners are not there to find fault; they're on your side;*

❑ Second, *they're genuinely interested in what you have to say;*

❑ Third, *most presentations get easier as they proceed—and all presentations eventually come to an end;*

❑ Fourth, *when your remarks do end, you will know that the next time will be easier.*

I've been asked: "Are there people who are just constitutionally incapable of overcoming speech anxiety?" My answer: very few, if any.

For example, some years ago, I attended an introductory course given by a representative of Dale Carnegie Associates. At the first session, an executive woman gave a presentation where her knees knocked, literally. A man who had achieved some success in business and politics was afraid to look at his classmates; he mumbled his words to the floor. In the second session, the woman gave a much improved talk; she won the "personal progress" award for that class. In the third session, the erstwhile mumbling man was the runner-up for the same award.

What produced these amazing transformations? A talented instructor and supportive classmates played a role. But the real reason was this: The man and the woman were gaining something they'd never had before, experience in public speaking. They surprised themselves by surviving the first session. After that, it just got easier for them.

Q: Are there any "mental games" we can play to minimize our speech anxiety?

A: Let me give you a few:

❑ *Prepare your talk thoroughly—and practice it assiduously, but don't let it become an obsession.* When your preparation and rehearsals are done, put the talk in a corner of your desk— and a corner of your mind. Then, keep it there until your step up before the audience.

❑ *Don't allow yourself to think negative thoughts, only positive ones.* If you find yourself worrying about your presentation, give yourself a pep talk. Tell yourself that you're a talented person...that you have an important message to deliver...and that you have as much intelligence and courage as anyone else who gets up in front of an audience. *Recognize that the work you've put into your presentation ensures that you've done everything you can to make your remarks a success.*

❑ *In the hours before your presentation, keep busy.* Have something to do that's important enough to consume your attention and not let it wander to the forthcoming speech.

❑ At the event where you're to speak, *listen carefully to what any speakers preceding you have to say.* Don't ignore them and think about your own remarks. Keep focusing on the world around you, and that will keep you from excessive inwardness and concern about the task ahead.

Q: But what can I do about the physical symptoms of speech anxiety? Sometimes as I'm waiting to speak, I find it hard to breathe. My neck muscles get stiff. My throat gets as dry as a July day in Kansas. I start to sweat. How can I deal with these things?

A: *Two points:* The more you follow the "anxiety avoidance" approaches I've suggested, the fewer physical symptoms you'll have. Also, there are simple exercises to minimize each of those symptoms.

❑ *On breathing problems: As the time approaches for you to speak, breathe deeply every 30 seconds or so.* Breathe so that your abdomen visibly inflates. This will relax you and make sure you have the oxygen necessary to speak effectively.

❑ *Stiff neck:* Alternate between (1) *rolling your head rhythmically in a circular motion* and (2) *hunching your shoulders.* These exercises will loosen any tightness in the back of your neck and any constriction in your throat.

❐ **Dry mouth:** *Be sure there is water available for the speaker,* something that should be on your prespeech checklist. If there's water nearby, you probably will find you don't need it. If it's not there, you may begin to feel as if you're in the Sahara Desert. If you're waiting to speak and you find your mouth feels desiccated, try one of the following: Rub your bottom lip vigorously against your top lip or run your teeth against your tongue. Both these techniques will generate saliva.

❐ *Sweating:* In the case of speaker's anxiety, this is a case of the body's cooling mechanism responding to someone who's (emotionally) "hot under the collar." To counteract the effects of sweating, put on talcum powder and a liberal application of antiperspirant. Also, wear lightweight clothing, and as your time to speak approaches, think about drinking an ice-cold beverage on a cool day. In many cases, the sweating is a product of mental processes and you can counteract it through redirecting your thoughts. If you start worrying about a few beads of sweat, you might find them turning into a torrent. In the words of legendary baseball pitcher Satchell Paige: "Think cool thoughts." And carry a handkerchief!

Q: When I get up in front of an audience I start perspiring profusely. Any additional thoughts on this?

A: Performers on stage call this "flop sweat." You might look at it as *unearned perspiration.* It's sweating that's caused not by exercise or a too-hot room, but by anxiety. Dealing with flop sweat is like overcoming insomnia. The more you think about your sleeplessness, the harder it is to get to sleep. As soon as you can start thinking about something other than your insomnia, you'll probably fall asleep. (As Dale Carnegie says in one of his books, in the annals of medical history, no one has ever died from lack of sleep. Ditto "flop sweat.")

Q: Speaking of baseball, I remember that Yogi Berra supposedly said one time that "90 percent of baseball is 80 percent mental?" So you're saying, in a serious way, that public speaking is a lot like Yogi Berra's description of his sport?

A: Yes, good speaking is more than a product of our vocal cords, or our "stage presence." Its origin is in your head and your heart. In our minds, we talk ourselves into being afraid. But by the same token, we can use our minds to determine that we have nothing to fear.

Q: What about the use of prescription medicines to overcome fear?

A: The key word is **prescription**. *Don't self-medicate with alcohol or drugs you may have in the medicine cabinet.* If all else fails, consult a physician, perhaps a psychiatrist. On occasion, doctors prescribe a beta blocker for anxious speakers. This class of drugs blocks adrenaline from being picked up by the body's adrenaline receptors.

Q: Are there any other nonmedical ways of overcoming speech anxiety?

A: There's an important technique called visualization that I'll discuss in the next section.

Tip: The time to start overcoming your fear of public speaking is right now. Use the information in this section to analyze the reasons for your fear (e.g., lack of experience; low self-esteem). Then develop a plan of action that will help you to overcome your fears. Finally, follow the action steps in your plan tenaciously. *Develop that plan today; start working it; and stay on schedule.*

1.3 Visualizing Your Ideal Presentation

Q: You mentioned "visualization." Exactly what is it?

A: For those who use it, visualization is a godsend. It involves forming a clear mental picture of what you want to accomplish. It's a technique used frequently by athletes. When they're faced with a difficult feat, they form a picture in their minds of themselves achieving it.

The theory behind it is simple: Before you can *achieve* something you have to believe you can do it. But before you can *believe* it, you have to *conceive* how to do it. Conceive. Believe. Achieve.

Let me give you a personal example from sports. One day I was playing golf in Vermont. On one par-4 hole I hit my second shot just over the putting green, leaving me about 60 feet from the hole. It was a difficult "chip" shot. The green ran downhill, and the ball would roll very quickly.

Before hitting the shot, I visualized exactly what I wanted to do. I had to hit the ball about 10 feet in the air. Then, because of the contour of the green, the ball would roll slightly to the right and then to the left. I visualized myself hitting the ball solidly to a certain spot and then having it roll down the hill into the hole.

What happened in actuality? I hit the shot solidly, and it landed right where I wanted it to; it rolled first right, then left; it seemed to pause at the hole, just before dropping in.

The fascinating thing about this technique is that it works, and not only in golf. It can be a vital factor in making individuals effective presenters.

Visualization is something like dreaming while we're awake. A talented young professional golfer named Melissa McNamara was once asked what was the source of her abundant energy. She replied, "My dreams. I think about the things that I want to attain. I have visions of where I am now and where I want to be. When I have a sense I'm not moving toward my goals, I work harder." In her comments, Ms. McNamara suggests an important point: our dreams, or visions, can come true—if we make them do so.

Q: You suggested before that visualization could help diminish speech anxiety...

A: Use visualization this way: *see yourself giving your next presentation.* See yourself standing confidently before an audience highly attentive to you...speaking with knowledge and conviction...providing the kinds of details that enliven a talk...and crisply summarizing the benefits your listeners will gain if they do what you tell them (that is, heed your "call to action").

In short, *picture yourself giving the presentation of a lifetime.* Picture yourself as you are, with a recognizable physical appearance and speaking voice. But picture yourself looking and speaking the best you can. *What you will visualize is the real you in a new role: reaching for the ideal, striving for your personal best.*

If you use visualization, it can help you improve your presentations and overcome speech anxiety. It will do so by removing a lot of uncertainty you might feel about presentations. It will give you a clear image of what steps you need to take to turn your "ideal" presentation into a real one. It will make you more confident about your abilities. In other words, *if you can picture it, you can perform it.*

Exactly why visualizing presentations helps speakers is a question for the most insightful of psychologists and cognitive scientists. But in a practical sense, *why* visualization works doesn't matter. The crucial point is that it *does* work.

Good Source of Information: If you want to learn more about the use of visualization to improve various personal traits and business practices, consult Stephen Covey, *The 7 Habits of Highly Effective People* (Simon & Schuster Fireside Book, 1990.)

Tip: If you have any doubts about how visualization will help your presentations, experiment with it. For instance, if you have to make an important phone call (say, to a customer), try visualization. Picture how you want the conversation to go, how you want to sound, how the other party might respond to your questions and suggestions. In other words, use your imagination to prepare a scenario for something that's about to happen.

Will it go precisely the way you planned? Probably not exactly. But you'll be surprised how much the visualization will give you confidence, direction, and control over the situation.

1.4 Being Your Own Best Instructor

Q: Visualization sounds like the speaker's version of a magic "bullet." Are there other ways it can be used to help me become a better public speaker?

A: Visualization gives you a personal benchmark—a "best performance"—against which you can measure your current performances and your future aspirations. It can help you assess the areas of public speaking in which you need improvement.

Specifically, you can contrast the "picture" of yourself in your head with that you hear on audiotape and see on videotape. It's important for you to have these electronic records of your remarks. They can point up what we're *actually* doing as compared to what we might *think* we're doing.

Remember, speaking in public is not part of our genetic make-up. It's a *learned* activity. That means it's a skill we can sharpen—improve. We learn where *we want to be* through visualization; we learn where we are through reviewing tapes of actual speeches and presentations.

If your institution has an audiovisual department, it's usually easy to get someone to tape your performances or at least your practice sessions. But taping rehearsals at home is also a key to improvement. Just be sure to make the setting for taped presentations as lifelike as possible. (For example, don't practice giving your speech in an easy chair!)

Q: Could you expand on how I use the tape to improve?

A: Actually, this approach makes you your own speech instructor. The process is no different from videotaping yourself swinging at a golf or a tennis ball. You look at the tape and compare your actions to the ideal image you have in your mind. You'll be surprised what you discover. Golfers might find themselves swinging too fast; tennis players might discover an absence of follow-through. Speakers might find themselves looking like Inspector Clouseau in *The Pink Panther.*

Q: Really, what kinds of things are speakers going to find on the tapes?

A: As you know, when we first hear ourselves speaking on an audiotape, we're amazed. We ask, "Do I really sound that way?" What's happening is that, for the first time, we're hearing ourselves as others hear us.

On audiotape, you may find yourself doing some of the following: slurring words; failing to emphasize key words; trailing off at the end of sentences; speaking in a monotone; "umming" and "ahing"; speaking too softly—or loudly; or stumbling over the pronunciation of certain words.

On videotape, you may also discover that, among other things, you're staring at your notes or text rather than speaking words and phrases to the audience; slouching rather than maintaining good posture; failing to use your natural gestures and body language; wearing clothing that's not appropriate for public appearances.

In evaluating your taped performances, you will be contrasting what you hear and see with the visual picture you formed. In the areas where you fall short of your ideal, you will need to make adjustments. For example, you can work on looking members of the audience in the eye, on putting the proper emphasis on key words, and on articulating with more care. Then, you can judge the effect of your efforts at self-improvement by making another tape.

It's usually not necessary to hire an expensive speech coach to improve your performance. When most of us see tapes of ourselves, we're painfully aware of where we're deficient. When we spot shortcomings, it's up to us to make improvements. And "improvement" is defined as modifying our behavior—our actions—to make it more effective and appropriate.

When people take this systematic approach to self–improvement, they're generally amazed by their progress. If you're dedicated in your efforts, you can see dramatic improvements in a few hours.

Q: What if I see deficiencies, but I don't quite know how to cure them?

A: As you become more aware of your own style and techniques, you'll also become more alert to what other speakers are doing. In many cases, you can learn from their example. If your delivery, for example, is overly stiff, or formal, you probably won't learn much from an Albert Gore, who has the same flaw. But you can benefit from analyzing the easy, conversational style of a Bill Clinton (or, if you're a Republican, a Ronald Reagan).

And don't ignore tapes of speakers from days past. You can learn a great deal about pacing and the strategic pause from listening to tapes of Churchill. John F. Kennedy was a master of the short, intense sentence ("Let them come to Berlin!"). Douglas MacArthur was gifted at using unusual words and phrases to describe uncommon situations (as when he called the soldiers in Korea "splendid").

In short, if you hear or see a speaker using an effective technique, incorporate it into your own delivery.

Good Sources of Information

My book *Talk Your Way to the Top* has a chapter on using visualization as part of the process of self-improvement (Chapter 3, "Self-Analysis: Finding Out What's Broken and Fixing It"). Also, Cristina Stuart's book, *How to Be an Effective Speaker* (Nichols Publishing, 1988) is outstanding on effective speech techniques, and it would benefit any self-trainer to consult it. (See also sections 10.4 and 10.5 in this book on radio and television interviews.)

Tip: In conjunction with your self-training, visualize your "ideal" speaking performance at least two or three times over a like number of weeks. Each time you do so, *write in a notebook exactly what you see.* Make your description as detailed as possible. That will give you a permanent record you can use in judging, practicing, and enhancing your oral skills. (Unfortunately, visualization is a little like dreaming. If we don't write down dreams and visualizations soon after they occur, we forget them.)

1.5 Seeking Out Speech Opportunities

Q: I know that the more I speak, the better I'll get. But it seems to me that getting experience in speaking is like those "Help Wanted" ads that read: "Experience necessary." Sure, if you're a great speaker, everyone wants you to speak. But how does a neophyte get invited to speak?

A: Generally, they don't. *So you have to invite yourself.* At work, *volunteer to give presentations*—reports, award presentations, "going away" remarks, and introductions of other speakers. When you become known as an able, willing speaker, invitations will multiply.

If your company has a "speakers bureau," join it. These organizations consist of individuals who speak to community groups on behalf of their company and industry.

But don't just stop with opportunities related to work. Seek out occasions to speak in your community.

- ❒ If you have a skill others will want to learn, *volunteer to teach a course at night or on weekends;*
- ❒ If you're interested in politics, *run for office,* perhaps starting with the school board;
- ❒ If you don't want to run for office, *start attending—and speaking at—town meetings and at public sessions of your local government.*
- ❒ If you're a person who attends religious services, *volunteer to teach Sunday school or a youth class at your church or synagogue.*

Tip: Many people get their initial speaking experience through working with groups of young people: in churches or community organizations; Boy Scouts or Girl Scouts; and junior sports teams. A "pep talk" is a presentation. So is an awards presentation. Talking to young people and their parents (who generally ignore everything the speaker says unless it relates to their youngster) is a nonthreatening way to get experience in talking in public.

If you're community-minded, *join a civic group and volunteer to chair a committee;* that will put you in a situation where you will conduct meetings and present reports.

If you smoke too much, drink too much, eat too much, worry too much, or overindulge in some other way, *join a "recovery pro-*

gram" in your area. Most such groups strongly encourage their members to speak about their experiences.

1.6   Choosing Public speaking Courses

> *Q:* What about speech courses? What are they like, and which
> ones would you recommend?

> *A:* Basically, there are three main types of public speaking
> courses: classes at private and public educational institu-
> tions; courses taught by Dale Carnegie and Associates; and
> sessions conducted under the auspices of Toastmasters In-
> ternational.

I recommend strongly that you *visit a session at all three groups before you make a decision on which one to take.* Make sure the class is one that emphasizes practical experience in speaking. Above all, don't allow yourself to be pressured into taking a course that's not right for you.

Courses taught at educational institutions range, as you might imagine, from the mediocre to the magnificent. You will find the Carnegie courses and Toastmasters in all large (and most medium-sized) communities. Both groups have good reputations and seem to have consistent quality throughout most of the country.

The basic Dale Carnegie course in "Public Speaking and Effec-tive Living" costs (as of 1993) $950 for 12 weekly sessions of three and a half hours. Participants get the opportunity to speak for at least two minutes at each class. If you want information (and a call later from an instructor/sales representative) call 1-800-231-5800.

As for Toastmasters, it operates through more than 8,000 local groups located at corporations, government facilities, and military units. The fee for participation is nominal. You can get membership information by calling Toastmasters International at 714-858-8255, or by writing to: P.O. Box 9052, Mission Viejo, CA 92690.

> *Q:* Is there specialized training for executives—and, if so, what
> do you think of it?

A: There is such training, usually available in the larger cities. Generally, the sessions last for a day or two, and the cost ranges from about $1,000 per day on up. The best way to find out about the effectiveness of this training is to get the views of those who've taken it. It's instructive, however, that some executives who've taken the high-priced training still swear by Toastmasters and/or Dale Carnegie.

Tip: Don't forget: The public speaking course you want is one where you get to speak frequently. If you visit a course in which the teacher spends most of the time lecturing, head for the exit. In Dale Carnegie, you'll get to speak once—and often twice—at each session. At Toastmasters, the emphasis is also on speaking. When you're evaluating any course, remember: You're not there primarily to accumulate knowledge; you're there *to get good advice and to practice.* In learning to speak effectively, a little theory goes a long way.

1.7 Learning from Books and Other Resources

Good Sources of Information: I'd recommend that all speakers have at least five books on their shelves. You'll forgive me if I'm partial to my own work:

- ❐ STEPHEN R. MALONEY, *Talk Your Way to the Top* (mentioned previously). This book discusses many of the same principles contained in *Speaker's Portable Answer Book.* Where *Talk Your Way to the Top* differs is in its total concentration on identifying the techniques that make for decisive, effective speaking and on outlining a systematic approach for speakers to learn and use those techniques. The book has received wide acceptance in corporate–training programs. The comment I liked best from a reader (M. J. Genova, head of her own communications firm) was: "This book is written with amazing clarity and intensity."
- ❐ CRISTINA STUART, *How to Be an Effective Speaker* has been mentioned previously. This is a superb book that deserves to be widely read; it's clearly written, and it deals with subjects other speech books don't give much attention to;

see, for example, the chapter on "Finding Your Voice" (most of us don't like our own voice, she says, because "throughout your life you have heard [it] through the bones of your jaw, while everyone else (including the tape recorder) hears it straight from your mouth." Ms. Stuart's remarks on dealing with the media also are very helpful. Her section on "Visiting the Site" (where you're to speak) is a classic.

❐ DALE CARNEGIE, *The Quick and Easy Way to Effective Speaking* (Pocket Books, 1990) is the revised version of Mr. Carnegie's original 1926 book, *Public Speaking and Influencing Men in Business.* The book was revised and updated by Carnegie's wife, Dorothy, in 1962. As the dates might suggest, this book has a slightly old-fashioned quality. But it is an absolutely wonderful achievement. Dale Carnegie is especially good on two subjects: first, fear of speaking—he recommends courage and tells how to get it; second, impromptu speeches, where he outlines his "magic formula" for giving short, effective speeches.

❐ WILLIAM STRUNK, JR., and E. B. WHITE, *The Elements of Style,* Third Edition (MacMillan, 1979). Known as "the little book" or "Strunk & White," this volume is not really about making presentations. It is, however, probably the best short book ever written on how to write with style. Strunk and White emphasize that in communicating, a simple, direct approach is best. The authors prefer little words to big ones; they urge writers to "omit needless words"; they advocate the active voice rather than the passive. Almost everything they say in this timeless work is applicable to speaking in public.

❐ BRENT FILSON, *Executive Speeches: 51 CEOs Tell You How to Do Yours* (Williamstown Publishing Co., 1991). To obtain this book, prospective purchasers must write to the author (at P.O. Box 295, Williamstown, MA 01267). *Executive Speeches* is a motherlode of information about subjects such as: how to open and close a speech; how to write for an international audience; and how to deal with the media. As a writer, Filson is a true professional—animated, articulate, and artful.

Q: Wow! Reading those books will take care of my spare time for a while. But in case I really get carried away, are there other books you'd recommend?

A: Yes. You should take a look at the following:

❒ RON HOFF, *"I Can See You Naked": A Fearless Guide to Making Great Presentations* (Andrews & McMeel, 1991). A book that lives up to its title.

❒ JEFF SCOTT COOK, *The Elements of Speechwriting and Public Speaking* (Collier Books, 1989). Solid information on public speaking.

❒ KATHRYN HALL JAMIESON, *Eloquence in an Electronic Age: The Transformation of Political Speechmaking* (Oxford University Press, 1988). Brilliant, informative, and intellectually demanding.

❒ JERRY TARVER, *The Corporate Speech Writer's Handbook* (Quorum Books, 1987). Practical insights on speaking and speechwriting from a man who's superb at both.

As for speech collections: For great historical speeches, look at William Safire, *Lend Me Your Ears* (Norton, 1992). In addition, you should get ideas from Diana Booher, *Executive's Portfolio of Model Speeches for All Occasions* (Prentice-Hall, 1991). This book contains several actual speeches, as well as approximately 180 models written by the author.

Q: Isn't there a danger I'll get confused reading all those speech books?

A: Yes, there could be. Look at it in these terms: The way you should learn to play golf isn't to start out by taking ten lessons from the professional. Instead, take a couple of lessons, then play a lot. After that, you'll know what your problems are, and you can zero in with your instructor on specific areas where you need improvement.

To improve your speaking, read one or two of the core books; then go out and practice what you've learned. After that, read as many books and take as much speech training as you find helpful. But be sure to keep practicing what you're learning.

CHAPTER 2

Building a Foundation for Good Presentations

Athletic coaches never tire of telling us that big games are won or lost before the team ever steps on the field. The same is true of presentations, where the quality of the thought and effort that goes into preparing them usually determines success or failure.

Before you make a presentation, ask yourself some hard questions: Am I the right person to give this talk? If so, how long should I speak? What do my listeners know about me and my subject? What kind of information will I need in order to make my points effectively? How much time will I need to budget in order to prepare and practice my presentation?

The more thoughtful and complete your answers to these questions, the greater your chances for a successful presentation. That's because you will have ensured that you are the right person giving the right talk to the right audience. That's all your listeners can expect of you—and all you can expect of yourself.

2.1 Accepting, Rejecting, and Modifying Speech Invitations

Q: It seems to me that a lot of the presentations I listen to in business aren't really necessary. Sometimes I hear someone's remarks, and I think, "That's nice, but why am I listening to this." What's your opinion?

A: You're probably right. Pip Printing Company once estimated that the number of presentations (speeches, reports, sales pitches) given every day in the United States may exceed *20 million*. That seems like a lot. In fact, it may be more than the country needs.

Remember, generally you're *invited* to speak, not *ordered* to speak. Unless the invitation is one of those "offers you can't refuse," you shouldn't automatically say yes. In fact, before you accept or reject an invitation, you should ask yourself two questions.

First, is this presentation necessary? That is, does it make sense for anyone to give a speech on the assigned subject to the designated audience? Or is it just a case of, "I'm having a meeting, so someone has to say something?"

Second, if a presentation is justified, am I the right person to make it? That is, do my knowledge, experience, and point of view make me a good choice to address the assigned subject? Or is there someone else who should have this dubious honor?

Q: What do you mean specifically by "is this presentation necessary?"

A: *Don't give a presentation: (1) when you don't have anything significant to say; or (2) when some other form of communication would be more suitable.* For example, if you're just "presenting information," facts and figures, don't do it in a speech.

Why? *Because your remarks in a presentation go by so quickly that the audience can't assimilate extensive, detailed information.* If they concentrate on scribbling notes, they can't focus on your line of thought. If you want to present information, do it not through the spoken word, but in written form. *In other words, save your voice and send a memo.*

Essentially, this is a dollars-and-cents question. When you get people together for a presentation, you're taking them away from their jobs. You have to ask yourself: Is there a more efficient way to get my point across? For example, is my message something I can put in writing? Or on electronic mail? Or, if the group is a small one, does it make more sense to talk to each individual?

This leads to the second time when you shouldn't give a presentation: when your message is one the audience already knows. This happens all the time in business.

For example, during the "energy crisis" days, Senator Henry Bellmon of Oklahoma spoke to the executives of Phillips Petroleum Company. He spoke from notes; his subject was the energy crisis precipitated first by the Arab oil embargo of 1973 and later by the fall of the Shah of Iran. Bellmon's point was the need for the government to remove various regulations on domestic oil companies.

One problem: *Most of the executives he addressed knew more about the subject than he did.* As he spoke, Bellmon seemed to recognize the inappropriateness of his approach. During his remarks, he shuffled rapidly through his note cards. The man next to me whispered, "What's he doing with the cards?" I replied, "He's looking for another speech."

Ironically, if Bellmon had talked about what he knew best—his personal experience of the inside workings of Washington—he would have enthralled the audience. (As one cynic put it, "If you asked Madonna to speak on the 'Economics of the Modeling Business,' you'd really want to hear: What's it like to pose in the buff?")

Another example of presentations that would be better left undelivered: In a book written after he left General Motors *(On A Clear Day You Can See GM)*, John DeLorean describes a strange process. Before a GM manager could make a presentation to the company's executive committee, the remarks had to be cleared and edited by, you guessed it, the executive committee. So you had a situation where twenty or more high-paid executives sat for many days every year listening to reports they'd read (and approved) previously. If the goal was to give the presenters practice in speaking, it was an expensive way to do it.

Q: I know what you mean about giving a speech when some other form of communication makes more sense. But how can I really decide whether I'm the right person to give a specific presentation?

A: The questions you have to ask yourself are: Do I have the expertise—and the enthusiasm—needed to talk on this subject? Or is there someone else in our organization who's better suited to make the remarks. *If so, suggest that person to the individual making the invitation.*

Also consider turning down an invitation when the subject is one you don't care about. If you're not really interested in your subject, you'll convey that attitude to the audience.

Q: All this talk about turning down speaking invitations strikes me as not realistic. Most of the "invitations" I get to speak come from my boss. Isn't refusing the boss a way to get a short, unhappy career?

A: It's true that *some orders come disguised as invitations.* If your boss is not the kind of person who takes no (or maybe) for an answer, you may determine that it's unwise to "take a rain check."

But there's an alternative: *you can usually influence the direction a presentation will take.* For example, suppose your boss says, "Jones, I want you to spend five minutes reviewing the financials from last quarter." You know that would be duller than last week's baseball scores. So you say, "Certainly, boss. I hope you wouldn't mind if I concentrated on the results in areas that suggest the greatest opportunity for growth."

The boss might then say, "Be my guest. Anything to breathe some life into those numbers." In other words, if you're handed a dull topic, try to put some shine on it. You'll enjoy it more, and the boss might even learn something.

Q: What about just going ahead and modifying the topic? Is that ever permitted?

A: Frankly, *it's almost always permitted.* Generally, the person who asks you to speak actually wants a good talk on an area related to your supposed subject. Granted, if you're asked to speak about "profits," don't speak exclusively on "sales."

But what will happen, for example, if you talk about the fact that sales are declining in direct proportion to the rise in profits? You will be: (1) congratulated by the person who asked you to concentrate your remarks on profits; (2) promoted.

Tip: If you're given an especially unpromising subject, discuss that fact candidly with the person making the invitation. Suggest improvements that will broaden your speech's appeal—make it more enjoyable for the audience. Invariably, the person asking you to speak will be sensitive to audience response. That's because it's the meeting planners and program chairs who "get the heat" for bad presentations.

2.2 Deciding How Long to Speak

Q: Why do most presentations—especially speeches—go on too long?

A: You may recall "Parkinson's Law," which stated: "Work expands to fill the time allotted for completion." There's a similar "law" for speeches—call it "Maloney's Law": "Speeches expand to fill the time allotted on the schedule." In other words, if we're told we have 10 minutes on the program, we'll speak for 10 minutes. Unfortunately, however, if we're told we have an hour and a half to speak, we'll do it.

Long speeches are a case of historical precedent overcoming present-day realities. Three hundred years ago, it was common for speeches (in those days, mainly sermons) to last three hours. In the seventeenth century, speakers may have had more powerful vocal cords, and audiences longer attention spans. Also, sermons were a form not only of spiritual fulfillment, but of entertainment. As recently as 20 or 30 years ago, the one-hour speech was common, both among businesspeople and politicians.

Today's long-winded speakers haven't received the message: *modern audiences don't like long presentations.* They also don't like long presentations one after another from dawn to dusk, which is a fair description of today's business conferences.

Q: How long should a presentation last?

A: I bet you think I'm going to say: "It depends on the nature of the presentation." But I'm not. *A speech should last between 10 and 25 minutes.*

Admittedly, in the hands of a genius like Abraham Lincoln, it's possible to make a great speech that lasts less than 10 minutes. He did so, for example, with The Gettysburg Address. But most of us will have trouble making substantial remarks in less than 600 seconds. That's especially true if we're making a point that might be unfamiliar to the audience.

On the other hand, remarks of more than 25 minutes are paddling against powerful social and cultural tides. Sermons are now 10 to 15 minutes rather than three hours long. Television shows—always sensitive to audience's attention levels—last about 22 minutes, not counting commercial time. Similarly, the average business speech now lasts around 20 minutes. Presidential inaugural addresses typically take about 15 minutes. Even the President's State of the Union message usually goes on no more than 35 minutes.

Frankly, if Presidents can discuss the state of the entire union in a half hour, why should it take longer to discuss "Marking Strategy in the Southeast" or "What the New Accounting Standard Means to Our Company"?

Q: What about people who always seem to speak longer than necessary? What's their problem?

A: Invariably, they misconceive what a speech should be—and what it can accomplish. Generally, these are people trying to feed a seven-course meal to an audience that wants a tuna sandwich. It may be true, as speakers often believe, that they have information their audiences need. But in that case, the answer is not to present a bloated, over-long speech. Instead, it's to get that information to the audience in some other form.

A speech is not a spoken version of a last will and testament, a final opportunity to address an audience. A speech is an occasion to make *certain* points and to encourage *certain* actions. If there are additional points to make, there will be other opportunities to make them. Thinking otherwise leads inevitably to a presentation obese with information and directives.

In 1988, at the Democratic National Convention, Governor Bill Clinton of Arkansas nominated Michael Dukakis for President. Clinton's nominating speech was very long—almost endless. During the remarks, some delegates fell asleep; others read newspapers; still others shouted insults ("Get off the stage!") at the Arkansas Governor. Finally, when Clinton uttered the words "In conclusion..." hundreds of delegates burst into applause. (I hope the moral of this story is not that if you make an incredibly long, numbingly boring speech at a national political convention, you too may become President of the United States.)

Tip: What if the program director says you have 45 minutes or, worse, an hour or more, to make your presentation? Answer: Tell the director thanks, but that you don't need all that time. Indicate that you can make your presentation in 20 to 25 minutes. If necessary, add that you'll be happy to take questions after the presentation. Why do program directors sometimes appear to want speakers to go on interminably? Because they're wedded to the schedules they've created so arbitrarily—to fill time—without regard for the speakers' vocal cords or the listeners' bottoms.

Caution: Many senior managers make their speeches too long by telling themselves: "This stuff I'm adding is important. They have to know every last detail. So it has to be in my speech." This is a certain recipe for boring your listeners; crowding out the truly important points you're making; and undermining your authority. *Present only as much information as you can reasonably expect the audience to assimilate.*

2.3 Learning About Listeners

Q: I know speech consultants always say that it's essential to find out everything there is to know about the audience. But why is this so? Speakers know what they want to say, and presumably the audience knows what the topic is. So why the need to inquire into the audience's beliefs, attitudes, and so forth?

A: You have to remember *the purpose of a speech: It is to get the audience to do something.* A speech should influence behavior, get your listeners to act.

On the one hand, *if they're already doing what you're advocating,* already behaving in the way you want them to, *there's no reason to make the presentation.* You literally would be "preaching to the choir."

On the other hand, if the audience is not doing what you're advocating, you have a reason to speak to them. Your remarks will not be effective, however, unless you know why your listeners have not been doing what you are about to recommend.

Do they, for example, have a tradition of inaction? Or are they committed to beliefs other than the ones you hold? Are they just ignorant of certain facts? Have they remained inert only because no one has ever applied the proper leverage? That is, are they just waiting for the right leadership—for you and your remarks?

Q: I think I see what you mean, but can you give me a concrete example of how not knowing an audience's beliefs can undercut a speaker?

A: Take the case of a company I know that had a tradition of mediocre service. Traditionally, they'd left "service" up to the company's sales representatives. When that approach no longer worked, the company mounted a big motivational effort in presentations to emphasize serving the customer's needs. One problem: The effort met with a lot of employee skepticism.

The company conducted an attitude survey to find out what was wrong. They discovered that there had been much lip service given in the past to "customer service." People had "heard it all before" and so were tuning out the message. Others frankly believed that customer service costs money; they had trouble reconciling calls to serve the customer with other calls to keep down expenses. A third group believed that "the customer" was not the end buyer of the product, but was in fact the independent sales representative!

With those kinds of audience beliefs, a simple "serve the customer" message would not work. What did the company do? It made sure that presentations on service dealt with audience skepticism and confusion. The presentations emphasized three things: (1) the total sincerity of the company's commitment to buyers of its products; (2) the fact that an emphasis on customer service would *reduce* expenses; and (3) the identity of the customer as the person who signed the check for the product.

Q: I see your point: We shouldn't assume our listeners share our backgrounds and beliefs. Could you outline the kinds of things it's important to know about our listeners?

A: Here's a list that you can add to depending on your specific needs:

❑ *Who will introduce you?*

❑ *Are there people who will attend whom you should mention in your remarks?*

❑ *What other speeches or written documents on your subject has the audience heard or read previously?*

❑ *What will other speakers (if any) on the program will there be—and how will their statements square with yours?* (You might have to call the other speakers and find out.)

❑ *What are the educational backgrounds and work experiences of your listeners?* (Presumably, you would frame remarks differently to senior managers than you would to hourly workers.)

❑ *What biases or misinformation does the audience have that will interfere with their acceptance of your message?*

❑ *What interests or needs does the audience have that will dovetail with your remarks?* (For instance, if your audience is concerned about, say, worker safety, how will your proposals help them to stay safe on the job?)

Q: What about when you're talking to a diverse audience—economically, socially, or politically. How can you target remarks to that kind of audience?

A: A good question. Sometimes audiences aren't homogeneous. In that case, I'd advocate that you not dilute your remarks and try to have something for everybody. Select the people you're most interested in reaching, and then direct your remarks to them.

Here's a related point to consider: A talk to a specific audience may be aimed, in reality, to a much larger group that will read (or, more often, hear) the remarks. For example, one politician said he spoke "in the name of all the people who do the work, pay the taxes, raise the kids, and play by the rules—the hard–working Americans who make up our forgotten middle class."

One journalistic critic of the candidate noted that many people in the audience didn't fit the candidate's definition of his listeners. The writer said many of them were either political activists, or celebrities, or millionaires who had bought their way into political office, along with others who did not really fit into "the forgotten middle class."

If asked privately, the candidate might have agreed partially with the critic. He probably would have added, however, that the criticism missed the point. He was not speaking primarily to the audience in the hall; *he was speaking instead to the larger audience of middle-class Americans watching on television.*

On certain occasions, the real audience for a speech may be the community, shareholders, elected officials, other companies in your industry, or customers. A speech to 50 employees might be directed to—and distributed to—10,000 shareholders.

Tip #1: If your time is short and you need to find out what your audience thinks about your subject, conduct your own survey. Call up five or six people who are going to be in the audience. In general terms, discuss your theme, your main points, and your call to action. Find out how they react—and why—to the issues you raise. Also ask them what other points they'd like you to cover. This type of "survey" should take an hour or less, and it may help you to improve your presentation substantially.

Tip #2: If you're going to make a speech in a town with which you're unfamiliar, you can learn something about the audience awaiting you by consulting *The Almanac of American Politics* by Michael Barone and Grant Ujifusa (discussed in section 2.5). I had to write a speech for a corporate CEO who was speaking in Des Moines, Iowa. I'd never been to that state or city, and I knew little about either. *The Almanac* told me that while Iowa's economy was declining generally, Des Moines' was booming. As the authors put it in the 1992 edition of their book: "It was as if Des Moines was absorbing most...of Iowa's psychic energy and economic imagination."

In telling me about Des Moines, the authors told me, indirectly, about the audience we'd be addressing. We prepared an upbeat speech that was well received.

2.4 Getting Information

Q: What is the role of *information* in a presentation?

A: *Speakers should use information to this end: to get their audiences to act.* The information is secondary to the speaker's advocacy of specific actions.

That said, however, using the right information can be to a speech what gasoline is to an internal combustion engine. It can be the fuel that drives your message. Your speech's effectiveness may depend largely on how efficiently you gather information and how creatively you use it.

It's crucial that you not overload your presentations with information, with facts and figures. Most listeners (and speakers) don't suffer from a lack of information. We're bombarded by it, as demonstrated by our overflowing "in boxes." If you want to experience a true feeling of inundation, just use your favorite electronic database and key in, say, "The Budget Deficit." You'll get a list of references it would take you a lifetime to wade through.

So the problem is not a lack of information. Rather, *it's targeting your search to get the right information.* To do so, you first need to know relevant information of use to people in business and the professions.

In the rest of this section, I'll list various reference sources that I've found useful. I'll also tell you where to look to find information sources that I haven't used with any regularity. (At various other points throughout *Speaker's Portable Answer Book*, I'll direct you to information sources on specific subjects.)

Q: Could you first give me a couple of examples of how you'd use information from reference sources in speeches?

A: One way speakers can use information from reference books such as the ones I mention is to find unusual facts and figures that support points they're making. Take, for example, the facts I used in working with a pharmaceutical company executive on a presentation. One of the issues he was confronting was whether the American people had to spend too much money for prescription medicines (about $50 billion a year at the time).

In looking through *Statistical Abstract* (described later), I found that Americans also spent roughly the same amount of money on each of two products not exactly conducive to good health: tobacco and alcoholic beverages. In addition, the *Abstract* illustrated that prescription medicine's percentage share of health–care expenditures had been declining for many years. Using these facts allowed us to put the money paid for medicines in a context helpful to our point of view.

Another example: A major oil–company executive asked me to help him with a marketing speech. He was pitching the use of a liquefied petroleum gas, propane (used in the past for cooking and heating), as a motor fuel. One point we wanted to make was that timing is important for a product to be successful.

In paging through the *New York Public Library Desk Reference*, I found a couple of examples of very bad timing. The parachute, for example, was invented in 1797, 106 years before the Wright brothers made the first successful flight. Moreover, the patent for a gas-driven automobile was granted in 1806, 47 years before the development of a workable gasoline engine!

These strange facts gave us a humorous, but pertinent, opening for the speech.

Q: Before you start listing information sources, tell me this: Is TV a good source of information for people who have to make presentations?

A: Not in the most important sense. People who watch a lot of television—and who don't read books, magazines, and newspapers—also don't make interesting presentations, or care much about listening to them. Printed material stimulates thought. TV seems to have the opposite effect; it encourages passivity, conformity, and an inordinate concern with the adventures of people regularly featured in supermarket tabloids.

Good Sources of Information: I find the best ideas for presentations come from daily newspapers, especially *The Wall Street Journal* and *The New York Times*. Books are also a good source of ideas. Also, for business presentations, I've found issue-oriented magazines such as *Fortune* and *Business Week* very useful.

As for *reference books*, the grandaddy of all such works is Eugene Sheehy, ed., *Guide to Reference Books*, tenth ed. (American Library Association, 1986). Sheehy's (periodically updated) volume will direct you to more than 16,000 reference books.

But for most people, the most useful source is Sherwood Harris, ed., *The New York Public Library Book of How and Where to Look It Up* (New York: Prentice-Hall, 1991). This is an indispensable work from representatives of a library that each year answers millions of information requests. *How and Where* calls itself "The ultimate one–volume reference to the best, most up-to-date and readily available sources."

It's not exaggerating. The book will tell you everything from which reference books deal with the federal government to where to call Gambler's Anonymous, from where to find information about heraldry (*A Dictionary of Heraldry*) to where to find out information about business mergers and acquisitions. *How and Where* is organized around six general sources of information: reference books; telephone sources; government sources; picture sources; special (library) collections; and electronic databases.

An inexpensive book that provides useful help in finding information and "expert sources" is Robert Berkman, *Find It Fast* (Harper & Row, 1987).

If you're looking for a book that answers *frequently asked questions about everything under the sun,* again the NYPL comes to the rescue. Consult *The New York Public Library Desk Reference* (Webster's New World/Simon & Schuster, 1991). Like its sister publication discussed previously, this is a superb reference work. It provides answers on everything from which horses won the Triple Crown to the content of major Supreme Court decisions, and on and on. The book is a cornucopia of fascinating facts.

If you're looking for *statistics about the United States,* you want to consult a yearly publication by the United States Bureau of the Census: *Statistical Abstract of the United States: The National Data Book.* (Washington, DC). This book is available in most libraries. You can get your own copy by calling the office of The Superintendent of Documents, United States Government Printing Office: 202-783-3238.

Statistical Abstract contains an amazing amount of statistics about social, economic, and political trends. It has information about various major products and markets. It also tells, if you're interested, how many tons of nectarines the United States produced from 1987 through 1989.

As for *statistics and other information about the rest of the world,* a readable, well-organized source is John S. Wright, ed., *The Universal Almanac* (Andrews and McMeel, pub. annually).

If you're looking for another readable almanac with very good visuals, see *The Economist Book of Vital World Statistics* (Economist Books, 1990). This book contains a fine introduction by economist Robert J. Samuelson.

You also can't go wrong with Mark S. Hoffman, ed., *The World Almanac and Book of Facts* (Pharos, pub. annually). The book advertises itself as containing "more than one million up-to-date facts."

If you're looking for *information about elected officials and politics in the United States,* then the book for you is by Michael Barone and Grant Ujifusa, *The Almanac of American Politics* (National Journal, updated after every national election). This is the bible of American politics, with information about United States Senators, Representatives, Governors, states, and congressional districts. Newsman Jim Lehrer (of *MacNeil/Lehrer News Hour*) calls *The Almanac* "the single best reference there is for Congress and Washington specifically and the country generally."

He'll get no argument from me. This is a wonderful book of facts, insights, and personalities. It's especially valuable when you have to make an out-of-town speech. It will tell you about the political/economic/social climate of the area you're visiting. *The Almanac* has short, information-packed descriptions of each congressional district.

What if you are looking up dates of historical events? I'd send you to *The New York Public Library Book of Chronologies* (Simon & Schuster, 1992). Another book of modern chronologies (post-World War II) I've found useful is *Timelines: What Happened This Day in History* (Addison–Wesley, 1990).

Do you need a book that *deals with historical figures turning a certain age?* What you need is a work by Anthony and Sally Sampson, *The Oxford Book of Ages* (Oxford University Press, 1988). Here, by the way, is what Winston Churchill said on reaching 75: "I am ready to meet my Maker. Whether my Maker is prepared for the ordeal of meeting me is another matter."

Finally, I've found *electronic databases* marvelous tools for finding information quickly. (Unfortunately, I've never found them to be inexpensive sources; to use major on-line databases can cost from 25 cents a minute to about $5 a minute.) The best place to look for information on how to find and use electronic data bases is *The New York Public Library Book of How and Where to Look It Up*, pages 281–361.

Another good reference on commonly used *interactive services* (America Online, CompuServe, GEnie, Prodigy, and The Sierra Network) is *Fortune*, November 2, 1992, pp. 108–114. The article gives number of subscribers, prices, and features of the various services. Services and prices are changing fairly rapidly in this area, so it's good to look for updated information in business publications and computer publications.

2.5 Preparing and Practicing

Q: I know what you're going to say. I should practice my presentations before I give them. But the problem is that I'm so busy I barely have time to prepare my remarks, let alone practice them...

A: Let's be candid. *If you don't have time to practice, you shouldn't accept the invitation to speak.* Consider this: Athletes who don't practice don't play very well. Actors who don't practice (rehearse) perform poorly. And so it is with speakers. If you don't practice, it will be evident to the audience.

It's like tuning up your car. Yes, you might get away without doing it—for a while. But, eventually, you'll have problems. The car will stop running. In the same way, your "untuned" presentations will develop their own form of "transmission" trouble.

Practicing is the act of perfecting your presentation. It's where you discover problems with your remarks, some of which just aren't obvious in reading through a text. In fact, practice sessions generally are where you first "hear" what you're going to say, and discover where your talk needs strengthening.

In practicing, you gain confidence in your ability to speak effectively. When you have a good practice session, you discover that giving a particular presentation is something you do well. That knowledge dissolves any residual "fear of speaking" that you might have. *After all, there's no reason to fear doing something that we've already done well.*

Q: I get your point. Where should I practice my remarks? At home? At work? Alone? Or with someone else?

A: In your practice sessions, you should try to simulate the actual situation you'll face at your presentation. If possible, try to practice in the same room where you'll deliver your remarks. That may acquaint you with some unforeseen problems. For example, you might find that the acoustics or lighting are bad, or that the lectern is too low or too high, or that there's a chain saw competition scheduled to take place next door. It's a lot easier to deal with these problems ahead of time than when you're giving the speech.

If you don't have a chance to practice at the site where you'll speak, at least visit it. When you do, go through a checklist of "what ifs." Consider what things might go wrong, and make sure you are prepared for any eventuality. If there are problems with the site, raise them with either the individuals in charge of the meeting or those responsible for the room.

Overall, it's a good idea to practice with someone (your "designated constructive critic"). This should be a person whose communication judgments you respect, and will make suggestions that will improve your presentation.

Q: Should I use a video camera to record my practice sessions?

A: Absolutely. Video shows us how we actually look—not how we *think* we look—in giving our remarks. That help us to spot areas that need improvement.

Tip: Practice sessions are a good time to try new techniques. If you've noticed, for instance, that your taped presentations seem to be a little bland, try a little exaggeration. Be flamboyant. Use more gestures. Hit your key points harder than usual. And then look at the tape to see the results. You might find that your "exaggerations" are exactly what your actual presentations need.

Caution: Don't ever think that you've practiced just because you've read your presentation silently. As part of your practice routine, read your remarks aloud. If you don't, you'll miss tongue twisters or other verbal problems (for example, words repeated too frequently, unintentional puns, and so forth) that are not evident in "silent readings."

3

Determining What Type of Presentation to Make

*T*here are various ways to make a presentation: speaking impromptu ("off the cuff"); referring to note cards; or speaking from a written text. In fact, it's conceivable that a single presentation could rely, at various points in the remarks, on all three forms of delivery. Generally, however, in any given talk, you will use one of the three methods.

The question is, which method will be most effective? This is only partially a matter of personal preference. You may *prefer* in all your presentations to speak impromptu (or, alternatively, to use note cards or a speech text). But this begs the question of *which method is appropriate to the occasion and your subject.*

To take an extreme example, if you're proposing marriage to your beloved, it's best not to rely either on note cards or a formal text. Similarly, if you are delivering a major policy speech for your company, you probably shouldn't try to "wing it." The question boils down to this: What kind of written support (notes or text) do you need to make your remarks coherently and effectively?

You are risking your presentation's success if you make false assumptions about your mode of delivery. Specifically, you shouldn't assume that speaking impromptu or using note cards demands less preparation (and practice) than using a formal text. In fact, the less written support you have, the more work you should put into your preliminary efforts.

As for written speeches, a lot of confusion exists about them. Remarks made from a speech text may be wooden, artificial, and unconvincing. On the other hand, they may be natural, conversational, and compelling.

Determining the method of delivery you should use involves many considerations. Your success with any method, however, depends primarily on the amount of effort you put into it.

3.1 Knowing When to Speak "Off the Cuff"

Q: When isn't it appropriate to speak from notes or a speech text?

A: On occasions when one or more of the following occurs:

❐ *When you're being asked to speak briefly* (2 to 3 minutes or so); this usually happens in businesses and organizations when you're asked to comment at meetings and other gatherings;

❐ *When you're speaking at an event where notes or a text would seem odd; for example, a wedding, a christening, an anniversary dinner, or a graduation party;*

❐ *When there are other speakers, all of whom are talking without notes or texts;*

❐ *When you're speaking about a subject the audience will assume you "know by heart."*

Q: What exactly are "impromptu" remarks?

A: *The American Heritage Dictionary* defines "impromptu" as "performed or conceived without rehearsal or preparation."

But that's a shaky definition. It suggests that a presentation can be given without forethought.

As I've indicated, "impromptu" remarks are those given in a situation in which notes or a speech text would not be appropriate. Such instances occur at ceremonial events, such as weddings, at "going–away" parties for co–workers, and at unstructured business meetings. Those are the times when individuals are asked to "say a few words." (And be sure to heed the admonition; your few words should almost never last more than a minute or two.)

But in most cases, it's possible to anticipate such requests. For example, at a wedding, it's customary for the best man, and sometimes for the fathers of the bride and groom, to give a toast. And it's also usual practice for individuals to be asked to say something at events saluting colleagues who are leaving. So if it seems likely, or even possible, that you'll be asked to speak on such an occasion, you should go to the event with a good sense of what you're going to say.

Don't count on stirring words flowing out spontaneously. The only person who wants to hear you "free associating" is your psychoanalyst. Seriously, if you don't prepare your impromptu remarks, they will come out unfocused. Even worse, unprepared speakers risk saying something embarrassing to the guest(s) of honor. Follow the Coast Guard motto: "Semper Paratus," always prepared.

Tip: The best time to speak impromptu is when you can use personal details—a personal anecdote that taught you a lesson and has significance for your audience. If your talk lends itself to this approach, try talking impromptu.

3.2 Giving Effective Impromptu Speeches

Q: You stress that impromptu remarks should be short, but my club had a well–known speaker who talked for 40 minutes—and didn't use a note...

A: And if you did the same thing, probably no one in the audience would need a sleeping pill. Don't judge yourself by the practice of professional speakers. One of them might give essentially the same speech hundreds of times. In fact, one speaker in the early part of the twentieth century gave the same talk, "Acres of Diamonds," more than 16,000 times. Clearly, he wouldn't have needed notes. He was extremely well–prepared.

Q: But take me through it once again on how you prepare "impromptu" remarks...

A: When you know you'll be called on, you prepare to speak off the cuff the same way you do for other presentations; you consider what points are appropriate, given the nature of the subject and the audience. Then you test—practice—your remarks on friends and colleagues, modifying them in response to the comments you receive.

The difference with the impromptu speech is that you won't have note cards or written remarks on which to depend. That means you'll have to outline, first on paper, then in your head, the points you want to make.

Q: Is there a form or a model for preparing impromptu remarks?

A: Yes, remember that almost everyone likes to hear a (short) story. So start your remarks with an illustrative story that fits the occasion. Then talk briefly about the significance the events in your tale has for you. Conclude by pointing to the larger significance the story has for others, the people in the audience. Story...significance to you ...significance to others. The three S's. Let me illustrate:

Suppose you're at a sales meeting designed to motivate salespeople to seek out new business. The theme of the meeting is the need to look at your products from the customer's point of view. You knew in advance the meeting would take place and that you might be asked to give your response to the meeting. When the time comes, you say:

[Story] *"Today's meeting reminds me of the toughest customer I ever had, the aptly named Mr. Grimsley. I used to think he had only one word in his vocabulary, and that word was NO! On the rare occasions when I'd get to see Grimsley, he'd sit at his desk drumming his pencil. When he wasn't looking at his watch, he was glowering at me. The famous Grimsley Glower.*

"One day I got lucky—or got smart, or both. Before he could bellow NO, I hit him with the magic words. I said, "Grimsley, I'm not here to TAKE your money. I'm here to SAVE you money. Give me two minutes to show you how. If I can't do it, you can toss me out of here." That got him. The pencil stopped drumming, and he stopped looking at his watch. I made my pitch, and he bought it. Today, Grimsley is one of my best customers.

[Significance for you] "What this story means to me is that even the toughest customer can be sold. The secret wasn't that J. B. didn't want to buy. The secret was that I just hadn't found the key to selling him.

[Significance for others] "The story of Grimsley is relevant to our meeting today—and to all of us. He was my customer, but all of you have your own Grimsleys. We know what our interests are: getting them to buy. But in order to sell them, we need to find out exactly what we have that they want and need. When we find that out, we can get out the order books."

Q: But what if you really don't have time to prepare your remarks, if the request comes as a total surprise?

A: Whether you have five days, five minutes, or five seconds to prepare, remember the three S's. Tell a *short story* related to the topic; tell what *significance* the story has for *you*; tell what *significance* it has for *others*. This approach gives you a way to order your remarks—and to do so quickly, if you have to; moreover, it uses something you know well—personal experience. It will work every time.

(The "significance for you" is a lot like the "call to action," which I'll discuss later at length in section 4.8. It tells what you did, and that bears on what you're going to ask the audience to do.)

Q: Are there any things to watch out for in making impromptu speeches?

A: *Pay careful attention to the appropriateness of any story you use that involves another person.* For example, the night you had

to drive the preacher home because he had too much
Christmas cheer might be hilarious to you. If told in public,
on the other hand, it might be deeply humiliating to the
preacher. If you have any doubts about the propriety of a
story you're using, it's probably best to choose another one.

Q: I take it that the key to impromptu remarks lies in the use of
personal experience...

A: As I said, whatever age we are, we like to hear stories—
focused, meaningful stories. Compare hearing a good story
with hearing a bunch of generalities. We'll probably forget
the latter in a few minutes or hours. But if we hear a compelling story, we might remember it for a lifetime.

For example, I once heard a young woman in her twenties
deliver a powerful, impromptu speech about her fear of the dark.
Why was she afraid? Because, as she explained, she had been
subjected as a child to "sadistic abuse" by a baby sitter. The audience
sat there fascinated as she talked. She pointed out how the techniques she was using to overcome her fear of the dark were pertinent
to anyone who had similar fears. It was a talk I will never forget.

3.3 Using Note Cards

Q: In what kind of presentations is it appropriate to use note
cards?

A: For the most part, they're not used at large–scale formal
presentations. They're generally most appropriate in sessions with audiences numbering twenty or less. The topics
discussed using note cards usually are those where precision
(in terms, say, of organizational policy or financial numbers)
is not crucial.

Q: What size cards do you recommend?

A: Generally, 3 by 5 cards, the small ones. Why? Because the 5
by 8 cards, being larger, tend to call attention to themselves.

One of the reasons for using cards in the first place is that they're relatively unobtrusive. In addition, there's a tendency to write something resembling a speech on the bigger cards. When that happens, the presentation starts to become a hybrid—one part "notes," one part speech text.

The exception to using the small cards would occur with speakers who have poor eyesight. They can put larger letters on the 5 by 8 cards. By the way, I strongly recommend that you print or type on your cards. It can be embarrassing if a speaker is standing up there sputtering while trying to decipher scribbled words on the cards.

Q: The CEO of our company likes to write out an entire speech on note cards. What's your thinking about this?

A: I'm not enthusiastic about this practice. What happens is that the speech text gets jammed into rather small spaces. That makes the speech hard to see, especially for speakers whose vision is less than perfect. Also, a 20-minute speech might require 50-plus note cards, and that's a large number to keep track of throughout a speech. If as a speaker, you have a huge pile of cards you're not fooling anyone into thinking, "Why, he's just speaking from notes."

Q: This question might seem odd. But what should be on the note cards? Words? Phrases? Sentences?

A: *In terms of sentences, I'd suggest having only two or three on your note cards: your opening sentence, the one with your call to action, and—perhaps—your last sentence.* Your first sentence sets the tone for your remarks, so it's extremely important. Generally, you should have committed it to memory. But as we'll discuss shortly, memories sometimes fail. So as a back-up, have the first sentence written on the card.

I'd recommend that most of your notes consist of words and short phrases, particularly the latter. What you want on your cards is the core of your presentation, the skeleton. For example, if you're talking about the national debt doubling in the 1980s, you might have one card with these words: *DOUBLING OF NATIONAL DEBT–1980s.*

If your next point deals with the growth in "entitlements" (payments for things such as Social Security and Medicare), your next card could read: *ENTITLEMENTS: SKYROCKETING COSTS.* Underneath those words you might have the following words indented:

Social Security

Medicare/Medicaid

Of course, you want your notes to be in the form you find most useful. That will usually require some experimentation. But remember two points:

☐ First, with few exceptions, *you don't want to have your notes in a form (sentences)that you'll be inclined to read;*

☐ Second, *you don't want to have your note cards filled up with words, making it hard to find your points at a glance.*

Q: There's a senior executive at our company who has an aide put together what he calls "bullets"—key points; then the executive grabs the "bullet paper" just before he gives a talk and goes in and "wings it." What do you think about that?

A: Not much. Socrates said "the unexamined life is not worth living." Maloney says: "the unrehearsed, unreflective speech is not worth giving." It's also usually not worth hearing.

Using note cards or "bullets" shouldn't be an excuse for not preparing or practicing remarks. In fact, note cards users should devote *more* time to their presentations, not *less*, than speakers who use formal texts.

Q: What other kinds of things should people avoid when they're using note cards?

A: *First, if you hold all the cards in your hands, there's a tendency to start shuffling them.* Listeners being human, they'll seize almost any excuse not to concentrate on your remarks. If you shuffle cards, they'll focus their eyes on them—and close their ears.

Second, don't lose your place and start searching through the cards as if you'd dropped your wedding ring in a snowbank. Before you speak, *number the cards and check that they're in order*; that should help prevent "card searches."

Warning: If you're using a lot of note cards, make sure that they're on a flat surface. There are few experiences more embarrassing for a speaker (or an audience) than to have note cards hit the floor and fly in all directions.

Tip: It's easier to forget to bring your note cards than it is to overlook a formal speech text. Therefore, some time before your presentation, put the note cards in a place that will ensure you'll bring them with you. For men, this probably will be the vest pocket of a suit coat. For women, it may be a purse.

3.4 Avoiding the Memorization Trap

Q: You don't advocate memorizing remarks—even though most professional speakers do commit their presentations to memory. Why are you against memorization?

A: There are two major problems with it. First, under the pressure of speaking in public, it's easy to forget a speech you've memorized; second, unless you're a professional actor, memorized lines tend to be presented mechanically, without the natural rhythms and emphases of conversation.

On the other hand, *it's helpful to memorize two or three lines in an impromptu speech: the first sentence, the call to action, and perhaps the last sentence.* The first line will get you into your introductory story. The last line will sum up the significance of what you've said and will get you off the stage.

Q: Let me press you on this one. You mentioned that professional actors memorize their lines. Moreover, you advocate practicing to a point where delivery of a presentation becomes second nature. Aren't you involved in a contradiction?

A: Actors learn their lines in a special way. They commit them to memory, but they do so in conversational language. Most "amateurs" memorize in a stiff, formal way, and when we deliver the lines they reflect that fact. Ironically, it takes a lot of training to be able to memorize lines and deliver them naturally.

(When my father attended elementary school in the Province of Quebec, boys who were "bad" had to stay late, memorize poems, and recite them to the teacher before they were released. My father memorized a great many poems. Now, many years later, he can still recite many of them. What's interesting is that *he recites these "punitive poems" not in his voice as it now is, but in the sing–song tones of his childhood.* He remembers them exactly as he memorized them 70 years ago.)

In advocating extensive practice with presentations, I'm pointing the way to a middle ground: a familiarity with your material that approaches, but does not include, memorization. Be *very* comfortable with your material, but don't take the next step, committing it to memory. Doing that would create tensions–and a dependence on verbatim delivery—that could diminish the quality of your presentations.

3.5 Knowing When to Use a Formal Speech Text

Q: Many experts advise against using a speech text, but you seem to take the opposite position. Why?

A: Some of those "experts" are afraid you'll give a mechanical, lifeless reading of the text. Others believe that the absence of a text encourages "naturalness." In fact, *there are many occasions when a speech text is not only desirable, but essential.*

An example would be if you're making remarks that outline company policies with legal implications. In such cases, misstatements and misleading ad libs conceivably could make your company liable for damages. That's one reason it makes sense to learn how to use a speech text.

Many of the experts who scorn such texts nevertheless have high praise for speakers who used prepared speeches: Abraham Lincoln, Winston Churchill, Franklin Roosevelt, Martin Luther

King, Jr., John F. Kennedy, Douglas MacArthur, Ronald Reagan, and so on. No one ever accused these people of delivering wooden speeches. It's just a matter of learning techniques that will make your prepared speeches animated, evocative, and natural.

Q: What kinds of talks generally have legal implications?

A: Examples would be current financial results of your department or company, government regulations that affect your business, and new policies that will be binding on your company. In those instances, it's important for you to present your information fully and accurately. At times your institution's legal staff may *insist* that your remarks be in writing—and that they be delivered as written—so as to protect the company from potential lawsuits.

Q: Would you list occasions—other than when I'm making a statement with legal implications—when I'd need to have a written text to read from?

A: If your talk meets one or more of the following criteria:

❐ *When you're introducing a guest speaker.* The written text will ensure that you give the details about the speaker accurately and that the introduction remains brief;

❐ *When you're aiming your remarks beyond the audience that initially hears them.* For example, you may want to distribute your remarks throughout your company, or perhaps to industry groups or customers. In such cases, it makes sense to have a written speech that you can duplicate and distribute. (Of course it's possible to make transcripts from tapes. But that can be time-consuming, especially in the extensive editing that's usually necessary when turning spoken remarks into print.)

During one of the energy crises of the 1970s, President Carter appointed James Schlesinger America's first Secretary of Energy. This was a crucial job because of the turmoil in the world's energy markets. Schlesinger's statements were watched closely by those businesses affected by Department of Energy policies, especially oil companies.

When Schlesinger delivered a major speech, his office received many requests for copies. However, those requesting speeches were told they'd have to wait until audiotapes of his remarks were transcribed. It turned out that Schlesinger despised the use of speech texts; instead, he spoke from rough notes. That meant there were no copies of his speeches immediately available for those who needed to know what he had said.

Eventually, Schlesinger capitulated to the realities of the situation. He began to use written texts, thereby allowing his office to make copies available to those who needed them.

❐ *When you're serving as a stand-in and delivering a speech prepared by or for someone else.* This happens rarely—in cases such as unavoidable travel or illness or a death in the original speaker's family. If the words you're going to be saying are not your own, the person you're substituting for should provide, if possible, a written text.

❐ *When you're sufficiently trained to deliver a prepared text in an animated, but conversational, style.*

Q: What's the worst thing a person using a speech text can do?

A: We've probably all seen speakers come to the podium and deposit a huge pile of papers there. Then, as their speeches proceed, the original pile slowly—very slowly—gets smaller, while the new pile grows larger at an equally slow pace. (The situation is even worse when the speaker transfers pages with a flourish.)

Take my word for it: Three minutes into the speech the audience will be concentrating totally on the two piles, one diminishing, one growing. After a while, the listeners begin to speculate, will this speech come to an end before the earth cools?

Q: I've attended those kinds of speeches. What's the solution?

A: Some listeners pretend they have to visit the rest room—and never return. But the solution lies with speakers. First, they need to keep their remarks suitably brief; second, rather than picking up pages and depositing them in the "used" pile, they need to slide them unobtrusively from left to right. (Quality office supply stores generally have special folders that make it easy to move speech pages. By the way, photocopy paper is easier to slide than heavy bond paper.)

3.6 Dealing With The Challenges of Formal Texts

Q: I agree that there are cases when a speaker needs a text. But a lot of the written speeches I hear are deadly dull—formal, lifeless, uninspiring. Why is that?

A: *A written speech should not sound like an essay—at least not in its final form. It should be simple and clear; it should be impassioned and provocative; it should be personal and anecdotal; above all, it should be conversational.* Even though it's written—especially because it's written—a "formal" speech should have an informal quality.

Most people are decent communicators—until they start writing on paper or punching keys on a typewriter or word processor. The writing courses we take in school convince us that the spoken word is inferior to the written. We learn the dubious view that natural English—with its subject–verb–object directness, its colloquialisms, its contractions, its sentence fragments, its emphasis on the first person singular—is somehow substandard.

That's why, when individuals write out their speeches, they sometimes sound like stuffy Victorians. They use words in speeches such as "albeit...consequently...henceforth...hereinafter...eleemosynary...contraindicate...counterproductive." Frankly, almost no one uses those words anymore except in institutional prose.

Q: Would you check off the things I can do to make my written speeches clear, conversational, and interesting?

A: Yes, when you write a speech, you should make sure you do the following:

❐ *Make it personal.* Why are most of us as speakers so hesitant to talk about what we know best: ourselves? Our best presentations invariably are about us—our job, our experience, our hard–earned views. But instead, we feel compelled to fill our speeches with abstractions and generalizations gathered from outside.

That's because we think a speech is somehow a series of points stitched together. Don't fall into that trap. Don't talk, for example, about "government regulations and their effect on business"; instead, talk about how a particular regulation affects *you* and your operations. Don't talk about "the principles of sales"; instead, talk about how you sell a particular product. In other words, don't neglect in your speeches the one subject on which you're truly an expert: yourself.

❐ *Make your speech detailed.* In speeches, as in art, *truth lies not in the broad outlines, but in the details.* Give life to what you say by appealing to the audience's senses of sight, sound, smell, hearing, and taste. For example, consider the description Yale Dean Edgar Furniss gave of a construction foreman named Finnegan. Dean Furniss said he was "an Irishman of middle age with a battered face of mahogany hue, with snapping eyes of piercing blue." He doesn't just *tell* us about Mr. Finnegan; he *shows* him to us.

❐ *Make your delivery animated.* Most people naturally speak with animation. But when they get a written speech in front of them, they tend to read it in a monotone. The best way to avoid monotonous delivery is to recognize the problem and to resolve to speak with emphasis and variety.

To stimulate an animated reading of your text, fill it with verbal aids and admonitions. For instance, keep your paragraphs short— one or two sentences—to avoid the tendency to start "plowing through" long stretches of text. Second, to encourage variations in your emphasis, underline key words. With the most important words in your speech, underline them twice—and give them double emphasis with your voice. Recognize that, as a speech unfolds, your energy tends to flag. So write messages to yourself in the margins, for example, "Emphasis!" or "INTENSITY!" or *"Hit this point hard!"*

❑ *Keep your words (diction) conversational.* Most truly memorable speeches consist primarily of one–syllable words. Think of Churchill's "blood, sweat, [toil], and tears" and "This was their finest hour." Or of Roosevelt's "The only thing we have to fear is fear itself." Or of Reagan's speech commemorating the Normandy invasion: "These are the *boys* of Point du Hoc. These are the *men* who took the hill." Inflated diction—big words—does not increase the significance of a speech; it only pumps in hot air.

❑ *Use subject–verb–object syntax.* You should keep your sentences simple. Most sentences in a speech should be straightforward ("declarative," as the English grammar books call them). For example, "I read the regulation. I saw it would complicate my job. And it would cost our company money." In speeches, you should avoid complex sentences—those that contain words such as "although...because...since...until." Such words tend to complicate sentences, making it difficult for audiences to get the sense of what you're saying.

The subject–verb–object sentence can be a powerful tool for clarity and sense in speeches. Look, for example, at the opening of a speech in which foreign correspondent and humorist P. J. O'Rourke talks in *Give War a Chance* (Atlantic Monthly Press, 1992) on the subject of "What I Believed in the Sixties": "You name it and I believed it. I believed love was all you need. I believed drugs could make everyone a better person....I believed private property was wrong....With the exception of anything my mom and dad said, I believed *everything.*"

❑ *Remember to pause.* The key to reading at an appropriate speed is to pause frequently, especially after each clause and sentence. Present your points at a pace that makes it easy for the audience to assimilate them. [See appendix "B" for various formatting devices that will help speakers pause.]

Good Sources of Information: One book that's helpful in giving ideas for simplicity and clarity in language is Strunk and White's *The Elements of Style*, mentioned earlier. For a book full of good information about speechwriting, see Jerry Tarver's *The Corporate Speech Writer's Handbook*, also mentioned earlier. My *Talk Your Way to the Top* discusses how "speech language" differs from the written variety. Rosalie Maggio's, *How to Say It: Choice Words, Phrases, Sentences, & Paragraphs for Every Situation* (Prentice–Hall, 1991) also contains helpful information.

Tip: To make your sentences clear, try to keep most of them to ten words or less. Done thoughtfully, this will not give your speech a "Me Tarzan, you Jane" quality. (In this tip, my first and second sentences each have 14 words. To make both sentences 10 words or less, I can break them up this way):

Sentence #1 will read: *Make your sentences clear. To do so, keep them about 10 words or less.*

Sentence #2 will read: *Will your speech sound like "Me Tarzan, you Jane?" Not if you edit your remarks well.*

4

Organizing Your Remarks Effectively

Organizing your remarks should not be, as it often is, a great mystery. You will have problems in organization when you structure your remarks architecturally, and not in terms of your communication objectives. You will not find organization difficult if you keep in mind two points: first, keep your listeners awake and alert; second, get them to do (or to think) as you want them to.

On keeping your listeners interested: They want to hear a good presentation. They want the points in it to be provocative, fresh, and insightful; they also want your remarks to build in interest and intensity. That's because (perhaps subconsciously) they want you to help them resist their natural tendencies to have their attention wander as time goes on. The point for you: Don't fire all your verbal ammunition in your opening remarks.

On getting your listeners to do what you want them to: Design your remarks as if they were a form of intellectual and emotional seduction. If you're just talking at your listeners—giving them information and not asking them to do anything—then you'll soon lose them. They'll decide at some point that they're undergoing information overload, and they'll tune you out.

In other words, *your organization should flow from your intentions.* In deciding how to structure your remarks, you need to ask two questions of each point: How will this order appeal to my audience? And, how will this order advance my argument? Each point you make should be a wedge that nudges your listeners in the direction you want them to take. If you approach organization in this manner, it should not be a problem.

4.1 Using Basic Organizational Approaches

Q: Are you saying that where a particular point in a talk belongs depends on its effect on the audience?

A: Right. When you're deciding whether to put "A" or "B" in a certain place, ask yourself: how will this appeal to the audience at this point? Ask yourself further: Is it too early to use this point? Will it have more effect later? In other words, organizing a talk is a case of having an imaginary dialogue with your listeners.

Q: Does the number of points I should have in my presentation depend on how long I'm going to talk?

A: That shouldn't be the case. In fact, I believe every talk (other than impromptu presentations, which we've discussed) should have three main points. Not two. Not four. *Three.*

That may seem arbitrary. But as many commentators have noted, there's something mystical—magical—about the number three. Why do we make three wishes? Why are there three persons in the Christian Trinity? Why are three medals awarded in the Olympics? Why are there three parts to most stories (beginning, middle, and end)? Why did humorist James Thurber say he always had three martinis (his answer: "One is not enough; two are too many; three are just right.")

The number three has a special appeal to the human mind and psyche.
In substantial presentations, a three–point organization almost always works best. Two points are—unlike Thurber's martinis—
somehow not enough. The two–point talk inevitably seems overly
brief. On the other hand, four points are too many. For some reason,
it's much harder for audiences to comprehend four points than it is
for them to grasp three. Also, the four–point talk tends to be too long.

The three–point organization imposes discipline on speakers.
It forces them to determine which arguments are their strongest.

Q: What's the simplest kind of organization?

A: Probably the kind that follows this pattern:

- ❑ First, start with an arresting opening, as I discuss in sections
  3 and 4 of this chapter.

- ❑ Second, list the points you're going to discuss—one, two,
  three—and then devote the body of your remarks to
  developing each point in terms of the audience's interests.

- ❑ Third, before your call to action, summarize the points
  you've made and their implications for the audience;

- ❑ Fourth, end with your call to action and a statement of the key
  benefits the action you advocate will have for your audience.

Q: So basically you're saying that simple forms of organization
follow the "first, second, third" approach. Won't that get
boring?

A: Not really. In the next section, I'm going to discuss creative
types of organization. However, even the most creative approach follows a sequential pattern. That is, one part follows
another.

In the "1–2–3" organization itself, there's a lot of room for
variety. Each of your points might consist of simple statements (for
example, "Seat belts save lives") and supporting information (for
example, "The National Safety Council estimates that wearing seat
belts could save 15,000 lives a year").

However, you could spice up your approach with anecdotes ("My cousin Mary survived a head–on crash because she was wearing a seat belt"), illustrations, and even audio–visuals. You might, for example, get a videotape of the spectacular Sioux Falls airplane crash. Half the passengers survived this terrible accident, in part because they were wearing seat belts.

A basically simple organization does not mean a presentation has to be dull.

Organizational problems in a presentation generally result when the speaker is giving the audience too much information. Suppose you want to talk about the nine ways your product is superior to the competition's or about the twelve obstacles to peace in the Middle East? In these cases, you're certain to do two things: (1) talk too long; (2) confuse your audience.

Your product may, in fact, be superior in nine ways. But if you ramble on about the subject, the audience may develop a strong liking for your competitors' products.

The purpose of a presentation is not to fill the audience with more information than it wants—or needs. The purpose is to get the audience to think—and to act—in the way you want.

So talk about three important ways your product is superior; similarly, talk about the three major obstacles to peace in the Middle East. This approach will keep your presentation short, focused—and effective.

4.2 Using Creative Organizational Approaches

Q: The simple approach to organization sounds like the best one from me. Why would I want to use what you call "creative approaches"?

A: As we discussed, one thing speakers want to avoid is having their audiences "settle down." That is, you don't want them to go into a listening mode that's akin to being on automatic pilot, giving your remarks polite attention, but nothing more.

If your topic is sure to be of interest to listeners, a simple organizational style will suffice. For example, if you're talking about a "corporate restructuring" (i.e., layoffs) to people worried about their jobs, you won't need a creative approach to organization. If you believe, however, that your listeners may be less than totally attentive to your remarks, organizing your talk in a novel way may help.

Q: What do you mean exactly by "creative organization"?

A: It refers to any organization that deviates from the "1–2–3," point–by–point approach outlined in the previous section. Let me give you several examples:

1. *The Q & A Approach:* Suppose you're talking to a group of prospective employees. You get the audience's attention with the following line: "I'm going to organize my remarks around three questions people in your position would love to ask—but are afraid to." You then use a Q&A format to develop your talk.

2. *The A & Q Approach:* This is a variation on an old Johnny Carson routine, where he provided a (humorous) answer in response to a (fictitious—and equally humorous) question. Suppose you're giving a talk on mistaken beliefs. Your first statement is: "Thirty million Americans." That's the answer. The question is: "How many adults in the United States believe the moon landings were faked in a television studio?" You could then talk about the implications of this mistaken belief and then go on to other such misapprehensions.

3. *The "Begin at the End" Approach:* You're informing fellow employees that your company has lost an important contract. You say: "I'm going to begin not at the beginning, but at the end: We lost the contract. Now, I'd like to go back point–by–point to the beginning—when we first sought the contract. I think this reverse order gives us some new insights into why our bid failed."

4. *The "Organization Is in Front of You" Approach:* You're giving a talk on teamwork in your organization. You build your

presentation around your audience, the team sitting in front of you. Going from person to person, you outline the special contribution each individual makes to the team.

5. *The Organize Around Audience Participation Approach:* This is a way of turning the tables, getting the audience to participate actively in the presentation. Suppose you're talking about various issues. You start by asking, "How many of you either have been involved in an auto accident or have a family member who's been involved in one? Please stand." This approach can be a compelling way to turn abstract issues into something concrete and personal for the audience.

For example, an article in *The Toastmaster* magazine told about a speaker addressing the topic of "Downsizing in the Nineties." The speaker "had all the participants stand up, then gradually sit down if they or family members had been affected by firings, layoffs, corporate takeovers, or staff changes. Eventually the entire group was seated." This is a good example of building a talk around the audience.

In another case, the CEO of Syntex, a pharmaceutical company, illustrated the tremendous part that prescription medicines play in health care. He asked members of an audience how many of them had received care in a hospital over the past year. Only a couple of hands went up. Then he asked, "How many of you take a little pill every day?" Almost every hand in the audience was raised. He went on to make his point: Pharmaceuticals are the core of modern health care.

6. *The Myth and Reality Approach:* Suppose your industry has a number of widely quoted, persistent critics. You organize your remarks around their criticism ("Myth #1") and your responses ("Reality #1"). (If you take this approach, don't get carried away. If you have a dozen or so myths and realities, your remarks could become tedious. So keep the myths to a relative few.)

7. *The Striking Visuals Approach:* Get up in front of the audience and don't say anything. Instead, show them a video, say, of the Sioux Falls air crash. Then, make your point (about seatbelts? airplane safety?). After that, show another striking visual, perhaps a police chase on a Los Angeles freeway, ending with a car crash.

The number of creative approaches to organization is limited only by the human imagination. Some of the best efforts in this regard are the result of tinkering by speakers. If you're not happy with your organization, start asking yourself, "What if?" You may come up with a novel, effective approach.

Good Sources of Information: Brent Filson's book, mentioned earlier, is strong on this point of creative organization. Also look at Ron Hoff's book, also mentioned previously.

4.3 Developing Attention–Getting Speech Openings

Q: What's the worst way a speaker can open a speech?

A: By saying, "It's a great pleasure to be here with you today." The second worst is to say, "Unaccustomed as I am to public speaking." (I believe the last person who uttered those words was attacked by the audience and beaten senseless.)

Q: I see your point about "unaccustomed," but what's wrong with saying it's a pleasure to be here? Everybody does it...

A: That's true, "everybody does it." But the "It's a pleasure" opening is a clanging cliché. Worse, it's one of those trite sayings that baldly conveys insincerity. It's like the statement, "Our greatest resources are our human resources," which employees generally interpret: layoffs are coming. In like manner, the "it's a pleasure" opening is one of those statements that many listeners tend to reverse; that is, they hear it as, "I'd rather be almost anywhere else."

To paraphrase Churchill: Food is a great pleasure; sex is a great pleasure; public speaking is hard work.

Q: So what should I say in my opening?

A: You've asked a hard question. Some thoughtful students of public speaking believe you should open by establishing "identification" with the audience, that is, by getting them on your side. These experts say you should start by (1) praising your audience; (2) pointing up your association with the group you're addressing (or with the values they represent); and (3) mentioning your association (if any) with specific individuals in the audience.

Consider the speech given by Winston Churchill to the United States Congress a few weeks after the Japanese attack on Pearl Harbor. Churchill became the first foreign statesman to address both houses of the United States Congress.

In focusing on his American mother, he produced an identification with the audience that is a masterpiece: "I feel greatly honored that you should have thus invited me to enter the United States Senate Chamber and address the representatives of both branches of Congress. The fact that my American forebears have, for so many generations, played a part in the United States and that here I am, an Englishman, welcomed in your midst, makes this experience one of the most moving and thrilling in my life."

He continued, "I wish indeed that my mother, whose memory I cherish across the vale of years, could have been here to see me. By the way, I cannot help reflecting that if my father had been American and my mother British, instead of the other way around, I might have got here on my own." Reportedly, the Congress gave Churchill a standing ovation.

For example, if you're addressing a local society of professional engineers, you might note things such as: your own longstanding membership in the group; your pride in being an engineer; your many friends and associates present at the meeting. Or if you're the department head speaking to your subordinates, you might mention matters such as: how you once sat in their place, thought their thoughts, experienced their frustrations, dreamed their dreams, and, like them, fought the good fight day in and day out.

I believe it's essential that speakers establish this kind of identification—bonds of belonging and belief—with their audience. Where I differ with some experts is in advocating that speakers not do this in their first words. I think it's the second thing they should do and that it should be done briefly and sincerely.

Q: So what should those initial words be?

A: The first words should be, "Thanks," followed by the first name of the person who introduced you. If you feel compelled to do so (and I hope you don't), you might add one sentence about your introducer, such as, "Gladys and I go back a long way." By this time, your audience should have quieted down and the glasses should have stopped clinking.

Your next words are extremely important. They are what journalists call "the lead, "(defined as the opening sentences of a news story). It does more than introduce the reader to what follows. It determines in fact if the reader is going to read the rest of the story. Like the speaker's first substantive words, the lead is an attention–getter. It is the hook that will keep the fish—the audience—from wriggling away (or, perhaps, dozing off).

Your opening words should be language that will knock their socks off. Say something that's just on the edge of being outrageous but that you can back up in the body of your remarks. Historically, this approach is more common in books than in oral remarks. Think of Karl Marx's and Friedrich Engel's opening words in *The Communist Manifesto*: "A specter is haunting Europe—the specter of Communism." Or of Jean Jacques Rousseau's words opening *The Social Contract:* "Man is born free, and everywhere he is in chains."

Some years ago, Al Hillegas, a senior vice president at U.S Steel, gave a speech on productivity. His opening words were the reverse of the then–conventional wisdom that productivity would result from capital investment in advanced equipment. Hillegas asserted that *productivity was a question more of people than of capital.* He then backed up his assertion by relating his experience at the Lorain (Ohio) Steel Works, one of the United States Steel's oldest plants but because of its people (and Hillegas' motivational techniques), its most productive.

Another example of a strong opening is that used by the head of a major insurance company in remarks made to a business club. His speech began: "John Paul Getty—who made money the way Domino's makes pizza—was asked once if he could sum up his business philosophy in a 15–minute speech. He said, 'I can do a lot better than that. I can sum up my secret to business success in six words.' He then said the following: RISE EARLY...WORK HARD...STRIKE OIL."

Q: Okay, you've pointed out that the opening words should be "knock your socks" off language; then the second phases of the opening should involve the speaker's *sincere* identification with the audience. Is there anything more that should be in the opening?

A: Yes, the final segment of the opening is where you give the audience a road map for the rest of your talk. In traditional terms, this is where you "tell 'em [your listeners] what you're going to tell 'em." Summarize the points that are the cornerstones of your presentation. Most emphatically, this device does not "insult your listeners' intelligence." It allows them to feel comfortable knowing the direction of your remarks.

Tip: In seeking imaginative ways to open their speeches, speakers need to learn from the example of good journalists. One book reviewer, for example, began with these words: "Sex, I gather, is a pretty popular topic." The imaginative opening invites the reader to continue.

Fred Barnes, of *The New Republic*, told me he spent a lot of time choosing the first word of his pieces. He believes that, if you don't get your readers right away, you will lose them forever. The same is true in presentations.

4.4 Maintaining Audience Interest

Q: It's my impression that an audience's interest is highest at the beginning of the talk and at the end. Is there any way to keep people from going to sleep in the middle of the talk?

A: Your impression is correct. The audience's attention curve is high at the beginning, declines through the middle of the talk, and generally rises sharply at the end. What happens in many speeches is this: presenters start out with a bang with a good opening statement, followed perhaps by an anecdote or some humor. Then, they shift into a lower gear, perhaps earnestly—sometimes endlessly—arguing their thesis, while the audience's attention lags. Finally, the speaker concludes by challenging the audience to take certain actions, and the listeners perk up in response to this personal appeal.

What's the answer to the problem of the boring middle? Perhaps it lies in the comment of a wonderful pitching coach (Ray Miller) of the Pittsburgh Pirates baseball team. When asked what he told his very successful pitchers, he said, "Change speeds. Work fast. Throw strikes."

How does this relate to speakers?

☐ *Change speeds*: Don't allow your delivery to fall into a monotone; and don't let your arguments proceed at a metronomic pace. At some points, speed up your delivery a little. At others, slow it down. Like the pitchers, don't let your "batters" (listeners) lock in on your "velocity." Keep them slightly off balance. For example, if you're talking about the problem of chemical pollution, you might suddenly ask for a show of hands: "How many of you use chemicals on your lawns to stimulate growth and control weeds and pests? Raise your hands." The resulting mild commotion will jar awake any snoozing listeners.

☐ *Work fast*. This doesn't mean to read your remarks at faster–than–conversational speed. It does mean to keep your remarks moving forward. Don't digress; don't let your energy flag; and don't lose your momentum.

☐ *Throw strikes*: For speakers, this means to use your "A" material, your presentational "high, hard ones." If you're using arguments, make sure they're good ones, compelling and thought–provoking. If you're relating personal illustrations or anecdotes, make these stories "drop dead" perfect.

4.5 Winning Over Skeptical Listeners

Q: My company makes chemicals, and sometimes I'm asked to speak to environmental groups. Most of them listen politely to what I have to say about our company and its environmental policies, but I don't seem to make any converts. Any suggestions about speaking to skeptical audiences? Are we wasting our time talking to our opponents?

A: Answering your last question first, no, you're not wasting your time. In a world where sharp disagreements are increasingly the rule, it's important that we not ignore our opponents or critics. Otherwise, we won't build the public support and understanding we need to conduct our operations effectively.

The key in speaking to skeptical or hostile audiences is to find the common ground you share. You'll never speak to a group with whom you have *no* interests in common. Here are some suggestions for proceeding in this kind of presentation:

❏ *Don't be defensive; don't apologize for your views, but show proper respect for your listeners' views.*

❏ *In the first part of your remarks, highlight the areas of agreement that exist between you and your audience,* the views or interests that you hold in common.

❏ In the body of your remarks, *don't try for an "instant conversion" of your listeners. Instead, explore in logical, nonemotional terms how you can expand the areas of agreement you share with the audience.* (For example, if you're representing a chemical company before a group of environmentalists, talk about real, measurable progress your company is making in dealing with the problems of hazardous waste.)

❏ *In your call to action, ask for the group to make common cause with you (and your organization) on areas of mutual interest.* For instance: "I urge you to keep hazardous chemicals in your home behind lock and key. That will prevent a possible tragedy and keep your family safe." The more you can make *your* problem *their* problem, the more opportunity you have to get your points across.

For example, some time ago, Phillips Petroleum Company gave a number of speeches on natural–gas pricing. The company's goal was to build support for an end to federal price controls on this fuel. At the time, gas produced, distributed, and sold within a single state (intrastate gas) could be sold at free–market prices. On the other hand, gas transported across state lines (interstate gas) was subject to federal price controls.

Phillips made the point that this dualistic approach to natural–gas prices made no economic sense. However, this logical argument did not change many hearts and minds. The consumers who purchased intrastate natural–gas had abundant supplies (and relatively low prices). Consumers who purchased interstate natural–gas had occasional shortages, but even lower prices. Thus, there was little public support for changing the pricing policies on natural–gas.

Like other gas producers, Phillips had a difficult communications challenge. In several speeches to nonindustry groups, it used an interesting approach. It put the natural–gas pricing "monkey" on the listeners' back. It did so by posing this hypothesis to the audience: Suppose you inherited a natural–gas well from your long–lost uncle in Oklahoma. Your first thought is: "I'm rich."

But then you find out something disturbing. The gas well your neighbor across the street owns is on an intrastate pipeline. Your neighbor gets $2 per unit of gas.

But even though you're right across the street, you have the misfortune to be on an interstate line. So you get only $1 for your gas. It costs you no less to produce your gas than it does your neighbor; it doesn't generate any less energy. But the government tells you it's worth only half as much. Is this fair? Does it make any sense? Does it make you mad?

What Phillips did was to make its problem into the listeners' problem. Interestingly enough, audiences who had hypothetically "inherited" a gas well tended to become indignant about their imaginary mistreatment by the federal government.

❑ Try the same approach: *invite listeners to stand in your shoes, and you may gain some allies.*

To reiterate: *Throughout your remarks, show respect for your critics' views.* Neither through words nor implication should you suggest that your audience "doesn't know the facts" or has any impure motives.

In taking this four–part approach, you're doing two things: first, by emphasizing a rational approach you're lowering the "emotional temperature" of the debate (and the audience); second, by not being an "organizational ogre," you're helping earn the audience's respect.

Remember, *it's hard to despise someone's views if you like the person.* (That was one of the main secrets behind Ronald Reagan's popularity. Many people who hated his politics liked the man. His easygoing, sincere style of communications tended to disarm critics.)

Q: Like you, I've seen meetings on television where some members of the audience tried to disrupt the speaker by shouting, demonstrating, and so forth. What should I do if I ever face a situation like that?

A: That's something few speakers will ever face. *If you ever should find an audience that won't give you the basic courtesy of listening quietly, perhaps it would be best to pick up your presentation and leave.*

However, remember that any discourtesy you might face usually will involve, at most, a few members of the audience. There are techniques for quieting obstreperous people. Here are some possible situations and reactions speakers might make:

❑ *Situation*: Someone gets up in the middle of your speech and asks you a question. *Reaction*: Say "Pardon me. There will be plenty of opportunity for questions after I finish my remarks." Then continue with your remarks. If the questioner persists, say: "Please give me the courtesy of letting me express my views, and then I'll give you the same courtesy." (At this point, the audience will be forcefully telling the disrupter to sit down.)

❐ *Situation*: You're speaking, and a group of demonstrators get up and ostentatiously walk out. *Reaction*: Pause until the demonstrators have left and then say: "A wise old colleague once told me: 'Don't worry if people walk out on your speech. You should only worry if they start walking *toward* you.'" (The audience will chuckle, and you can go on with your remarks.)

❐ *Situation*: In the Q & A session, one individual tries to hog the limelight, asking questions that are really accusations. *Reaction*: After you've answered one (or, at most, two) of this person's questions, say: "I'll be happy to come back to you later, but please be courteous enough to let other people have an opportunity to ask questions." (See section 8.2 for additional information on handling difficult questioners).

The key in any difficult situation with presentations is to be polite and to ask firmly for politeness in return. Don't hesitate to use words and phrases such as "courtesy" and "fairness" and "right to be heard." These (somewhat old–fashioned) terms have a way of shaming, and quieting, disruptive individuals. As an invited guest, you do have a right to be heard, and audiences recognize that individuals seeking to deny that right are out–of–bounds.

Q: When I talk to skeptical audiences, I give them a lot of statistics about how little chemical pollution actually exists. But my numbers don't seem to have much effect on the audience. Could it be that they don't believe me?

A: Yes. Statistics have very little emotional effect. Moreover, people really do believe the old line about the three forms of prevarication: "Lies, damn lies, and statistics."

Don't use more than two or three statistics in any presentation. Moreover, let me reiterate: in the case of skeptical audiences *try never to use figures from your own company or industry.* Your organization's statistics may be solid, but hostile audiences tend to disbelieve any numbers they hear from their opponents.

If you're talking to an environmental group, say, use *their* statistics if they have any that are useful. If not, use statistics generated by academics in the universities, generally a credible source. As a third alternative, use government statistics. Many people distrust the government, but they usually respect its fact-gathering abilities. (See also section 5.9 on the general use of statistics.)

4.6   Fine-Tuning Your Delivery To Listeners' Responses

Q: Let me tell you about a speech I gave the other evening. It was after dinner; the room was warm; and my speech probably ran a little long. About two thirds of the way through it, I looked out at the audience, and at least two people had fallen asleep. A lot of the others could barely keep their eyes open. I hurried my way through the rest of the speech—before everybody started snoring. Was that the right thing to do?

A: Well, at least it was the *humane* thing to do. Perhaps it should be asking enough of a speaker merely to *deliver* a speech well. But in fact, that's not enough. The speaker also has to prepare and deliver a speech in such a way that the audience *receives* it well.

How can you gauge that? The audience will tell you—and not only with its applause, or lack thereof.

Speakers have to go beyond reading their speeches. They also have to *read their audience's response.* Do your listeners look puzzled? That means you're not getting your point across. Are they restive? That generally means you're taking too long to get to your point. Are your listeners shaking their heads in disagreement with points? That means it's time either to bring out your best arguments or to get off the stage before they start coming for you.

On the other hand, are your listeners apparently in vigorous agreement with you? That means it's probably time to start to move quickly to your conclusion and wind up the speech.

Q: But isn't your speech—especially a set text—what it is? Doesn't the audience have to take it or leave it? How can you change it in midstream?

A: You have to build some flexibility into your speech. If you have five points why the audience should take a certain action, and they're obviously ready to take it after three points, then you should either lop off the last two points or summarize them quickly.

Some people will find it difficult to modify their text. But at least they should be able to adjust their delivery in response to "signals" from the audience. If the audience is nodding off, for example, you shouldn't let their lethargy be catching. Instead, you need to put more passion and emphasis into your voice.

Or, if your listeners' facial expressions indicate they don't get a point you're making, then ad lib a simplified explanation of your point.

Q: Boy, this "reading the audience" sounds really difficult...

A: What makes it difficult is the fact that it is an audience of diverse individuals. If we're talking to one person—one of our children, our spouse, a friend—we "read the audience" without even thinking about it. We look into the other person's eyes and we see when there's puzzlement, astonishment, disagreement, or some other response. We do it as a matter of course.

Most of us have much more difficulty reading responses when we're addressing not an individual, but a group. When there are many faces, many pairs of eyes, it's somewhat more difficult to interpret reactions to what we're saying. Part of the problem is our normal speech anxiety; it's difficult to focus on others when we're feeling anxious.

As we gain experience in speaking, however, the "speech anxiety" tends to melt away. As that happens, it becomes easier to gauge our listeners' reactions to our words. At that point, we can make our presentations truly responsive, fine–tuning them as we speak, improvising when necessary.

Tip: When you're preparing your remarks, anticipate possible audience responses. For example, if you're making a complicated point, put a "check mark" (or a "happy face")in the margin. That will mean to check the audience's facial response. Do they get your point? If so, continue on. If not, use some clarifying words.

Also, mark in your text where you expect an audible response from the audience, say, applause, or laughter. You should pause briefly at those points, so that your listeners' response doesn't drown out your words. What if the audience doesn't laugh or applaud? In that case, shorten the pause and continue on with your presentation.

4.7 Avoiding the "Tailing-Off" Conclusion

Q: What's the *least* effective way you can conclude a presentation?

A: The worst thing you can do at the end of your speech is to say "Thank you." Speakers mean it as a courtesy. But thanking your audience for listening to your remarks is something like thanking a waiter for bringing the silverware: It's the waiter's job to serve the customer; it's the speaker's job to speak; it's the audience's job to listen.

When the presenter says "Thank you" it's really a disguised apology. The implication is that the person speaking is unworthy of the listeners' attention. What we have is a premature "thank you" made by the wrong person.

In fact, *it's the speaker who deserves thanks, the speaker who is the guest, the speaker who has spent the time and energy preparing remarks and addressing the audience.* A speaker should get three "thank you's"—first, in the introduction; second, when the audience breaks into applause at the conclusion of the speech; third, when the master of ceremonies expresses the group's gratitude after the speech.

Some presenters are nervous about omitting the "Thank you" at the end of their remarks. "How," they ask, "will they know the speech is over?" There's no doubt when Beethoven's"Fifth Symphony" is concluding, and there shouldn't be any about when your remarks are ending. Your remarks should build to a climax—a crescendo—that encourages the audience to take the action you're recommending.

Q: Let me press you on this point. I hear a lot of speakers conclude by saluting the audience for "being so attentive," or, humorously, for "resisting the temptation to nod off." What's wrong with these pleasantries? Don't they build rapport with your listeners?

A: The approaches you describe are "tailing–off" conclusions. Rather than building energy, emotion, and commitment, such comments deflate them. If speakers make fun of their presentations, should they expect the audience to take them seriously? What's more, if speakers really fear they might put their audiences to sleep, they should prepare better presentations.

You don't build rapport with your audience by making fun of your speech—or your speaking skills. You get your listeners' support by emphasizing what you and they share: affiliations, aspirations, experiences, views, and interests. You gain credibility, moreover, by the strength of your convictions, the breadth of your insights, and the skillfulness of your presentation.

So, *avoid self–deflating conclusions; don't even imply that the audience has wasted its time listening to you.*

Tip: Build your identification with your audience in the first third of your remarks, preferably, in the first minute or two. *When you get past that point, avoid all temptations to praise or thank the audience. When you get to your concluding paragraphs, you and your audience should be in harmony. At that point, urge your listeners to do something, to take a specific action that will benefit them.*

In other words, don't keep "casting your line" after you hook the fish. Instead, gradually, skillfully reel it in.

4.8 Ending with a Call to Action

Q: Do most business speeches end with a "call to action?"

A: Some do. Most don't. Unfortunately, most business speeches end either in generalized observation or in aimlessness and anticlimax. The result is that the speech's message soon disappears from the listeners' mental universe.

Q: You've pointed out that the closing—the conclusion—shouldn't be an anticlimax. So how should you conclude a presentation?

A: *The closing—the concluding paragraphs—is where you call the audience to action.* It's also where you tell them what benefit they'll receive by taking a particular action. If the speech has been successful, the audience will be ready to act, to behave in specific, positive ways.

Because people's emotions drive them to action, your conclusion should have an emotional tone. Generally, that means you should use words that appeal to the heart more than to the head. Use reason where it serves your purposes, but go beyond it when you want people to act.

Don't be afraid to call for sacrifice, idealism, or altruism. Challenge your listeners. Urge them to do what's right. And show them how it's in their best interest to follow your lead, heed your words.

Q: Somehow I just can't see myself talking in those terms to my company's engineers or accountants. They're not a bunch known for their appreciation of emotional appeals...

A: *Audiences don't want soothing talks that meander along the road to nowhere.* Don't underestimate your listeners. They've heard enough dead–end reports. Instead, *they want to know what they should do. They want to know how they can use their knowledge and experience to bring about constructive change.*

In short, listeners don't need a *speaker* as much as they need a *leader.*

Some speakers might argue: "But my subject doesn't lend itself to that kind of a talk." What they really mean is: "I'm not a leader." Any talk you give should have a point, a reason for being. It shouldn't be merely an intellectual exercise. *If the talk doesn't encourage people to act, what is its purpose?*

The essence of business and the professions should be *the use of knowledge to encourage productive actions:* Usually, those actions involve developing products, selling them, and supporting those activities. Speeches that recognize that fact reflect the real nature of business.

> *Q:* Let me play the Devil's advocate. I seem to recall that one of your heroes—Dale Carnegie—said the "action" speech was only one kind. He said there also were speeches to inform, to convince, and to entertain...

> *A:* Dale Carnegie was a wise and wonderful man. But in this instance, I disagree with him. A speech that seeks only to inform falls short of its potential, which is to move people to action. Our listeners need a specific kind of information: the type they can use to improve their job performance, their company's prospects, and their society.

What about the "speech to convince"? Yes, we need to demonstrate the validity of our points of view. But for what purpose are we convincing an audience? We're not doing so only to win adherents to our views. We're doing it *to get listeners to act on their newfound convictions.*

Finally, what of the "speech to entertain"? That type of presentation was a lot more common a generation or two ago. In those days, there was a strong demand for after–dinner speakers who could make audiences chuckle and do so without causing indigestion.

But the speaker–as–entertainer is an endangered species. Even the best such speakers have a hard time competing with the entertainers we see on television.

Admit it: When all we can say about a speech is that it was "entertaining," we're generally indicating it was pretty much a waste of time.

> *Q:* I'm still not clear on your point about the "call to action." Can you give me some general examples?

A: Sure. Perhaps it's a speech asking people to give blood. Or to contribute to the United Way. Or to resolve to stop using business phones for nonessential personal calls. Or to come up with solid suggestions for improving productivity. Or to write letters to elected officials on a proposed piece of legislation.

Q: What kinds of calls to action are the most effective?

A: *The more specific the action—and the sooner it can be carried out——the better. The more general the call to action, the less effective it is,* and the more quickly the audience forgets about it. For instance, suppose a financial officer gives a speech describing a dramatic rise in expenses at the institution he serves. The call to action is: "So let's all do everything we can to keep expenses down."

What effect is that kind of pallid request going to have on the corporation's big spenders? What reason has the CFO given them to keep expenses down? As for those responsible souls in the audience who want to cut expenses, what practical advice have they received to help them? None.

How might our CFO–speaker have made a more effective call to action? Here it is: "It's urgent that we keep expenses down. Otherwise, we can't compete effectively or operate profitably. Our careers and livelihoods are at stake.

"So here's the action I want you to take: Within one month, all department heads must have a report on my desk. The reports will outline how each department proposes to reduce expenses over the next 12 months by at least 15 percent. Areas you should examine are: savings from additional vendor discounts...savings from head–count reductions through attrition...savings from reductions in business travel and entertainment...and savings produced through the use of computer technology."

As this example demonstrates, *don't leave any doubt about the action you propose.* Give your words teeth. If you're asking, for instance, that the sales force generate new business, you might tell them to call ten new prospects by the end of the week and 250 new prospects by the end of the year. Tell them to give the results to their supervisor. Don't forget to add the benefits: more business for the company, increased market share and greater opportunity for repeat business, and—most important—more commission money for the sales staff.

Tip: Remember, the best actions are those your listeners can perform right on the spot. For example, if your appeal is to give blood, tell them: "I urge you to go right now to the Bloodmobile next door. Give the gift of life; your unselfish action just may save your life someday, or the life of a loved one."

Or, if you want the audience to write their elected representatives, say: "I'm handing out stationery and envelopes, along with a pen. Experts tell us the best letters to political officials are handwritten ones. So let's use the points we've discussed to write that letter...in the next 15 minutes. If you need any help, ask me or my assistant."

Remember: *Your listeners will never be more ready to act than they are at the conclusion of your remarks.*

5

Choosing Your Words Carefully

When I used to teach English composition in college, some of my students would occasionally remark that I "hadn't understood" what they were trying to say in their papers. I would tell them: "The reader is *always* right." My point was this: We don't write for ourselves, so it's up to the writer to make sure the reader understands what's written, to express ideas clearly.

In oral communications, if you're the speaker, you can't assume a high level of attentiveness on the part of the audience. That means you have to choose words and grammatical constructions carefully so that your points will be understood. To do otherwise is to defeat your purpose of gaining your listeners' support for the action(s) you advocate.

In speaking, your goals are clarity, simplicity, and freshness. In this regard, follow Churchill's advice. He said, "Short words are best, and the old words when short are best of all." He knew that the purpose of speaking was not to impress others with our

vocabulary. It is to amaze them with the clarity—and forcefulness—
of our expression.

As parents, teachers, and managers all know, it's easy to be
misunderstood. The best communicators are those who put in the
difficult—but ultimately rewarding—efforts necessary to "indicate,"
in the words of a popular song, "precisely what you mean to say."

5.1 Making Your Point Clear

Q: You emphasize being clear in communications, and I agree. But
aren't there a lot of concepts in business, engineering, and so
on that are just too difficult for lay people to understand?

A: Unless it's Einstein's Theory of Relativity you're talking
about, I disagree. When people claim their subject is too
difficult to be made intelligible, they're really confessing
their own laziness.

People will not support that which they do not understand. So it's absolutely necessary to find understandable words to describe what
we do and what we mean.

Consider the example of Nobel-prize-winning theoretical
physicist Richard Feynman. He never doubted that intellectual
brilliance was compatible with clear thinking and writing. Once he
was asked if some concepts in theoretical physics were so arcane
that they couldn't be explained to first year students. He replied,
"That would mean we don't really understand it." In other words,
if you understand it fully, you can explain it clearly.

Q: What special challenges are there in oral communications
that we wouldn't find, for example, in reading written communications?

A: The two are quite different. Sophisticated writing deals in
subtleties. When we read an essay or an "in–depth" news
story, we may—or may not—understand it on first reading.
If we don't, we can always go back and reread it until we
understand it.

Conversely, we don't have that luxury with spoken communications, especially in presentations. In most cases, we can't ask the speaker for clarification. Even when it is permissible to interrupt a speaker, most of us hesitate to do so. We don't want to embarrass the speaker or call attention to our own lack of understanding. By the time the Q & A period rolls around, we've probably forgotten what our point of uncertainty was.

Q: Is this situation the result of poor listening skills?

A: Sometimes. More often, however, it's caused by the speaker's failing to speak clearly and intelligibly. *It's our job as presenters to make sure we're understood.* If our messages aren't clear, it does little good to blame the audience. That fact imposes some special demands on presenters.

❏ First, make certain your key ideas are presented clearly. To do so, use simple language and everyday words whenever possible. Don't try to impress the audience with your intellectuality.

❏ Second, examine your remarks for the presence of jargon ("shop talk") and other words and phrases familiar in your business field but not otherwise in common use. Then, translate this material into ordinary English.

❏ Third, when you make crucial points in your remarks, pause, *and then repeat the point verbatim.*

❏ Fourth, question the assumptions underlying your remarks. Do your words and concepts mean the same thing to your audience as they do to you? (This is the reason that so little is resolved in debates about matters such as abortion. Key words, e.g., "fetus," have profoundly different meanings to the two sides.)

❏ Fifth, *read key portions of your remarks to friends or colleagues. Then ask them to paraphrase what you've said.* You may find the results interesting.

As a speech consultant to many businesses, I've found an amazing disparity between what speakers think they're saying and what audiences think they're hearing.

For example, when I worked with executives in the metals industry, they always talked about the need to improve productivity. By this, they referred to the need for employees to work smarter and to produce more products in less time and at lower costs. To these executives, productivity meant about the same thing as "efficiency."

We discovered, however, that our union employees interpreted the word "productivity" much differently. They equated it with an assembly line "speed up," with working harder, longer, and faster (with perhaps less concern for safety and product quality). To them, productivity meant not more products at lower unit costs. It meant instead fewer—and harder—jobs.

To deal with this type of situation, present your ideas with utmost clarity and simplicity. Spell out exactly what you mean–and don't mean–by a word such as "productivity." Point out precisely how improving productivity can provide greater job security and eventually *more*—and better-paying—jobs. (If you can't make this kind of compelling case for productivity, then don't waste your breath talking about it.)

Remember: People tend to interpret our remarks in terms of their own experience and prejudices. When presenters are dealing with sensitive topics, they should make every effort to prevent misunderstandings. When they do so, their messages will be heard and understood.

Q: What about using analogies to explain abstract concepts?

A: Let me quote a point made by a columnist for the Boston *Globe*: "The best way to understand something really big is to reduce it to a meaningful scale" (Alex Beam, Boston *Globe*, July 12, 1992). Most people have trouble grasping large numbers, long distances, and vast spaces. Try to find ways to simplify information so that people can grasp it.

As an example: Public relations consultant Gerry Hickman once participated in a discussion about health–care expenditures. Some people in the conversation were emphasizing the overall cost of prescription medicines purchased by the Veterans Administration (VA).

In seeking to define the relative significance of the numbers involved, Hickman said: "Look at total health-care expenditures as if they were the size of a beach ball. On that scale, VA expenditures on prescription drugs would be the size of a marble." (If you were giving a talk on this subject and wanted to use some theatrics, you could hold up a beach ball in one hand and a marble in the other.)

Good Sources of Information: For people committed to using words carefully, I'd recommend Strunk's & White's *The Elements of Style*, mentioned earlier.

Also have in your library Sheridan Baker's *The Practical Stylist*, Sixth Ed. (Harper & Row, 1985). Over many years, I've found this to be a readable, easy–to–use guide to matters of word usage and style.

If you're looking for synonyms, get Robert L. Chapman, ed., *Roget's International Thesaurus*, 5th ed. (HarperCollins, 1992).

If you want a combination dictionary, thesaurus, and almanac, you need Stephen Glazier, compiler, *The Random House Word Menu* (Random House, 1992).

As for dictionaries, there are many good ones. One I've found especially helpful is *The American Heritage Dictionary*, Third Edition (Houghton Mifflin, 1992). This volume offers guidance on contexts in which certain word usage is appropriate. It also includes significant information on regional usages.

5.2 Weeding Out Jargon and "Businesspeak"

Q: Would you define "jargon" and "businesspeak"?

A: Jargon is "shop talk." These words or phrases are those that have specific meanings to members of a certain profession. For example, in baseball a "duster" is a ball thrown by a pitcher at a batter's head. In the oil business a "duster" (or a "dry hole") is an exploratory well that finds no (or very little) oil or natural gas. To a maid, a "duster" has quite a different meaning.

Similarly, in the world of high fashion, the word "elegance" has a much different meaning than it does in mathematics, where it refers to consistency and cogency of a mathematical theorem.

"Businesspeak" refers to words (or, occasionally, phrases) that are: (1) polysyllabic; (2) worn out through overuse (and often, misuse); (3) subject to more than one interpretation—for instance, "implement" used as a verb. Does it mean "begin," "carry through," "give directions"?

In most cases, businesspeak involves using a supposedly more prestigious one when a simple word (or two) will do. That's the case with "prioritize," which means set priorities, and with "finalize," which means (to) complete, and with "component," which means part. The recently popular business phrase "on a going forward basis" means, at best, "in the future." Sometimes it's no more than linguistic dead weight (example: "In the 1990s, we'll invest $25 million on a going forward basis").

Q: The words you've used as examples are ones you hear all the time in business and government. What harm is there in using them, especially if "everybody does it"?

A: True, just about everybody uses jargon. The problem is that not everybody understands it. By definition, jargon is intelligible to a limited group, the people in a particular business or profession. Thus, there's no real problem using "shop talk" with our group—as long as they're the only ones in our audience.

The problem arises when we talk to "outsiders." These are people to whom the terminology of our profession is so much gobbledygook.

Remember: *when we make a presentation, we're not just talking to ourselves.* As always, the test is, will the audience receiving the communication understand a word or term we're using? To make our remarks understandable to general audiences, it's necessary to do some self–analysis. We need to think about the words we're using; we need to ask whether they will make sense to our listeners.

Q: But what about the category you've called "businesspeak"? Surely you don't mean to suggest that audiences won't understand words such as "implement" and "finalize" and "negatively impacted"?

A: With businesspeak, the main issues are to: (1) avoid the appearance of pomposity; and (2) avoid the use of words that tend to keep our listener's brains in neutral—that evoke no emotional or intellectual response.

Let me illustrate: If you're arguing against a certain proposal, you can say it's "contraindicated," or that to pursue it would be "counterproductive." To use those words makes your opposition sound almost official, linguistically certified. But what does "contraindicated" really mean? Does it mean that if a patient takes a certain drug, the result will be death? In a business context, does it mean the proposal will make the company lose its share of the market, or, worse, lose money?

If so, why not say it? If something is a *bad idea*, say so. If the facts and figures available don't support a proposal, say that. Why hide your real meaning behind a five-dollar word?

With general audiences, jargon and businesspeak are not terms that help us express ideas. Instead, they're substitutes for thought and communication. They are verbal counters we insert when we're too busy—or too lazy—to consider what we really mean.

As an illustration, take your use of "negatively impacted" (or its even more objectionable twin, "favorably impacted"). An impact is a collision; it's negative by its nature. By the same token, a "favorable impact" is like a pleasant toothache—hard to imagine.

Q: Could you give some more examples of the kind of language that you're counseling us to avoid?

A: In a style booklet I wrote for Aetna Life & Casualty (1990), I suggested the kinds of words businesses should avoid, or at least reexamine: Run a red pencil through...*innovate, maximize, quality* (used as an adjective), *market–oriented, facilitate, indicative, aggressively managed.* Take a stand against "cutesy" words and phrases such as *touch base, connectedness,* and *comfort level.* Avoid technical language (including "computerese") *input, output, throughput, feedback.*

Finally, let us never return to *"square one."* Let us make our last visit to *"re–visit"*; let us recognize *"win/win"* situations as losers; let us acknowledge that *"cutting edge"* has lost its sharpness; let us say "down with *'rachet up.'"* Let us affirm the artlessness of *"state of the art."*

My point was, these are terms that we use when we want to describe a situation, but don't want to think about its precise nature. They're lazy terms—ones of convenience, not *conviction*.

5.3 Keeping Clichés to a Minimum

Q: What's the difference between a cliché and a proverb?

A: Clichés are expressions that once were fresh, but now are worn out, have become trite, because of overuse ("a tough old bird"). Proverbs are pithy statements that express an enduring truth ("A bird in the hand is worth two in the bush"; or, "A watched pot never boils.")

Where clichés have a bad reputation, proverbs tend to have a neutral (even slightly favorable) status. The difference seems to be largely a matter of intention: people who use clichés are mainly unaware that they're doing so; the opposite is true with proverbs. (If you use a lot of proverbs, however, you might be revealing your age; they're much more popular with the older generation than with younger people.)

Q: Could you give me some more examples of clichés?

A: Well, as you know, with clichés it takes one to know one. And, as you also know, it takes all kinds to make a world. Also, they just don't make 'em like they used to. From sun up to sun down, we get the tried and true. We find out that a woman's work is never done. We get the nitty–gritty about the man of the hour. When the talk turns to business, we find out what the Big Guy at the top is doing to improve the bottom line.

Q: Stop! I'm convinced. Clichés can be deadly. But are they mild irritants–or something worse?

A: The difficulty with clichés is that they represent language that has lost its power to penetrate our consciousness, let alone move us. When speakers string clichés together, they lose credibility with audiences.

The fact that clichés are so available can make us lazy. We look at the dark clouds and decide they're "ominous." We look at the rain and say it's "healing." We look at the sunrise and decide it's "glorious." We look at last quarter's losses and start talking about "red ink." When we fall into this kind of language, there are no surprises, no new angles on reality, no striking insights.

Look at those dark clouds again. What color are they? Do they look like three–day–old bruises? Is the "healing" rain really a liquid pain? Is the sunrise a visual alarm clock inviting us to a day we'd rather miss? Are last quarter's losses small–a caution light rather than a stop light–or are they massive, perhaps a corporate version of the Red Sea?

We find clichés in some strange places, including publications that have generally been relatively cliché–free. For example, in the June 29, 1992 *Newsweek*, Barbra Streisand published an article called *"Physician Heal Thyself,"* the first cliché in an essay replete with them. Speaking about her character in *The Prince of Tides,* Streisand says the movie is about: *"people who meet each other...at crossroads where...life–changing decisions are about to be made.* They sometimes decide after standing at the crossroads for a while *to take the same path.* Sometimes they decide *to go separate ways."* I've italicized the clichés in only one segment of the piece. They undermine any sense of conviction we might otherwise perceive in the passage.

Q: Are clichés just a language version of dead weight, or do they have *any* use in presentations?

A: I'm going to surprise you. An occasional cliché does not undermine a presentation. In fact, audiences do not expect clichéless speeches from "nonprofessional" presenters. Clichés become offensive *when they're overused.* For example, sportscasters who tell us "these two teams don't like each other" should be pitched out of the press box.

Clichés can be very effective when speakers use them consciously and then turn them on their head. Dolly Parton was once asked if it bothered her to be called a "dumb blond." She replied, "Well, I don't *think* I'm dumb." She added, "And I *know* I'm not blond."

In another case, a corporate CEO cautioned against concentrating only on "the bottom line." He said, "Let's have more emphasis on the *top line*." He added, "Remember, without the *top line*, there is *no bottom line*."

A sports broadcaster once described a football player as "tough as nails." He then redeemed himself by adding, "Tough? He looks like he could take his bare hands and *drive* the nails."

As these examples demonstrate, clichés, appropriately used and consciously modified, can be a source of humor and insight. Used without forethought, however, they're verbal sleeping pills.

Good Sources of Information: To read more about clichés and proverbs, consult two fairly recent books: Richard A. Spears, ed., *NTC's Dictionary of Proverbs and Clichés* (National Textbook Co., 1993) and John Simpson, ed., *The Concise Oxford Dictionary of Proverbs*, 2d ed. (Oxford University Press, 1992).

5.4 Using Conversational Language

Q: As you've indicated, a speech is a relatively formal occasion in our society. So why shouldn't a speaker's language be relatively formal?

A: In an oral presentation, formal language sounds artificial and pretentious. "Therefore, dear gentlemen and gentle ladies, we must formulate our options, taking care to prioritize them as we go about the business of making judicious choices." It just doesn't work.

Q: What steps can I take to make my language more conversational?

A: Every one of the following tips will help you toward that end:

❐ *Use short, familiar words* (e.g., "medicines" or "drugs") *rather than long, unfamiliar ones* (say, "pharmaceuticals"). Other examples: use "likes" rather than "predilections"; "complete" or "finish" rather than "consummate"; "spend less" rather than "economize"; "lie" rather than "prevaricate"; "profits" rather than "net income."

As an illustration of conversational language, consider the remarks made by an evening news anchor on the occasion in 1992 when H. Ross Perot reentered that year's presidential race: "Ross Perot jumps back in.... So suddenly it's a three-man race." The broadcaster also referred to "Ross Perot's on–again, off–again...campaign." Besides the conversational language ("off–again, on–again"), we note the use of dramatic diction: "jumps...suddenly...race."

❐ *Use candid language rather than euphemisms.* If you mean "have sex," don't say "make love"; if you're "firing" people, don't say you're "laying them off," or "downsizing," or, worse, "putting them in the mobility pool" (as one company put it); if you're "criticizing" someone's performance, don't call it "counseling."

❐ *Use contractions.* If in everyday speech you'd use "I'd" rather than "I would," stick with your normal usage. Other examples are "I'll" rather than "I will"; "we'll" rather than "we will"; "you'll" rather than "you will"; "he's" rather than "he is"; "she'd" rather than "she would"; "can't" rather than "cannot"; "shouldn't" rather than "should not."

❐ *Avoid words you might find in print, but that you rarely hear in everyday speech.* Examples would be "ascetic...aesthetic... pneumatic...dichotomy...deify....misanthropy...misogyny... deregulate...deracinate." The problem with using these words in speech is that, since we pronounce them so rarely, it's easy to mispronounce them. (Also stay away from the word "must," which we almost never hear except in business and political speeches. When you hear a speaker saying the country or the company "must" do something, you know it probably won't be done.)

❑ *Avoid syntax appropriate in written constructions, but less so in spoken ones.* Stay away, for example, from statements containing words such as "because...unless...although...since," and the like. In speech, these words (subordinating conjunctions) introduce constructions that are difficult to understand.

❑ *Use occasional sentence fragments.* (For a good example of this, see the speech by Wendy Liebmann in Appendix A.) Fragments such as "Not so" and "Just the reverse" are effective ways to introduce variety in speeches.

❑ Avoid transition words heard infrequently in speech. These include "thus... consequently... subsequently... however... nevertheless...moreover," and the like.

❑ *Use transition words common in spoken language,* such as "and...but...so...what's more (in place of "moreover"), and the like. (One transition word President Reagan favored was "well" as in "Well, let me tell you about that..." It fit in, well, with his folksy image. Lee Iacocca sometimes used "yeah" and "okay" as transition words.)

❑ *Use questions, including rhetorical ones.* For instance, consider the following (exasperated) comments by writer and social philosopher Irving Kristol: "Whoever expected that the creation of a Welfare State in an affluent economy would be accompanied by an incredible increase in criminality, so that our streets would be blanketed with fear? A sharp increase in teen–age pregnancies? In drug addiction? In the creation of a dependent, self–destructive 'underclass'"? (*Newsweek*, June 15, 1992)."

Tip: The best place to hear conversational language used well is by network newscasters on television. Tape one or more of their news programs and listen carefully to the language. You'll find it's especially straightforward and colloquial. Note also the way the announcers vary the pitches and emphases of their voices to keep the attention of the audience.

Caution: If you're tempted to use slang in your presentations, be careful. Some words, for example, "hooker" and "pimp" might be offensive to some more tender–minded members of your audience. Other words and phrases that have their origins in the teenage subculture (e.g., "chill out," meaning, roughly, "relax") and may be unfamiliar to most of your listeners.

5.5 Learning the Language of "Blunt Eloquence"

Q: In your book *Talk Your Way to the Top* you strongly advocate that speakers use a type of language you call "blunt elo-quence." Could you give a capsule description of what it is, and why and when you think presenters should use it?

A: In that book, I said the classic example of "blunt eloquence" was General Colin Powell's statement when a reporter asked how the coalition forces would deal with Iraq's army. Most listeners expected a long answer. Instead, Powell said: "First, we're going to cut it off." He paused briefly and added: "Then, we're going to kill it."

Blunt eloquence refers to statements that are short, pointed, forceful, and saturated with confidence. It's a style used throughout history by successful leaders–in politics, government, and the military. It reflects their ability to boil down their thoughts; it demonstrates their commitment to vigorous action.

The best place to use blunt eloquence is when you're defining the essence of a situation; when you're seeking to demonstrate leadership; and when you're pointing out the actions people should take to deal with the issue you've described.

Blunt eloquence is the language of decisiveness. In fact, when we say someone is decisive, we're generally not referring to specific actions. Instead, we're talking about their use of *language*–and their *attitudes*–more than their *actions*.

Q: Can you illustrate what you mean by that? I've always heard that "actions speak louder than words...."

A: Let me use a couple of political examples. Many historians tell us that President Kennedy's two and a half years in office were not successful in terms of programs recommended and passed by Congress. They see the Kennedy presidency as mainly passive. Yet most of us remember JFK as a "man of action."

Why? I think it has a lot to do with *his image of youthful vigor*. It's even more a reflection of his ringing words about a "New Frontier" and "a new generation of leadership." Of sailing, touch football, "PT 109," and a host of energetic speeches and press conferences.

We could say much the same about Churchill during World War II. Of course his political and military actions were a central factor in defeating the forces of Naziism. But our view of Churchill's decisiveness rests largely on his words. When, in response to rumors that the Nazis were about to cross the English Channel to invade Britain, Churchill said: "We are ready." Then he paused and continued: "So are the fishes." It turned out the invasion never took place, but Churchill's words ("We will never surrender!") still ring.

If a historical statement is memorable, it probably illustrates the principles underlying blunt eloquence. Examples: General MacArthur's "I shall return." Also, Franklin Roosevelt's statement on Italy's invasion of France: "The hand that held the dagger has plunged it into the back of its neighbor." Even Richard Nixon's "Your President is not a crook." Or take the statement of Republican political operative Lee Atwater when asked how they would deal with Michael Dukakis: "We're going to strip the bark off him."

Q: Can you give any more contemporary examples?

A: Yes. When President Reagan characterized the Soviet Union as "an evil empire," he was engaging in blunt eloquence.

Q: Let me make a statement that's not very blunt–and not very eloquent. Then would you try to turn it into blunt eloquence? The statement is: "We are suffering an erosion of market share and a decline in profitability in the Midwest region. Our strategy is to assess the reasons for this situation and to develop measures designed to regain market share and restore the area to profitability."

A: Anytime you start a sentence with "Our strategy is to assess," you're in trouble. It sounds indecisive, bureaucratic.

Here's how your statement might sound in bluntly eloquent terms: *"In the Midwest, competitors are stealing our customers and siphoning our profits. We're going to find out how. And then we're going to take back those markets—and those profits."*

Your statement has 42 words; mine has 30 words. You use a lot of big words (profitability, strategy) and elaborate phrases ("restore the area to profitability"). My statement is more colloquial. Beyond that, it emphasizes actions: "stealing...siphoning off...take back." Your statement is cerebral and tentative. My revision is more emotional and confident. In one sense, the two statements say roughly the same thing. But the revised statement says it with more confidence and conviction. That's the essence of blunt eloquence.

Q: Where can I find examples to study—and copy?

A: They're all around us, on television, on the radio, in our daily conversations. Here are two examples I heard in one day:

Eleanor Holm: Olympic gold–medal–winner swimmer in the 1932 Olympics, talking about her movie debut as "Jane": "One reviewer said that, during the love scene with Tarzan, I looked as if I were about to spit in his eye."

A talk show host: "If a woman calls a man 'hot,' she means he's sexy. But what if a woman calls a guy 'cute' or 'sweet'? That means he's a dead man."

On a television show popular in the early 1990s, one young man asked an older man if he should tell his girl friend that he kissed another woman. The older man told the younger one: *"Bury it. Bury it with a shovel, and then bury the shovel."* This is blunt eloquence— but with a comic twist.

Tip: Blunt eloquence is usually not a product of first drafts. Instead, it comes forth when you're revising statements, that is, when you're trying to cut down on verbal flab and give your remarks more punch. In this regard, it's like the subject in the next section: sound bites.

Caution: If you use blunt eloquence, be prepared to back up your statements. If you don't, people will indeed assume you're "all talk."

5.6 (Sound) Biting the Ear That Heeds You

Q: We read and hear a lot in the media about something called "sound bites." What are they, and what do you think of them?

A: Sound bites are closely related to blunt eloquence. They're short, pithy, quotable comments. They generally contain 25 words or less. They're designed to appeal initially to the ears of journalists, especially those selecting "news" for television. Many people associate sound bites with elected officials, who are not averse to saying things that will get them on their local news programs.

Some critics of sound bites, apparently longing for the days of Lincoln–Douglas debates and the two–hour sermon, condemn the technique. They call them "McNuggets [of wisdom]," which is, come to think of it, a good "bite" itself. The critics' theory is that pithy phrases are replacing reasoned argument with slogans, with one–liners.

Of course, discourse that is nothing more than sloganeering is not worth much. However, nostalgia for the days—if they ever existed—when people had time to sit through endless political monologues is misplaced. If you'll pardon the pun, sound bites have received a lot of bad press.

But there's absolutely nothing wrong with sound bites when they represent a striking insight or a vigorous summary of a position.

A good sound bite is a joy to hear. Speakers who use this form of verbal shorthand demonstrate that they're making a genuine appeal to listeners. That's because sound bites almost never appear by accident. They're the result of thought and editing by the speaker, who is following the old dictum of poet Alexander Pope: to say "What oft was thought, but ne'er so well expressed."

Q: Are sound bites something that require the talents of a professional P.R. person or speechwriter?

A: Not at all. I remember one time I was in a small–town office–supply store; I said to the manager that I wanted a receipt for a small, tax–deductible purchase. He said, "Good idea. It's not how much you get that counts. It's how much you get to keep."

The same day I was at my local golf course where a tournament was taking place. One middle–aged woman golfer, unfamiliar with the course, asked the assistant pro if he had "any advice." Without a pause, he replied: "Don't throw any clubs—and don't use any bad language."

Later that week, I went to church, and the pastor observed of the Kingdom of Heaven: "You can't buy your way in."

Some years ago, my grandmother talked about a woman who had been insulted on a New York subway. Turning to my grandmother, the woman said: "When they spit in your eye, say: 'It's raining!'" (That woman should have met Columbia University history professor James Shenton. Commenting in *The Wall Street Journal* on an effort to get New Yorkers to be gracious to tourists, he said: "[E]xpecting New Yorkers to be courteous is...to deprive them of their identity.")

Sound bites all.

Q: But what's the trick to creating good sound bites?

A: There are at least four approaches to creating sound bites. First, there are those that emphasize verbal surprise, the unexpected word. One example is the comment about a certain boyishly enthusiastic politician who was popular with men, but not with women: "He's every woman's *first* husband."

Corporate executive Robert J. Buckley, Sr., was a master of this kind of verbal shocker. In an interview, he referred to the many promotions he'd had when he worked at GE. He said, "I went up in that company like my last name was *Electric*."

Another example of the verbal shocker occurred when an accountant friend of mine was preparing a speech. In his first draft, he wrote this line: "Most people regard a visit to their accountant as necessary, but painful." In his second draft, he wrote: "Most people regard a visit to their accountant like a visit to the proctologist—painful, but necessary." With the inclusion of the word "proctologist," he had added wit—and the unexpected. In the third draft, he moved the key word to the end to give the line more punch: "Most people regard a visit to their accountant as necessary, but painful—like a trip to their proctologist."

The second type of sound bite turns an abstract concept into a memorable verbal picture. We see this in a statement by political analyst Ann Lewis. Discussing the decline in power and authority of the Democratic and Republican parties, she said they reminded her of the old French Foreign Legion movies. "You see this fort, and it looks fine from the outside. But when you go through the gate, almost everyone inside is dead."

The third variety rests essentially on a play on words: An economist was criticizing the banking regulators for refusing to let the banks take risks in loaning money. He said, "No risk means no business." Well-done puns also make good sound bites. When columnist William Safire was asked about his love of irony, he replied, "I have a lot of ironies in the fire."

The fourth type is what I'd call the creative put-down of an inflated reputation. General Schwarzkopf did this in his televised criticism of Saddam Hussein's deficiencies as a military strategist and tactician, ending with: "Finally, he's not a soldier." Another example is the line one college professor used in the Boston *Globe* to describe physicist/philosopher Stephen Hawking, author of the mind-numbing *A Brief History of Time*: "[Hawking] may be the only world celebrity whose admirers don't know what they're admiring."

Q: What's the most famous sound bite of all time?

A: They don't conduct polls on that, but it might be Albert Einstein's "I don't think God is playing dice with the universe."

Tip: Creating your own sound bites can be very enjoyable, but it's generally hard work. Or perhaps "hard play" is a better phrase. Look at publications that feature "sound bites"; *The Wall Street Journal* is a distinguished example. Examine each "bite" and infer the mental process that went into creating it. You'll find that sound bites result from playing around with—editing—material, with the writer or speaker looking for an unusual angle and showing a willingness to experiment.

5.7 Helping Listeners "See" Your Points

Q: Could you give an example of "verbal pictures"?

A: I heard a commercial on a New Hampshire radio station. It started out this way: "Picture this. Steaks sizzling on the grill. Children splashing in the pool. Friends sharing lemonade and laughter on the patio..."

Verbal pictures are those that set the scene for your listeners. They are evocative, appealing to the senses: hearing ("sizzling...friends laughing"); smell ("steaks"); taste ("lemonade"); sight ("children splashing"); and touch. The repetition of sounds adds to the sensuous quality of the statement.

Poets and fiction–writers (the good ones) rely heavily on verbal pictures. If you want to find some outstanding uses of pictorial language, read Donna Tartt's splendid novel *The Secret History* (Knopf, 1992): "Trees creaking with apples, fallen red on the grass beneath...the heavy sweet smell of them as they rotted on the ground and the steady thrumming of wasps around them." Notice how this passage appeals to our senses of sound, sight, smell, and even taste. This use of verbal pictures enhances the memorability of the words.

Verbal pictures also play a big role in Tama Janowitz's *The Male Cross–Dresser Support Group* (Crown, 1992). This is a delightful novel about a single woman who "adopts" a street urchin. Here's how she describes their playful wrestling matches. "It was the highlight of my day. His velvet skin, as soft as the tanned hide of a jacket made from unborn deer or fetal pig...his boyish, innocent odor, that of new meadow grass in spring and capped with the stale sugars of bubble gum, fermented orange pop...the heavy salts of popcorn bagged with artificial cheese, the stickiness of his dirty face..."

Q: But is there really a place for this kind of evocative language in, say, a business talk?

A: If there isn't at least a small place, there should be. Most business talks are TOO DRY. They shuffle generalizations and abstractions. At their worst, they're stiff and lifeless, dried–up things that flutter away like mealy leaves (or, as Emily Dickinson called it, "leaf meal").

We are not cognitive machines. In fact, most of what we know we learn through the senses. That's why we like verbal pictures; they appeal to those senses. They wake us up, make us more alert, get our imaginations working.

Q: Maybe I've been doing business talks for too long, but I don't even know if I can do pictorial language...

A: Yes you can. Just let your imagination blossom. Think about something you enjoy; then start breaking it up into its sensory details.

Q: Well, to tell the truth, I really like a cold beer after working in the garden...

A: Let me help you. Suppose you're talking to a business group about a complex problem you've solved. You then say: "How did it feel? It felt just like a cold beer on a hot summer day...after digging weeds in the garden. You know, the sweat's stinging your eyes...and your skin feels prickly from the heat. Then you crack open that beer, and the condensation runs in thin little lines down the bottle...and the cold bottle hits your warm, dry lips...and it goes down cool as a fall morning. Anyway, that's how solving that problem made me feel."

Yes, it would be a digression. Would the audience like it? What do you think?

Q: I think they'd enjoy the surprise. I see what you mean. Take some thing or event that appeals to us, and then describe it in such a way that it appeals to the audience...

A: Sometimes you surprise me with your perceptiveness.

Tip: Whenever you find your remarks becoming too abstract (and detached from everyday experience), try to insert some pictorial language. You'll find your audience, which perhaps had been nodding off, perk up its ears. For example, suppose you're saying: "The federal government announced the unemployment rate has risen from 7.7 percent to 7.9 percent. The rise in the rate means an increase of 70,000 in the number of jobless Americans." You might follow up this intellectualized approach with a pictorial image. "What do those numbers mean in real–life terms? They mean more hungry children...their stomachs grumbling...their tears running down their faces, while their parents bang their fists on empty kitchen tables."

5.8 Using Reason in Presentations

Q: I've noticed you emphasize the role emotion plays in speeches. But most speeches in business are relatively dispassionate—logical and factual. Do you think these speeches are on the wrong track?

A: I'll be daring and say "yes." In so doing, I'm not making an argument for irrationality. In a presentation, our arguments should make sense, should not be far–fetched. But we need to recognize the limits of a purely factual, logical approach to our subjects. The problem with most business speeches is that they fill up our heads but not our hearts.

The Irish poet William Butler Yeats said: "I always think a great orator convinces us, not by the force of reasoning, but because he is visibly enjoying the beliefs which he wants us to accept."

Throughout history, men and women have been willing, rightly or wrongly, to die for flag, family, and fatherland. They aren't willing to do so for a 15 percent return on equity, or a 5 percent increase in market share, or a 3 percent reduction in expenses. They are not moved by reasoned arguments for cost–effectiveness or by discussions of the need to "enhance shareholder value." (They may be moved by such discussions if the abstract concepts are personal-ized, made pertinent to their own lives and concerns.)

Q: Aside from questions of poor delivery, does the emphasis on rationality explain why there are so many boring business speeches?

A: It's not rationality alone that bores audiences. It's the excess of information. It's one of those speeches that tells us more about a company's "fixed costs," for example, than we'd ever want to know. It's the piling up of numbers without telling us either (1) what they mean; or, (2) what we can do to affect them.

Q: Is there a way to be reasonable and still move an audience to action?

A: Most emphatically, yes. It's to appeal to something called "common sense." That's rationality stripped down to its essentials. The appeal to common sense works especially well when the issue you're dealing with is an emotional one. (Why? Because *violating common sense is one of the few remaining taboos in modern society.*)

Let me give you an example: Suppose you're a manager talking about the need to keep down your labor costs per unit of product. And suppose your audience is a group of skeptical union members, who assume that cost–cutting will fall on their shoulders, not on management's.

How can you discuss this emotional issue effectively? You can take the "common–sense" approach. Lay out the problem simply and systematically. Here's a good six–step approach:

❐ *Emphasize that the audience knows as well as you that high–cost producers eventually start to (1) lose money; (2) lay people off.*

❐ *Point out that the audience is well aware that there are four ways to reduce costs:* (1) to cut back on management compensation and perquisites; (2) to reduce the cost of supplies; (3) to cut back on labor costs, through wage reductions or layoffs; (4)

to increase productivity. *Emphasize that there are no other avenues to take that will ensure the survival of the company and the jobs of its employees.*

☐ *Note that management compensation will be reduced, commensurate with any reductions in compensation for hourly workers.* (If you're not ready to take this step, expect hostility from the audience.)

☐ *Indicate what actions are underway to get the cooperation of suppliers to reduce costs.*

☐ *Note also that the company will stress measures to improve productivity and will encourage and listen to worker suggestions.*

☐ *Note that reductions in worker compensation and in the workforce will also be necessary to achieve the required savings.* (If possible, suggest these cuts will be restored as soon as economic conditions dictate.)

In this case, the common–sense approach will not win you the love and admiration of the workers. After all, you're cutting their compensation and perhaps laying off some of them. You are, however, presenting the issues in an honest, reasonable fashion. That will tend to defuse some of the emotion surrounding the issue.

That emotion, however, will erupt if all the sacrifices are aimed at the hourly employees. "Equality of sacrifice" may not make sense in classical economics. *But the concept of fairness is central in any discussion of this type.* It's also crucial that you hit hard on solutions other than labor cutbacks, including tightening the screws on suppliers and increasing productivity.

At its best, the rational approach has little to do with the recitation of dry arguments. It has everything to do with proceeding intelligently, with respect for the sensibilities of your audience. If reasonable people might disagree with the solutions you propose to a situation, say so. But make a strong, common–sense case for the course you choose.

Tip: The more intense the emotions surrounding the issues you're discussing, the stronger the need for a reasoned, common–sense approach.

5.9 Using Statistics Selectively

Q: In most business presentations, the speakers cite a lot of statistics. I suspect you're not enthusiastic about throwing in a lot of numbers. But business is about dollars and cents, about revenues, market–share percentages, earnings, year–to–year financial changes. How can you avoid statistics?

A: You can't, and you shouldn't try to. But if your presentation is nothing but a recitation of statistics, you've got a problem. *Listeners can assimilate relatively few numbers. After that, they start mishearing the statistics; they get confused; ultimately, their minds go blank.* There's probably no more exquisite form of boredom in human life than listening to someone recite numbers.

The point is: *the fewer statistics you use, the more effect each one will have.* In addition, the more time you'll have to *tell what the numbers mean.* People really don't want pure information. They want to know the *significance* of the information they're getting. Even more important, they want to know how they can use the information to make their jobs–and their lives–better. Telling them that is the real duty of the speaker.

Q: What's the most effective way to use numbers in a presentation?

A: The best way is to use statistics comparatively. It's a fallacy that numbers are meaningful in and of themselves. They have relevance—significance—only when they're used comparatively. For example, suppose you observe that car accidents each year claim the lives of more than 45,000 Americans. Your listeners may nod, but secretly they're wondering: "Is that a lot?" Suppose you then add: "That's more fatalities than we had in the entire Vietnam War. It's as if we wiped out an entire city the size of Burlington, Vermont, or Athens, Georgia, *every year.*"

Or suppose you're saying that your company had profits last year of $80 million. Suppose you then put that number into perspective by saying: "Eighty million dollars is more than we had in *revenues* ten years earlier."

Q: You've emphasized the need for presentations to move the audience to action. But my company is strong on statistics and suspicious of what we call "anecdotal evidence." Aren't you asking me to downplay statistics and emphasize anecdotes?

A: Look at it this way: *statistics are compilations of verifiable anecdotes.* The fact is that it's the "anecdotal" approach that moves people to act. Statistics are nothing more than the sum of their parts. In business and government, we throw around some big numbers. For example, in the early 1990s we were talking about the fact that the number of Americans without health coverage was about 35 million. That kind of number is almost overwhelming. Audiences tend to ask: Who are these people? Do I know any of them? And what can I do about such a vast problem?

But what if you talked about one family you knew who didn't have health coverage? You could talk about the terrible choices they had to make between eating and getting health care. You could talk about how an illness devastated this family financially. You could talk about their anguish and hopelessness. Yes, you'd be playing on the audience's emotions, but it is those feelings that will rouse the audience to do something.

Or consider another example. Most companies talk about the need to control overhead. Unfortunately, they usually make one of two mistakes: Either they content themselves with vague admonitions to cut costs, or they impose across–the–board cuts in funding.

One corporate controller took a better approach. She mentioned the amount of money that her company spent annually on overhead—a large number. Then she put the figure in perspective. She said that every single dollar that went out for expenses was the equivalent of "$40 in revenue." Her point was that, if each individual could reduce expenses by one dollar, that action by 40,000 employees would be the equivalent of adding $16 *million* in revenue.

By using an example to illustrate a problem, you haven't falsified the situation. Instead, you've made it compelling by giving it a human face.

Tip: If you have a lot of numbers to discuss, give them in simplified form. Instead of saying, for example, how many millions of barrels of oil the United States imported ten years ago versus today, say something such as: "So in that period imports have nearly doubled." Or, in another context, say, "Expenses have been cut in half." Or, "accidents have been cut in half." Audiences find it much easier to assimilate this kind of comparison than they do large numbers.

5.10 Harnessing Emotion in Presentations

Q: I know how you feel about emotion. But the question occurs: Doesn't the use of emotion lead to rash decisions?

A: You can reason a horse to water, but you've got to make the horse *want* to drink. In your question, you're confusing two different things. Yes, we should make business decisions rationally and logically. And yes, we should rely on facts, not on emotions, in making those decisions. But in a larger sense, business doesn't deal only with facts and figures. It also deals with motivation, with commitment, and with human psychology.

Show me an individual not moved by emotion—by the pull of the heart strings—and I'll show you Mr. Spock from *Star Trek*. Speakers in business and other institutions miss out when they undervalue emotion.

Reason and logic may convince people of the rightness of your arguments. But we don't want our listeners merely to agree with us. We want them to act on that agreement. And emotion drives people to action.

Think about it: We've all yawned at long, boring lectures about American history. And then, on a patriotic holiday, we see the flag and the veterans go by. When the band strikes up "The Star–Spangled Banner," a chill goes up our spine, and our eyes start to fill with tears. What is it that produces that response? It's emotion.

Q: But I still don't see the exact circumstances where I could use appeals to emotion in a business speech...

A: You can find those circumstances when your remarks deal with subjects that are deeply meaningful to your listeners. When we don't touch on areas of great concern to our audience, we need to reexamine our remarks. Perhaps, as presenters, we secretly believe that work and jobs are, in essence, boring or trivial.

But is that really true for most people? They spend 40 or more hours per week at work. Their jobs consume a great proportion of their lives and their thoughts. Jobs are linked to our sense of human worth, to the well–being of our families, and to the future of our nation.

Because people's jobs are part of the core of their being, it makes sense, in many instances, to use an emotional tone in speaking about work. When it's appropriate, appeal to workers' affection for their jobs, appeal to their sense of professional competence, to their pride in their industry. Remind them that their work is the foundation of the abstraction we know as "our country."

Q: I assume you don't want to rely on emotion throughout a speech, because it would leave the audience drained. Where in a speech does emotion work best?

A: *Emotional appeals work best in the conclusion of presentations.* Build slowly throughout the presentation to an emotional conclusion. But if you start your speech with an emotional tone, you may drain the listeners before you get to your call for action.

Caution: Appeal to your listeners' emotions, but don't toy with them. Emotional appeals will not work over and over again. For example, if you're "restructuring" the company (laying off workers), an emotional appeal (to pride, to the competitive spirit) might work well. But if, a year later, you have to "restructure" again, employees will respond more cynically.

In that case, the emotional approach will not work. That's the reason most professional sports coaches don't give pep talks. The athletes have become jaded. They've heard more than their share of emotional appeals from past coaches. In other words, don't go to the well too often.

5.11 Using "Speech" Techniques in Writing

Q: Is there any carry–over between writing speeches for the ear and writing regular material—memos, reports, and so on?

A: As we've discussed, an essay is different from a speech. A quality essay—in magazines such as *The Atlantic* or *The New Yorker*—will have more words than a speech. In addition, it will make greater intellectual demands on a reader than a speech will on a listener. The essay will be more suggestive, more directed to the imagination. It will use some words that we normally don't find in a speech.

If it's a great essay, it will be one we'll want to re–read. By contrast, there are few speeches—other than, for example, the Gettysburg Address and some of Churchill's efforts—that we'd want to hear again.

Q: What about business writing—proposals, memoranda, and the like?

A: Most business writing is not very good; it's too abstract, too verbose, and too hesitant to make a call to action (or even, in some cases, a recommendation). Something happens to businesspeople when they take pen in hand or start tapping on a computer keyboard. They start trying to sound important; they choose words they'd never use in conversation; they turn inward and forget about the cardinal rule: *to communicate their thoughts clearly to their audience.* That's why memos written by otherwise intelligent people often are unreadable.

Why aren't more business documents written like the material in Connie Clark's book, *Service, Sacrifice, Loyalty: Guarding Freedom's Flame* (Veterans of Foreign Wars of the United States, 1992)? In describing conditions during the Korean War, she writes (on page 80): "Everything froze—weapons, food, even human flesh. Pancakes froze before they could be eaten, and hot coffee was cold before the soldier could get it to his lips. Weapons refused to fire, misfired, or just plain broke completely. Grenades wouldn't explode. Water–cooled machine guns were filled with antifreeze to keep them operating correctly."

How can we make business writing sound more like Connie Clark's? One way is to reconsider the unnecessary divorce we have between the written and the spoken word. In today's best business prose, writing for the eye is starting to converge with what we've thought of as writing for the ear. That's a positive development. It means business writers who want to communicate are emphasizing the simplicity and directness we find in speeches.

How can businesspeople learn to write better? They can do so by emulating the example of some of today's best journalists. These are not people feeding pablum to nonreaders. Instead, they're writers who have a passion for communicating their ideas to a broad audience. The following piece, written by Susan Trausch of the Boston *Globe* (September 30, 1992) is an example of what I mean. Her column is a political goodbye to her erstwhile hero H. Ross Perot.

"GOODBYE ROSS, WE'RE THROUGH"

If Ross Perot calls, tell him I'm sorting my sock drawer.

No dinner date. No lunch date. Not even a coffee at our little corner table in the Cafe for the Common Man. We had a brief flirtation last spring, but he had a problem with commitment.

He still does. He has a problem with sincerity, too, and a problem with honesty, and a problem with telling the country exactly what game he's playing five weeks before an election.

Coy was cute in March. "I don't know what's going to happen; that depends on the volunteers" sounded straightforward coming from the man who stumbled into the presidential race on the Larry King show. But it rings pretty hollow coming from the guy who dropped his people flat in July.

Watching Perot and King have their lovefest [last] Monday night, I asked the question that's hung in the air since the beginning of the craziness: So what's the plan?

Yeah, I know somebody wrote a book for him, and the book says he wants to slash the federal budget, increase taxes, and send the economy into the trash compactor. This is not a plan. This is shooting from the hip in the general direction of the foot.

But for the sake of argument, let's say that he really believes in this crazy plan. Then he should lay it out for us. How? When? What kind of hardship can the country expect? Will it be worth the sacrifice? What are you asking us to give you, Ross?

A political leader has to be able to do that. Sitting there smiling impishly and telling people to "read the book" is not saying anything. It's ducking the issue.

I hate politics as usual and seek out new voices proposing bold, if simplistic, solutions. But this voice is just plain irresponsible. This voice speaks from no core of understanding or depth.

I keep looking for growth in Perot and a sense that his campaign has matured beyond the folksy "aw shucks" aphorisms that brought him to our attention. But he's still telling us to "pick up a shovel and clean out the barn."

He's still telling us to call an 800–number and light up that switchboard. He's still talking about "those good, decent, hard–working American people" in a tone that makes me want to hit him with a pie.

He says he made a mistake dropping out in July but doesn't tell us why. He says he spent a day talking with "real people about real issues" when representatives of the George Bush and Bill Clinton campaigns came to call, but he gives no specifics.

He says he can take the heat now, but doesn't say what changed. He says he's back if we want him, maybe, but don't order the bumper stickers until the end of the week.

He must have promised King a job, because the talk show host smiled almost as much as Perot did and let the obvious questions pass.

King acted as though he were hosting a party, giving the old boy the convention he never had, complete with the introduction of family members.

My favorite was son Ross, who set a record flying a helicopter around the world. He did this because he heard an Australian was doing it and felt the title should go to an American.

Chip off the old block, says dad proudly. And again I wonder where the substance is hiding in these people and what is the point. Around the world in a helicopter? Is this the agenda?

We are a troubled country. Six months ago, I thought Perot was serious about addressing that. Today, I think he is yanking our chain and trying to make *Newsweek* magazine take back its "Quitter" cover.

Angry as I get about our political process, I do feel it has worked its will this time around and given us a clear choice. Both Bush and

Clinton have sweated through the system, imperfect though it may be. Perot hasn't even tried.

I think those "good, decent, hard–working American people" will see that.*

Comment: Agree or disagree with her political views, Susan Trausch's essay has many effective speech qualities: it's conversational ("yeah"; "yanking our chain"); pictorial and colorful ("a tone that makes me want to hit him with a pie"); alliterative ("Bush and Clinton campaigns came to call"; "sweated through the system"). Her piece uses sentence fragments and rhetorical questions ("How? When? Will it be worth the sacrifice?"); it relies mainly on short, declarative sentences ("We are a troubled country"); it uses repetition for effect ("He says...he says").

It even blends two clichés to achieve a fresh effect ("shooting from the hip in the general direction of the foot"). Finally, it's intensely personal, with the words "I" or "my" occurring more than a dozen times.

Above all, Trausch writes with marvelous clarity. She follows George Orwell's admonition that "good prose should be like a windowpane." Her line of argument is sometimes subtle, but it's never difficult to follow.

Ms. Trausch does not have a specific call to action. Her point, however, can't be missed: Pull the voting lever for someone other than Mr. Perot. There's no doubt about where she stands.

In short, this is very good journalistic writing. It would also be a fine six–minute speech.

Tip: When writing material for work, apply some of the same tests you would to a speech. Ask: will the reader quickly understand my point? Does anything in the piece invite misunderstanding? Is it clear what action I'm requesting? (If you're not asking the reader(s) to act, is the information you're conveying truly important–and fresh–to the audience?)

---

* Reprinted by permission of the Boston *Globe*.

6

Knowing How and When to Use Humor, Anecdotes, and Quotations

There's a debate among public–speaking experts about using humor, anecdotes, and quotations in presentations. One side, recognizing the difficulty of using these devices effectively, counsels restricting their use. The other side emphasizes that the effective use of humor, anecdotes, and quotes can make a good speech into a great one.

I believe you should follow the advice of the second group: Use these devices, but make sure you use them well.

By using humor effectively, you can do more than amuse an audience. You can demonstrate that you have a balanced perspective—that you recognize that, like the moon, life has both a dark (serious) side and a light (humorous) one.

By using anecdotes well, you can "plug into" the appeal that stories have for listeners. In many cases, your audience will not remember for long what your arguments were. But if your anecdotes are good ones, the audience may remember them for decades.

By using quotes well, you can buttress your own points with the authority of prestigious figures from history, ancient and modern. Properly integrated into your remarks, apt quotations can indeed let you—and your remarks—"stand on the shoulders of giants."

6.1 Making Sure the Opening Joke Is Not on You

Q: What would be your advice for the neophyte speaker who wants to open a presentation with a joke or two?

A: Don't—unless your last name is Leno, Letterman, Crystal, or Hall.

Q: "Don't?" But isn't an opening joke a way of showing that the speaker's a regular guy? Isn't it an ice–breaker?

A: More often an egg–layer. Seriously, telling jokes effectively is a specialized skill. There are a lot of talented comedians going hungry as we speak. The public laughs at a Roseanne Arnold, a Billy Crystal, a Jay Leno, or an Arsenio Hall. But these people establish a high standard for humor. Most of us can't live up to that standard.

However, if you're willing to make the sustained effort necessary to find (or develop) good jokes and to practice delivering them, then go ahead and use jokes.

The success of a joke rests largely on its topicality and on the speaker's precise sense of timing. There's also a third factor: the audience's readiness to appreciate a joke. *When people go to hear a monologue or skit by a noted comedian, they're ready to be entertained, to laugh. Conversely, when they go to hear a CEO, an accounting manager, or a lawyer, they're not expecting the second coming of Johnny Carson.*

By the way, there's a reason that "roasts" are (sometimes) funny—even if the speakers generally are amateurish. People go to roasts expecting to have a good time. It's in the spirit of the evening to laugh—at good jokes and bad.

Generally, however, when the typical business speaker tells a joke, it reminds us of the old story about hearing a pig sing: We're not so surprised that it's done poorly as that it's done at all.

About your point on jokes establishing a speaker as a "good guy." Your gender reference is right on target. The "open the talk with a joke" set is almost entirely male. It's an affliction that female executives seem to have avoided.

In many cases, CEOs insist on beginning their talks with a joke. The message the speaker/jokester wants to send is: "I may have more money and a grander title than you, but I'm really a fun guy." The message, however, that the audiences may receive from an opening characterized by bad jokes is: "This guy must think we're bumpkins—always ready for a har–har, but incapable of intelligent thought."

Q: Boy, you're tough on what you call "the jokesters." Do you think it could be because you're a humorless sort?

A: I hope not. My aversion to (most) opening jokes doesn't extend to humor generally.

Here's how I see it: Suppose a speaker tells "a funny," and nobody laughs. Then suppose there's another joke, which is greeted not by hilarity, but by perplexity. What happens then? If the speaker is a seasoned comic performer, he or she makes a joke out of the failed jokes—and the audience roars.

But if the speaker is an ordinary soul telling a joke that misfires, there's a major problem. The opening disaster may—probably will—send the speech in the wrong direction. Listeners who start out embarrassed for its guest speaker are not good candidates to listen attentively, accept ideas, or respond to calls for action.

The problem with opening jokes is that the downside is so deep. In fact, if the jokes crater, the speaker ends up in the world's deepest hole.

Q: Well, I see where you stand. But do you have any advice for people who are, one, good at telling jokes; two, want to use them in speeches?

A: Make sure the joke relates to the main lines of the speech. Your listeners will be looking for the connection, and it will leave them dangling if it's not there. The linkage between joke and speech is helpful if the joke doesn't work. That way, it becomes not a joke, but rather a story that's a bridge to the larger message.

Q: What's the key to telling a joke well?

A: Make sure the joke deals with a current issue. Work hard on your timing—especially the pause before the punch line, which should be the last line of the joke. Before you deliver the joke "for real," test it on colleagues. Adjust your delivery as necessary. When you tell the joke to your audience, be relaxed, but mentally alert. In telling the joke, don't try to "rush" it.

Good Sources of Information: If speakers need to find current, topical jokes, there are several sources.

You definitely should look into the advisory services, seminars, and books of Robert Orben, who has written for Red Skelton, Dick Gregory, Jack Paar, and President Gerald Ford. Orben has written nearly 50 joke books, and many of them are available in paperback under the imprint of Wilshire Books and in hardcover by Doubleday. You can get information about using Orben's justly renowned services by writing to him at Apartment 1122, 1200 N. Nash St., Alexandria, VA 22209, or by calling 703–522–3666.

In addition, Ed McManus publishes a newsletter called *The Jokesmith*. He is an experienced, talented writer who has provided jokes to professional comedians. He's especially good on jokes relating to professions we don't normally associate with hearty laughs: accountants, human relations/personnel people, and lawyers, among others. You can contact McManus for information and to get his publications by writing to him at 44 Queen's View Rd., Marlborough, MA 01752, or by calling 508–481–0979.

Another fertile source of humor for speakers is *Current Comedy*, published twice each month and is available by calling 1–800–777–7098.

There are a variety of joke books by various authors. (Remember, however, that humor is like lettuce. It wilts if it's been around too long.)

One book full of good one–liners is Gene Perret's and Linda Perret's *Funny Business: Speaker's Treasury of Business Humor for All*

Occasions (Prentice–Hall, 1990). An example: "Our mail room is like mandatory retirement for packages." It's organized by subject.

You'll also want to look at Fred Metcalf, *The Penguin Directory of Modern Humorous Quotations*. (Penguin, 1986). It's organized alphabetically by subject and especially useful for Britons, Canadians, and Anglophiles.

Tip: Make sure your jokes are updated and made applicable to the particular audience and situation where they'll be delivered.

6.2· Showing a Sense of Humor in Speeches

Q: What's your favorite example of humor?

A: I've always been partial to a statement by Churchill. He once quoted a remark of the French generals who had lost to Hitler. They said Germany "would wring Britain's neck like a chicken." Churchill then reportedly raised his eyes and thrust up his chin, saying slowly, *"Some chicken...some neck."*

This is a classic use of a sense of humor. The situation faced by Britain and Churchill after Dunkirk was grave. The main thing stopping the Nazis was the resolve of the British people and their Prime Minister. Churchill could have responded gravely, with furrowed brow and jowls.

Instead, he made a (sardonic) joke out of his response. People who respond with humor to threats are people who are unafraid of bullies. In his response, Churchill made Hitler seem somehow less threatening. In calling attention to his jowly neck, Churchill made the German dictator seem slightly ridiculous.

We treasure a sense of humor in our leaders. When we have a President with a good wit, such as Kennedy and Reagan, we feel more comfortable with them. When John F. Kennedy introduced himself in Paris as "Jacqueline Kennedy's husband," he made many friends. In the face of speculation that he was "too old" to be reelected, Ronald Reagan may have saved his presidency by making jokes about his advanced age.

On the other hand, when our leaders lack a sense of humor, they tend to make us nervous. They seem too serious, too single-minded, too self-centered, too unmindful of the absurdities and uncertainties of the human condition.

Q: I take it that a "sense of humor" is not the same as an ability to tell good jokes.

A: It's not. At its best, a sense of humor is an ability to make light of ourselves and to see the incongruities of modern life. "Here I am, Chairman of the Board of the world's tenth largest industrial company...and I can't get the soft drink machine to work." We hear a remark like that, and we don't erupt in laughter. Instead, we think: Here's someone like us...an individual humbled by a coin-operated machine.

Think of humor in terms of the experiences you share with your audience. We all sit in traffic jams; we all endure the indignities of the Motor Vehicle Bureau; we all get to the Automatic Teller Machine just as it goes out of service; we all get phone calls at dinner time from people trying to sell us magazines we don't want. These are not side-splitting experiences. They are, however, humorous. Share them with audiences, and you're sharing your sense of humor.

Q: Why is it that a sense of humor is so rare in presentations?

A: Many business speakers become prisoners of their own earnestness. They are SO serious about their subjects. They are consumed with the importance of the points they address. They become like the Puritan Malvolio in Shakespeare's play—the man who is asked by the freespirited (and spirit drinker) Sir Toby Belch: "Dost thou think 'cause thou art virtuous there shall be no cakes and ale?"

We need to leave room in our talks for the cakes and ale—and for the banana peels that lie in wait for all of us.

Q: Are there any books that discuss systematically how to use humor to enrich your life and to get ahead?

A: Interesting that you should ask. I'm working on one now. It will come out in early 1994 and be called: *Power Humor*. The book's emphasis is on using humor strategically, that is, to accomplish goals at work and in your personal life.

Tip: One way to gain a reputation as a humorist is to seize opportunities to come up with unexpected responses. My uncle, Bill Wagner, was a funny man, even when he was very ill with heart disease. One time the hospital admissions person asked him the usual questions. When she got to "Religion?" my uncle paused. He then said, "I was going to be an agnostic, but then I realized they didn't have any good holidays."

6.3 Creating Your Own Humor (Yes, You Can!)

Q: Your uncle was a creative humorist. But I think the chances of my creating my own humor are about like my chance of winning the U.S. Tennis Open—closer to none than to slim...

A: Don't underestimate yourself. Remember what I said about humor arising from our perception of the deviations from the norm that we find in everyday life. It's not completely accurate to say that we "invent" humor. Look at it this way: humor happens.

For example, a few weeks ago I was entering an interstate highway in New England. Another car was a few hundred yards ahead of me on the entrance ramp. Suddenly, the car stopped right in the middle of the road. The driver pulled out a map, unfolded it, and gazed at it intently. I stopped, and so did the cars behind me. I wondered, "If he decides he's headed in the wrong direction will he start back up the entryway?"

There was no accident; no one was hurt. Therefore, the incident was funny—not hilarious, but funny. It's a slice of life that most listeners can identify with—an aspect of modern life, in this case "in the slow lane."

Also, a renowned professional golfer was playing in a tournament on television. He got up to hit his ball to a fairway lined with golf fans. The result was a terrible drive, pulled about 50 yards to his left into a crowd of spectators. Miraculously, no one was hurt.

An announcer (Gary McCord) said the drive was one all public course players could identify with. When it became clear the ball had miraculously missed the spectators, the announcer added: "I didn't see any chalk–mark outlines [of bodies]."

A third example: A friend told me he called an insurance company for information about his claim. The "service" representative said he'd have to get back to my friend, who enquired, "Can't you just put me on hold and call somebody to get the information?" The insurance person replied plaintively (and incredibly), "Our phones aren't equipped to put people on hold." My friend said, "Then put the phone on your desk and go ask somebody for the information."

Stories such as these will not be unfamiliar to most people. We all drive on highways with people who seem oblivious to the existence of other motorists. Even good golfers hit shots that are awesome in their awfulness. And most of us encounter customer "service" that is really *dis*service.

When we tell such stories—and define their morals—our listeners won't guffaw and hold their sides. They will, however, smile a rueful smile and nod their heads in recognition.

Q: What about creating my own one–liners?

A: I talk about this in my book *Talk Your Way to the Top*, and I also discuss it in the section on "roasts" (section 11.6). There are certain formulas you can use to create one–liners. They include:

❐ *The "like" approach*: When you're describing something (or someone) you find humorous or odd, compare it to something even more absurd: For example, if your company's shipping department takes forever to get products out the door say, "It's like a traffic light that shows only red and yellow."

Or, if you're describing a company where financial and accounting people are rewarded more than their manufacturing and marketing counterparts, say, "It's like a baseball team that pays the official scorekeeper more than the starting center fielder." The key to this approach is to formulate the situation you want to describe and then let your mind range through possible likenesses—the more outrageous the better.

❑ *The use of hyperbole (exaggeration)*: A steel executive once said of a bar mill his company had sold: "It hadn't made a profit within the memory of any individual now living." In fact, it had, but the audience laughed.

Other examples of hyperbole as humor: "He was such a dedicated accountant that on his honeymoon he brought along a calculator." "Our approach to customer service used to be: 'Let it ring. If it's important, they'll call back.'" (As an alternative, combine hyperbole with the use of "like": Example, "My approach to closing sales used to be like Nolan Ryan's—lots of strikeouts.")

❑ *The insertion of an unexpected word or phrase*: One senior vice president at a major company had a running battle about language with the company's lawyers. At one point he was asked for his comments on a compliance manual put together by the company's legal department. The senior V.P. noted that the document invariably capitalized the words "company" and "manual." His comment: "The words 'company' (in the second and subsequent uses) and 'manual' are not capitalized," he added, "in non–Communist countries." The Law Department had the last laugh: the completed document kept the offending capital letters.

Remember, you're not trying for belly–laughs. You're aiming for a smile (but won't turn down laughter if it occurs).

Q: Where do you get ideas for your own humor?

A: Humorous material is all around us. Sometimes, only a little exaggeration is necessary to turn what we hear, see, and read into a chuckle. For someone who is a consistent critic of television, I hate to admit it, but I get many ideas from TV—and not from the comedy programs. For example, one day I was watching the *CBS Morning News* and the anchor-woman used two analogies in reading the news. I thought about her analogies and decided there was something faint-ly ridiculous about them. That perception led to my writing an article for the *Speechwriter's Newsletter*. The relevant para-graphs follow:

> *In their efforts to reach the "Average Person," the network people have discovered the value of analogies. Thus, we hear a lot about balance of payment deficits three times the size of Mickey Rooney's alimony costs, jalapeño peppers large enough to eventually necessitate the services of a dozen gastroenterologists, hailstones as big as medicine balls, etc.*

> *Recently, however, this trend has accelerated. For ex-ample, on one segment of "CBS Morning News," the following events occurred. First, the anchorwoman announced in her cheerful, blond manner that the IRS has commenced sending out the 1040s to an expectant audience. She observed—cheer-fully and blondly—that the forms, if stacked one on top of another, would rise to a height of 56 miles. I found myself wondering: who would stack them? Wouldn't it be cold up there? What on earth would the stacker's ladder look like?*

Readers told me they found this funny. Why? Because it exag-gerates the pretensions of news readers. Instead of the (dubious) "soft–ball sized" hail (seen apparently only by weatherpeople on *CNN* nowadays), I make it the size of a medicine ball. As for the anchorwoman's stack of IRS forms, this was an (absurd) effort to make the news "listener friendly." The humor I found lay in the fact the more one pictured her analogy, the funnier it became.

What about the "cheerful, blond" comments. Are they gratuitous? Not if one knows the morning news shows, with their well–documented bias toward blonds. Also, in television school, anchors seem to learn that cheerfulness is never inappropriate.

That's why they're cheerful even describing plague, pestilence, and political perfidy. The world may be collapsing, but why should that wipe the winning smiles off their faces?

Tip: One of the best humorist–speechwriters in the United States is Landon Parvin, who formerly wrote speeches for President Reagan. In *Speechwriter's Newsletter*, Parvin says that the secret to creating humor is to take reality and exaggerate it. "The humor," he adds, "lies in the truth."

6.4 Knowing When—and How—to Use Quotations

Q: What are the pros and cons of using quotations in my presentations?

A: You should use quotations the way that porcupines proverbially make love: "very carefully." On the plus side, judiciously used quotes bring in expert opinion to support your viewpoints, to lend substance and authority to your remarks. They allow you to borrow from what nineteenth–century poet and essayist Matthew Arnold called "the best that has been thought and said."

However, quotations used inappropriately can disrupt a speech by sounding a false note. Overused, they can make the audience wonder, like the Puritan maiden Priscilla Smith, why you "don't speak for yourself."

When a speaker uses a quote that doesn't fit—that doesn't seem "right"—it has a curious effect on an audience. It creates for them the image of the speaker rummaging around in *Bartlett's*, searching for a quote. The misused quote doesn't reinforce the speaker's point. Instead, it distracts the audience and subtly undermines the speaker's credibility.

Q: When I try to signal to the audience that I'm quoting, do I have to use the words "quote/unquote"? When I do that, it sounds kind of odd...

A: Good point. The audience can't see the quotation marks in your script, so you do have to indicate when your quotes start and when they stop. "Quote/unquote" is one possibility. You can say, "As Franklin D. Roosevelt said, quote, 'The only thing we have to fear is fear itself, nameless, unreasoning fear,' unquote." The use of "quote/unquote" does distinguish Roosevelt's words from your own.

However, to use that approach breaks your verbal flow—takes away the magic—from the spell you should be weaving. It's like sneezing during a romantic interlude.

So try this technique: "Franklin Roosevelt put it this way, 'The only thing we have to fear is fear itself, nameless, unreasoning fear.'" Then pause and say, "That's how Roosevelt defined the problem." With this approach, you tell the audience when you're quoting Roosevelt and when your words are your own again. And you do so without jarring your listeners.

Depending on your context, it's sometimes possible to handle quotes in another way. When the quote is in a tone different from your remarks, you can refer to the fact that you're quoting and then let the quote "close itself." It will be obvious from the context when you are no longer quoting.

For example, take the example of Robert J. Buckley, Sr., former head of Allegheny International. He spoke about an article indicating that high unemployment always accompanied low inflation. Buckley pointed out that this did not have to be the case—as it was not in the Reagan years. Buckley then added: "I'm reminded of what Mark Twain said about one of his acquaintances: 'It's not what he doesn't know that concerns me. It's what he knows that's not true.'"

Twain's colloquial humor contrasted with the more formal approach Buckley was using, so it was clear to the audience when the quote concluded.

Q: In what specific instances should I avoid using quotes?

A: In five cases:

❏ *Never use quotes to "pad" a speech you think is too brief.* Doing so makes your quote have the same effect as the statement we sometimes hear on TV: "And now a word from our sponsor." As Professor Jerry Tarver puts it, "I've never heard *anyone* complain that a speech was *too short*."

❏ *Don't use quotes—other than humorous ones—when you're making brief, informal remarks.* Quotes almost always introduce an element of gravity in speeches. Why? Perhaps because we're used to hearing them mainly in formal talks—sermons, addresses by elected officials, and the like.

❏ *Avoid quotes that aren't in keeping with your personality or background—or the audience's.* Historian Arthur Schlesinger can quote Nathaniel Hawthorne or Woodrow Wilson without sounding a false note, but could Eddie Murphy? Generally, quotes from the Roman historians Pliny and Plotinus won't go over well at social functions held by Local 230 of the Boilermaker's Union.

❏ *Don't use quotes that are overly long—say, more than 25 words.* A quote that goes on and on can be as painful as a 12 year old's recitation of "The Gettysburg Address." Remember, the *audience* didn't come to hear an extended version of Socrates' views about Athenian democracy; the listeners *came to hear your insights.*

❏ *Refrain from quoting anyone whose name or words might draw gasps or boos.* For example, it would not be politic to quote Judge Clarence Thomas as an authority at a meeting of the local chapter of the National Organization for Women—or Ralph Nader at a meeting of the National Association of Manufacturers.

Q: So I guess the main points are to use quotes in more formal talks, to use quotes that are appropriate to the speech and the occasion, and to rely on quotes that are in keeping with my personality and education?

A: Yes. Your best quotes will come from your own experience and reading. When you encounter some quotes you may want to use, write them in your notebook for future reference.

In my work as a speechwriter for a major oil company, I'd sometimes suggest to the CEO that he use a specific quote. He'd always ask: "How would I have known that?" A good question, because he didn't want to sound inauthentic in his remarks. He wanted quotes that he would have encountered *in his life or his reading*, not ones that would sound as if they were provided by public relations advisors.

In looking for usable quotations, don't ignore the correspondence you receive. President Reagan used to quote letters written to him by the American people. He also quoted correspondence from soldiers and their parents, from schoolchildren, from mothers and fathers, and from various other citizens. Reagan knew that we all love to "read" other people's mail. In your job, do you get letters from customers and others that would be instructive for your audiences? If so, quote away.

Good Sources of Information: For *current quotations*, try the large daily newspapers: *The New York Times, The Wall Street Journal* (which has on occasion an editorial page section called "Notable and Quotable"), *Washington Post, Los Angeles Times, Chicago Tribune*, and other large dailies and the weekly or bi–monthly magazines: *Time, Newsweek, U.S.News, Fortune, Business Week, Forbes*, and so forth. Network news or interview shows as well as CNN and C–Span are also good sources for contemporary statements.

If you're looking for books of *quotations by historical figures*, consider the following: the mother of all quote books is Justin Kaplan, ed., of John Bartlett's *Bartlett's Familiar Quotations*, 16th ed. (Little, Brown & Company, 1992). This massive work and its predecessor editions have been around for nearly a century and a half. It contains quotes from Bud Abbott (as in "Hey, Abbott!") to Emile Zola, a listing that runs not only from A to Z, but "from the ridiculous to the sublime." The book also contains an author index and a quotation index, as well as cross–references. One negative I find in *Bartlett's* is that it's so loaded with information it can be overwhelming. Some critics also find Kaplan's choices influenced by "political correctness."

A book that emphasizes *twentieth century quotes* is James B. Simpson, *Simpson's Contemporary Quotations* (Houghton Mifflin, 1988). *Simpson's* is organized by categories (e.g., "Wit and Humor") and indexed by sources, subjects, and key lines. It's very good for "business" quotations. Overall, the book is a delight to page through.

A volume devoted to *quotations by United States figures* is *The New York Public Library Book of Twentieth Century American Quotations* (Warner Books, 1992). The volume is arranged alphabetically by subject ("Age" to "Work") and has an author and source index, as well as a subject index.

Another recent compilation of quotations is Angela Partington, ed., *The Oxford Dictionary of Quotations*, 2d ed. (Oxford University Press, 1992).

For *quotations relating to business and managers*, I'd recommend three books: Lewis Eigen and Jonathan Siegel, *The Manager's Book of Quotations* (AMACOM, 1989); Joe Griffith, *Speaker's Library of Business Stories, Anecdotes and Humor* (Prentice–Hall, 1990); and Louis E. Boone, *Quotable Business* (Random House, 1992).

If you're looking for a *dial–a–quote service*, call "Ideabank," which provides (for a fee) quotations for speakers and speechwriters, at 914–241–4978.

There are many books coming out featuring *quotations by women*: Rosemary Maggio, ed., *The Beacon Book of Quotations by Women* (Beacon Press, 1992). With emphasis on modern figures, Maggio's book features women listed alphabetically (from Maya Angelou and Hannah Arendt to Oprah Winfrey and Virginia Woolf). For quotes by earlier female figures, as well as by twentieth-century women, see the massive work (and labor of love) by Eve Partnow, *The Quotable Woman: From Eve to the Present* (Facts on File, 1992).

If you're looking for *a quote book that can be read cover–to–cover*, there's a fascinating work by Paul F. Boller, Jr., *They Never Said It: A Book of False Quotes, Misquotes, and Misleading Attributions* (Oxford University Press, 1989). Boller points out that Horace Greeley didn't really say, "Go West, young man." And Mark Twain didn't say, "Everyone talks about the weather, but no one does anything about it." Will Rogers didn't say it either. Charles Dudley Warner, editor of the *Hartford Courant* and a Twain contemporary, apparently was the source. (Of course, the possibility exists that before Warner said it, he heard it from Twain. Such are the uncertainties of history.)

If you need *references for quotation books I haven't mentioned*, as I suggested in section 2.5, a good place to look for reference books on any subject is in *The New York Public Library Book of How and Where To Look it Up.*

Tip: The best quotes to use are short ones–a sentence or two–from well–known figures. If the audience is familiar with the quote, (1) you don't have to indicate where it begins and ends, and (2) you don't have to interrupt your remarks to identify that person. Examples of such quotes: "As Churchill put it, 'This was their finest hour.'" "Or, as John F. Kennedy stated, 'Let us never *fear to negotiate*, but let us *never negotiate out of fear.*'" "Or, in the words of the Old Testament, 'The race is not always to the swift.'"

6.5 Finding and Using Anecdotes

Q: What's your favorite anecdote?

A: I've always loved Abraham Lincoln's story about the man who was tarred and feathered and ridden out of town on a rail. When someone later asked him what the experience was like, he said, "If it wasn't for the honor of the thing, I'd rather have walked."

I've used this story many times since I heard it ten years ago. The context I've used it in has usually dealt with my experience as a business manager. Many of the "honors" relating to that position—as with Lincoln's position as President—seem to contain their share of indignity, of tar and feathers. For example, managers get the "honor" of passing on minuscule salary increases and of casting aside loyal employees whose services are "no longer needed." Like all good anecdotes, the Lincoln story blends humor and realism.

Q: Why use anecdotes at all in a speech?

A: I'm not in favor of using lots of anecdotes in a presentation. One is usually enough, two or three at the most. Otherwise, they start to become tedious, to interfere with the line of argument.

Properly used, however, anecdotes add spice to a presentation. They give it concreteness and, most important, memorability. We tend to forget generalizations quickly. However, stories—good, pointed stories—tend to live on in our memories. Years after a speech, we may have forgotten everything but a telling anecdote.

Q: What kinds of anecdotes DON'T work in a speech?

A: First, long ones. Second, stories without a clear point—that is, "shaggy dog stories."

On length: Beware of anecdotes that last longer than 45 seconds (about 75–80 words). If they go on beyond that length, listeners begin looking at their watches. Over–long anecdotes also tend to cause listeners "to lose their place."

On anecdotes whose point is not clear: Using one of these—especially if it's a long one—can destroy a presentation. You don't want the audience's main recollection of your speech to be: "The speaker told a boring story, the point of which escaped me."

Q: What's this about creating my own anecdotes? I've always thought of anecdotes as coming out of books.

A: Personal stories make the best kinds of anecdotes. Creating anecdotes is like creating humor. It's nothing more than telling stories about things that happen to us.

Example: We drive to work in a large city. We hear motorists inching along in an endless line of traffic, honking their horns at one another, cutting each other off, perhaps even screaming apoplectically at one another. What use would this story have? It could illustrate the frustrations of modern life; it could demonstrate the need for mass transit; it could show how too many automobiles and too few highways can undermine people's normal civility.

Another example: We make our morning phone calls. Three people we call are in meetings. In three other cases, we get recorded messages asking us to leave a message. In the last instance, we get someone who cuts us off with the statement, "I'm running to catch a plane." This story could form the centerpiece of a talk on the declining usefulness of the telephone as a business tool, or of remarks entitled, "Who's Minding the Store? Answer: Nobody."

These two self–created anecdotes are not exotic. They describe things that happen to all of us. By turning events into anecdotes, we give them a coherence, a meaningfulness, that helps clarify matters for our audience.

I worked with an executive who was an extremely effective user of anecdotes. Some of his stories relate to his strong advocacy of using computer technology to rationalize the retention of information. He is not a friend of filing cabinets, which he believes take up space and bury information.

He tells a story about visiting an insurance branch office with file cabinets and files stacked on the floor. He saw a small army of personnel climbing over files and rummaging through the cabinets. He asked the branch manager, "Why don't you store a lot of this information on computer tapes, or at least get the file cabinets organized?" The manager replied wearily, "Oh, we're too busy to do that."

This is a marvelous illustration of how people are too busy to make themselves less, well, busy.

Good Sources of Information: Look at the following: Clifton Fadiman, *The Little Brown Book of Anecdotes* (Little, Brown, 1985). It has four thousand–plus anecdotes from 2,000 sources. Indexed by names, subjects, and sources.

Look also at Joe Griffith's book, mentioned earlier, and at Peter Hay, *The Book of Business Anecdotes* (Facts on File, 1988), which is organized by subject.

7

Highlighting the "You" in Your Speech

*I*n companies and other institutions, many people seem to believe that work products are somehow generic—that they do not reflect the efforts of individuals. The phrase "no pride of authorship" is used sometimes as if it were a badge of honor. (Actually, it reflects an abdication of individual responsibility.)

The committee approach doesn't really work with presentations. A group may try—usually in vain—to prepare a presentation. But no group is foolish enough to think that it can *deliver* the remarks collectively.

There is, in fact, no more individual act than standing in front of an audience and speaking. Your subject, your appearance, your voice, your body language, your credibility, your rapport with the audience: these are the tools with which you construct your success as a speaker.

The solitary nature of speaking can be intimidating. For another perspective, however, you should find it profoundly exhilarating. How well you speak on a given occasion depends largely on the individual effort you put into making yourself a strong, forceful, convincing presenter. You become not only the proud *author* of your remarks, but also the main *actor* and *producer* in a dramatic encounter with your listeners.

7.1 Knowing That Content Drives Delivery

Q: Most instructors on speaking emphasize delivery. However, in *Talk Your Way to the Top* you took the view that the content of a speech—its message—is more important. Could you explain your thinking on this?

A: *Most speeches that fail do so before the speaker ever says a word.* They fail because the content of the remarks will not support—will not encourage—an outstanding presentation. *A great subject will not ensure a great speech, but it will make it possible.*

Think about the great speeches of history—from Pericles talking about Athenian democracy, to Lincoln about the Union and the Civil War, to Roosevelt about America's response to the Great Depression, to Churchill about the Battle of Britain, to Kennedy about the "New Frontier," to Reagan about America as a "City on a Hill." The *grand subjects* these individuals had led them to invest their speeches with great energy and imagination.

The "content versus delivery" question boils down to this: If we don't have something to say, it's impossible to say it well. With poor content, delivery becomes a frantic effort to apply cosmetics to a corpse. In contrast, a good subject inspires good delivery, makes the speaker want to establish eye contact; to speak with passion, confidence, and variety; and to get the audience to share the conviction and enthusiasm that underlie the speech.

A few years ago, I became acquainted with a woman who speaks frequently throughout the country. She addresses groups about the need to get drunk drivers off the nation's highways. This is a relatively new role for her. Until a few years ago, she would not even have thought about talking in public to large groups.

Then, something happened. Her youngest son was killed in an accident with a driver apparently intoxicated. Later, she joined Mothers Against Drunk Driving (MADD). She began to speak frequently. Her subject: her own experiences, the role of MADD, and the need for stronger laws against drunk driving.

Does she speak with passion and conviction? Has she "earned" the right to her subject? Are audiences moved to action by what she says? The questions answer themselves. This woman is an effective speaker *because of what she has to say*. Her delivery is effective because she believes so profoundly in her message.

Q: Can you give me some advice on how I can make my messages more interesting and compelling, so that I can deliver them well?

A: Speak on matters you know from *personal experience*. Unless you're an expert on America's fiscal deficit, don't spew out a lot of second–hand generalizations about "The National Debt." Unless you're an expert on the urban poor, don't talk about "The Problem of the Underclass." In the latter case, you'll give a better talk if you discuss a single poor person you know—perhaps someone you've worked closely with in a charitable endeavor. Give some details on how this person became poor and perhaps what is being done to raise the individual out of poverty. And then tell the audience to take an action that will do the same for other individuals.

The point is this: *We are not experts on the matters that form the subject of many presentations. We are experts on our own lives—our personal histories, our families, our communities, our jobs*. To the extent possible, those are things we should talk about.

In fact, that's what our audiences want to hear from us. They don't want us to pontificate on broad national issues. They want to hear us talk about matters on which we have first–hand knowledge and about which we feel some passion.

So when you get a general topic to speak on, ask yourself this question: How can I adjust this subject to reflect my own expertise and interests? If you're asked to speak to a general audience on "The Financial Accounting Standards Board's (FASB) Role in Establishing

Generally Accepted Accounting Principles," don't fall into the trap of doing so.

Instead, focus on one or two of FASB's principles in your own business life. Are the standards sound ones? Can you give examples of how they complicate your work? How do you overcome those complications? What can the audience do to help overcome any problems you identify?

In other words, when you're given an invitation to generalize, ask instead how you can personalize. When your topic is something meaningful to you, it's much easier to deliver it effectively—to speak with conviction.

7.2 Evaluating and Enhancing Your Voice

Q: When most of us first heard our voice on a tape recorder, it was a painful experience. But isn't your voice a little like your nose—something you can't change without the equivalent of major surgery?

A: Far be it from me to suggest a "voice job." In fact, it's not necessary—nor probably even desirable—that male speakers sound like professional actors or broadcasters. Alfred Kahn, Cornell University economist and the father of airline deregulation, has a "New York" accent, never stands up straight, talks a mile a minute; but he's a much sought–after speaker, and a delight to hear.

Your goal should be to make only those improvements that are necessary to make you a more effective speaker.

Q: So should I just talk along with the voice I've got?

A: Generally, yes. If you have a severe speech defect or an accent that renders you unintelligible, you should seek professional help from a speech therapist or voice coach. Otherwise, you should stick basically with the voice you have.

But that doesn't mean you can't make improvements. To determine if you *need* improvement, you should seek out the opinions of others and make your own assessments about what adjustments are desirable.

Q: Exactly how do I go about making that judgment?

A: You have to ask two questions:

❐ First, *do audiences hear and understand what I'm saying when I speak?*

❐ Second, *does the way I sound detract from the credibility and the cogency of my message?*

You can make these determinations, first, by getting honest evaluations from friends and associates and, second, by making your own assessments of audio– and videotapes (refer to section 1.4).

A lot of minor voice problems we might have come as news to us when we first encounter them on tapes. Most such "problems" can be overcome quickly through minor modifications.

Q: What kinds of modifications?

A: Here are the types of problems you might discover and the adjustments you might consider:

❐ *Problem:* Your "volume" is too low for audience understanding, especially in the back of the room.
Quick Fix: Give more emphasis to the key words in your message; longer–term: learn how to speak less from the throat than from the diaphragm. (See also the next point.)

❐ *Problem:* Running out of breath before finishing your statements.
Quick Fix: First, recognize your tendency to take short, shallow breaths, and try to breathe more deeply; second, practice breathing in such a way that your stomach expands.

❐ *Problem:* Speaking in a monotone.
Quick Fix: first, underline (or put in **bold–face**) key words in your text; second, make sure the important words in your

sentences are at the end, where your natural pitch and emphasis will be higher; third, practice your presentation by using exaggerated emphasis, as if you were a dramatic actor in a theater.

❏ *Problem*: Overpronunciation of words, such as pronouncing the "t" in "often," or mispronunciation of certain words, such as saying "fa–kade" rather than "facade" or saying a French name "Lang–loy" rather than "Langlois."

   Quick Fix: First, replace every word in a speech that is not part of your normal conversation; that will include all words that offer any special pronunciation difficulties. Second, spell out the words—phonetically—in your text. Who's to know if your text has "offen" (the correct pronunciation) rather than "often"? Or "fa–sade" rather than "facade"? Or "Lang–lah–wah" rather than "Langlois"? Or "Mao Say Dung" rather than "Mao Tse Tung"?

A variation on the problem of overpronunciation is to misplace the natural emphasis on words. Ironically, this problem occurs many times when we're trying to avoid speaking in a monotone. Former Vice President Quayle sometimes had a problem with misplaced emphases.

For example, he said at one point: "Just **RE**...mem...ber the last time we had a Democratic President and a Democratic Congress." He drew out the first syllable too much. Doing so gave an unnatural stress to the "e" sound, making it physiologically impossible to put enough stress on the second syllable ("mem"). Thus, Quayle's pronunciation of "remember" had an artificial quality.

The most effective way to say "remember" would be to downplay the first syllable (making the vowel sound like the last syllable in the word "sofa") and to hit the second syllable, not the first. The Vice President's problems with pitch and emphasis made him a less effective speaker than he could have been.

Good Sources of Information: If you're looking for books that would be helpful for someone looking to speak more strongly and effectively, look at the works I mentioned earlier by Jeff Scott Cook and Cristina Stuart.

7.3 Dressing for Successful Performance

Q: Does a person's appearance help to determine how an audience receives a presentation?

A: If you're tall, slender, and handsome (or beautiful), for example, it helps. On the other hand, being short and fat didn't hurt Churchill. By the same token, being ungainly and homely didn't seem to sidetrack Lincoln's career. Good, sincere speaking can overcome most "handicaps."

Q: What kinds of clothes should I wear when I make a presentation?

A: It's hard to generalize, but *you should dress at least as well as the audience.* Unless the event you're addressing is truly "formal," however, men won't need a tie and tails, and women can forgo evening wear.

Overall, you should feel comfortable with what you're wearing—and so should the audience. After all, you're asking the listeners to pay respectful attention to you. Also, as we've discussed, you're going to ask them to take certain actions. In matters of dress, therefore, you should be respectful of the audience's tastes. That means no cutoffs if you're being inaugurated as President—and no leisure suits if you're chairing the company's annual meeting.

However, if you're speaking at an event where everyone is in shirt–sleeves (say, in a meeting room), then don't be afraid to roll up your sleeves. Likewise, if you're saying a few words at the company picnic, even a polo shirt and Bermuda shorts may be appropriate. Overdressing on such occasions—"I'm the CEO and thus can't be seen without my gray pinstripe and power tie"—can send a message of exaggerated self–importance.

Q: Can some clothing be distracting?

A: Bulls–eye. You don't want to dress in a way that distracts the audience from your message. In frank terms, female speakers don't want audiences to concentrate on their cleavage; likewise, male speakers don't want listeners to sit there counting chest hairs. It's a good idea to dress somewhat conservatively—to leave the red and green plaids for another day (perhaps an address to the Hibernian Society or "The Friends of Red Buttons").

If we dress inappropriately, we risk having the audience *look* at us—rather than *listen* to us. I'm sure most of us have attended presentations where we ended up wondering: "How could anyone let him out of the house in *that* tie?" Or, "What made her think blonds looked good in chartreuse and teal?" Or even worse, "If he keeps waving his arms, is that toupee going to make it through the speech?"

Q: Aren't you asking for the impossible: for people with *bad* taste to exercise *good* taste?

A: There you've got me. When you're getting dressed for a presentation, it might be good to seek an outside opinion. Ask a friend, your spouse—or a "significant other"—to evaluate your apparel. On matters such as the appropriateness of ties and jewelry, ask your most candid co–workers for an opinion.

Q: Any advice for last–minute checks before giving a presentation?

A: Only one commandment: Be sure to visit the rest room. Other than that, it's a good idea to check to make sure your hair isn't standing on end and, if you're wearing a tie (or lipstick), to make sure it's on straight. (Members of an audience watching a speaker with a crooked tie have an almost irresistible urge to walk up and straighten it.)

Good Source of Information: Even though it was first published in the mid–1970s, a still–useful book on how authoritative, powerful people dress is Michael Korda's *Power: How to Get It, How to Use It* (Warner Books, 1991). It also happens to be a helpful book on the next subject, body language. Korda's *Power* should be on every speaker's reading list because of its clear–eyed discussion of how successful people look and act.

Tip: When you're choosing clothing, consider the temperature of the room where you're speaking. Also, take into account if there are any special conditions that might raise the temperature (e.g., an especially large crowd; lights for videotaping; lack of air–conditioning). In fact, when you're due to speak in a potentially hot room, always have in place someone who can turn up the air–conditioning.

That's why it's a good idea to dress in (appropriate) lightweight clothing. If you tend to perspire heavily, it might also make sense to spray yourself liberally with antiperspirant; also, wear clothing that doesn't highlight perspiration stains; finally, keep your handkerchief handy.

As a general principle: *I've never heard a speaker complain that a presentation room was too cool.*

7.4 Using Body Language to Send the Right Messages

Q: What is "body language?"

A: It refers to the messages sent by your movements and expressions. For example, if you're answering a question and either you don't look the questioner in the eye or have your eyes darting right and left, the movement sends a message, in this case, that you're either very nervous or lying. Another example: People who stride straight ahead at a more rapid-than-average pace convey a sense of power and authority; by contrast, individuals who meander along convey a sense of powerlessness and indecision. Our body language reflects our inner feelings and convictions. Although they might not be aware they're doing so, audiences "read" this language.

Q: What are the main areas where people have trouble with body language?

A: There are four of them: general posture, hands, feet, and eyes (which we'll discuss in the next section).

❒ Posture: *Avoid rigidity (the "Buckingham Palace Posture"), but stand up straight.* You should feel as if you are attached firmly, but not rigidly, by invisible strings suspended from the ceiling. You should be on a podium, if possible, as this reinforces your aura of authoritativeness.

❑ Hands: *If you're talking to a group of people, you should keep them at your sides—except when it's appropriate to gesture with one or both of them.* Don't fold your hands in front of you (known as the "fig leaf" position) or behind you. Also, don't rub them together—known as the "undertaker's sales pitch."

❑ Feet: *Plant yourself as close to the center of your audience as possible—and don't move your feet.* (If the meeting organizers want you to speak at a lectern that is placed to one side or the other, talk to them ahead of time about moving it to the center—the "power position." Also, you want to be fairly close to the group you address; being too far away is like standing on second base and trying to talk to someone in the bleachers.

Some people try to "work off" their nervousness by shuffling their feet—even by pacing back and forth—but this is a very bad idea: It makes listeners nervous and distracted.

Q: It sounds as if having good "body language" is largely a matter of common sense—and of what my mother used to call "good posture"...

A: Actually, most of what you need to know could be summed in the aphorisms about posture and "public speaking" that you heard from your mother, father, and teachers: "Don't slouch—stand up straight"; "speak up—don't mumble"; "don't shuffle your feet"; "don't fiddle with your tie"; "don't stand so far away when you're talking"; "look me in the eye when you talk."

Having authority, as Michael Korda discusses in his *Power* book, is largely a matter of things such as technique and tone of voice. We can gain authority by positioning ourselves correctly in relation to other people and speaking firmly and confidently to them.

Don't forget: *How* we say something depends mainly on *what* we have to say. The poet William Butler Yeats once asked, "How can we tell the dancer from the dance?" His point is that the dance is an outgrowth of the dancer. The same is true of body language. It's an outgrowth of the speaker's emotional and intellectual "investment" in the remarks. It's not a separate subject. You couldn't have a useful course in "body language" that didn't relate it to speaking and listening.

If speakers are passionately committed to their subjects, generally they will stand up straight; they will talk directly to their entire audience, not just to part of it; they won't mumble into their shirt fronts; they will show in their posture and gestures their confidence—their conviction—in the importance and rightness of what they're saying.

Q: When I look at tapes of my performances, I know I'm committed to my subject. But I still stand up there like the proverbial cigar–store Indian. How can I learn how to use gestures?

A: The good news is that you can *learn* a lot about how to use appropriate gestures. The even better news is that most of us already know a lot about them. The problem comes about when we restrain our natural tendency to use gestures, when we think, for some reason, that they're inappropriate or unnecessary.

But if someone asks you how big the fish you caught was, what do you do? You indicate its size with your hands. You do the same things when you're talking ruefully about the short putt you missed on the eighteenth green. And when you're discussing the size of a professional basketball center you stood next to, how do you do it? You stand on your tiptoes and raise your hand up over your head. These are natural—almost spontaneous—gestures.

The more comfortable you are speaking in public, the more natural you will find it to use gestures. They will be an outgrowth of your efforts to paint verbal pictures for your listeners. You will find yourself using your hands to drive home points; to indicate relative sizes; and to indicate your attitudes and emotions about the subjects you're discussing.

Q: How can I practice using gestures?

A: It's a variation on the idea of painting verbal pictures. Make up—and talk out—stories that contain a lot of movement and outsized physical details. For example: *"I was walking up a steep hill when I saw a strange couple. He was about four feet–two inches tall. She was at least six–foot–ten. He was riding a unicycle. She was pushing a huge baby carriage, which ran over my toe, pitching me off the sidewalk into the road. A car bore down and I had to leap back onto the sidewalk. I yelled at the woman, 'Watch out where you're going.' She turned to me and then stuck her thumbs in her ears and wiggled them at me."*

As you speak the words, indicate every physical detail and movement with gestures. Practice by creating your own action–filled stories. This will make it easier for you to use gestures and to create verbal pictures in your presentations.

Good Sources of Information: In addition to Korda's book, consult Julius Fast, *Body Language* (Pocket Books, 1971).

Caution: If you're using a prepared text, don't spend any more time than necessary looking down at your script. To do so sends the wrong messages: It says that you're reticent, deferential, and that you lack confidence in what you're saying. (In the 1984 vice–presidential debate, candidate Geraldine Ferraro looked at the top of her lectern when she wasn't responding. Many people thought she was consulting notes. She wasn't; she had no notes.) In one of the 1992 debates, President Bush kept looking at his watch. Did he have an important appointment? Perhaps a job interview?

7.5 Standing Still on Stage—or Walking Around?

Q: You've talked about the need to stand in one place. However, what if you have to stand in one place for a long time? That's hard on the speaker—and the audience. Any thoughts?

A: A few years ago, Tom Peters wrote a book (*In Search of Excellence*) in which he advocated "management by walking around." In the case of a typical presentation (less than half an hour), it's probably best for the speaker to stay in one place. Otherwise, it's easy to get off–center and to start talking to one segment of the audience while ignoring the rest.

After the presentation—for example, during the Q & A—speakers should consider moving around. Speaking from a lectern for an hour or more is an excellent way to lose an audience. *Variation is a key to learning.* So if you're obligated to speak to people for a long time, try to vary everything—including your speaking position.

In conducting a Q & A, you may move *slightly* off–center, perhaps first to the right, then to the left. You may also want to walk a row or two into the audience. (Most of the people in the first two rows will turn to see you.)

Generally, however, don't walk to the back of the room, because everyone will have to turn around to see you.

Q: How will I know whether to "walk around" or not?

A: By the response of your listeners to what you're saying. If you notice their eyes glazing over, it's time to vary your routine—and to get moving.

Have you noticed what happens when you stare at one object for a long time? You start to become transfixed, and your attention turns inward. If you see your audience becoming mesmerized, it's probably time to "change your location."

For example, what if you're teaching a class that lasts an hour or more? Here's one approach that was successful. In the 1960s, I attended the University of Rochester. One professor there, Ralph J. Kaufmann, was an exceptional teacher. He also was an exemplar of the speaking–while–walking–around approach.

A graduate seminar I took met for three hours—a long time for a class to stay awake and alert. When Kaufman lectured, he would sit for a while. Then, he would stand and walk to one side of the classroom and then the other. At times, he would wander over to the window, fiddling at times with the curtain rod while he spoke. He was always on the move.

At one point, a student asked, "Dr. Kaufman, why are you always moving around?"

He replied, "I was a student before I was a teacher. And I know it's not easy to pay attention over a long period. So I walk around. And when I move, your eyes go with me. That tends to keep you alert and listening."

7.6 Learning The Proper Role of Eye Contact

Q: One thing I always hear in discussions of public speaking is that it's extremely important to maintain eye contact with the audience. Do you agree?

A: Yes, with one significant qualification. *Eye contact is not a magic technique that somehow will rescue a poor speech.* Looking members of the audience in their eyes—and wanting to do so—should be a *result* of a strong message and good preparation.

Without involvement in your subject, without a commitment to share your ideas and insights with the audience, without adequate speech preparation, eye contact is nothing more than a mere device.

Think back to childhood. Why were we sometimes unwilling to look our parents in the eye? Perhaps because we were ashamed of something we had done—or left undone. We knew even at an early age that "the eyes never tell lies," so we averted our gaze. On the other hand, we had no such problem when we had nothing to hide, so our gaze was clear and steady.

It's the same with speakers. When they're proud of what they have to say—and when they've done all in their power to say it well—they don't have to worry much about eye contact. They want to get their message across. Believing in their message, they have no hesitancy to look into their listeners' eyes.

Eye contact should be more than a stage technique. It should be a reflection of our confidence and commitment.

Q: If I have trouble taking my eyes off the text while I'm speaking, is there some way I can begin to "wean" myself from the text?

A: One technique that works well is this: *As you approach the end of each sentence look up at the audience.* You'll be able to retain in your mind the words at the end of the sentence, and the brief glance upward won't cause you to lose your place.

Q: I hear what you're saying. But where exactly do I look? Specifically, if I'm talking to dozens of people, which ones do I look at? One or two people? Everyone?

A: You don't have to give each person 15 seconds of eye contact. Instead, *as you speak, look into the eyes of several people throughout the room.* Concentrate on those individuals who seem most interested in what you have to say. If you do that, you'll come across just fine.

Concentrate on establishing eye contact with various people by communicating your points in a forceful—and sometimes impassioned— way. By doing so, you'll be making real points to your audience; you'll be talking person to person.

You might make a statement directed to one person in the audience; then you can make your next point to another individual, if this approach makes you comfortable. Or you might make part of the point to one person and another part to another individual.

By the way, don't worry too much about *maintaining* eye contact with specific listeners. If you do, some listeners might wonder why you're staring at them.

Tip: One way to force yourself to establish eye contact is to *choose your "contactees" before your presentation.* Say to yourself: "I'm going to make this presentation to Joe, Elizabeth, Andy, Sue, Ralph, and Jim, among others." You'll base your choices on the fact that you know these people and feel comfortable with them. You might even note in your text at certain points: "Talk to Joe...talk to Elizabeth."

7.7 Getting and Maintaining Credibility

Q: What is "credibility?"

A: It's the same as "believability."

Q: Can you give me an example of how business executives, for
example, *lose* credibility?

A: A lot of time it's because they forget one of the most
famous of the Yogi Berra–isms: "The game's not over
till it's over." In their duties, executives sometimes have
to announce bad news, earnings declines, layoffs
(called "restructurings," but meaning layoffs), plant
closures, and so on. They'd much rather announce that
the bad old days are over—that happy days are here (or
on the way) again.

But premature announcements of good news can be overtaken
by events. So the normal human tendency "to look for the silver
lining" can lead to credibility problems. Unless you're absolutely
certain the bad news bears have returned to their lairs, be cautious
in your optimism.

Trying to foresee the future often leads to credibility problems.
During the energy crises of the 1970s, oil company executives were
always being asked to predict the price of gasoline. Many did,
against the advice of their public–relations advisers (including me).
Why were we against these predictions, especially when they were
about all the media were interested in hearing from the oil companies? Because they were a Catch–22.

Suppose the executives said the price of gasoline would be
below a dollar. If that prophesy turned out to be true, critics would
say, "I told you so. The industry controls the price of gasoline." If
the predictions turned out to be wrong (as they usually did), critics
would say either (1) "the executive misled us"; or (2) "the executives
didn't know what they were talking about." To protect your
credibility, leave the foretelling of the future to the people who've
invested in crystal balls.

Another point: Because we *hear* what people say and generally *don't see what they do*, words can speak louder than actions. *But it's absolutely crucial that our actions not conflict with our words.* If you're telling people, for example, to give blood, be sure you're ready to roll up your own sleeve. Audiences will forgive you almost anything except hypocrisy.

Q: Are there some things we can say that are *in*credible on their face?

A: You've got a good point. *Some things people say in presentations are instantly reversed—disbelieved—by listeners.* That is, the audience assumes just the opposite of what they hear.

For example, a company I worked for announced the layoff of thousands of people. Simultaneously, a company "human resources" publication came out. Its first words were, "Our employees are our most important resources." That statement, which is usually disbelieved by employees anyway, was especially absurd given the company's situation. If employees were "our most important resources," why were we getting rid of them?

Company spokespersons often fall into two traps: first, giving insincere praise ("let's put in a pat on the back for the employees"); second, setting goals they can't meet ("therefore, our intention for the next decade is to realize a 20 percent compounded return on our shareholders' equity"). Don't give praise unless you mean it. And don't make promises unless you're certain you can keep them.

Q: I'm fascinated by the notion that there are some things we say that are almost *always* disbelieved. What are some more of these things?

A: Maybe the most famous one is: "The check is in the mail." In businesses, any statement that implies that profits are not the organization's primary concern ("Our most important priority as a company is training our work force to meet the challenges of a new century").

In nonprofit or government agencies, any statement that implies continued employment is not the employees' central goal ("Our only purpose in life is to advance the public interest").

In elective politics, any statement that implies reelection is not the overriding concern ("I don't want you to send me back to Washington unless you believe I can be an agent of meaningful change").

Most listeners respectfully ask that we not insult their intelligence. In presentations, don't say things you don't believe. Tell one good-sized "whopper" to people, and they'll never trust you again.

Q: Credibility obviously is a matter of being consistent and cautious in statements. But is it also a question of things such as tone of voice, of sounding "sincere"?

A: As usual, a good question. People do judge us on the way we sound. A juror who had been the last holdout on a jury that convicted a woman in a murder case reportedly shook her head and said, "But she had such a *nice voice*." Let's face it: the most successful con-men (and con-women) in history must have been very credible in some ways. Otherwise, they wouldn't have been so successful.

The other side of the coin is that some people who are sincere aren't perceived that way. What can they do to rectify that? They can follow the advice in this book, which emphasizes being direct and forceful. When they don't know an answer, they can admit it. In fact, most of us tend to equate credibility with imperfection. When someone is too "perfect," too "slick," we find that person to be *in*credible.

Tip: When you're making an important point, be sure you use the right words. One Republican congressman criticized his Democratic colleagues, saying: "they're not likely to accept a Republican plan unless they've changed it and put their 'imprimature' on it." He meant "imprimatur," a Latin term meaning permission to print. When we misuse words, we undermine our credibility. People say, "How can I believe this speaker when the words being used don't make sense?"

8

Maximizing Your Speech's Effect

A great deal of effort goes into preparing, practicing, and delivering your presentations. But when your final words are uttered and the audience's applause has died out, some important work remains. In fact, the ultimate effect of your remarks can depend on the work you do *after* you have delivered your formal presentation.

For example, the question–and–answer period can strengthen the impression made by your remarks—or it can weaken it. The keys to a successful Q & A are: to resist being defensive (especially in the face of pointed questions); to resolve any concerns listeners may have about the course of action you've urged on them; and to reiterate the main points—and the call to action—you've made in your remarks.

Beyond the Q & A, you can maximize your speech's effect in a variety of other ways, including: finding out how listeners responded to it (so you can make improvements in your next effort); retooling the speech to make it appropriate for delivery to other audiences; making it available in printed form to interested individuals; and preparing "speech releases" and newspaper articles based on your remarks.

Properly distributed (and modified), a speech originally given to fewer than 100 people may reach an audience of thousands—even tens of thousands. This will greatly amplify your voice and multiply the influence of your speeches.

8.1 Understanding the Role of the Q & A

Q: The Q & A period sometimes seems to be the "tail of the dog." A lot of times it seems to be an add–on to the presentation, without any clear purpose...

A: You're right. A lot of Q & As seem disorganized and disconnected from the remarks that preceded them. When that happens, it's generally the speaker's fault. If the remarks have been good, thought–provoking ones, there should be some good questions. If the speaker has anticipated the questions, as should be the case, the answers will be brief and pointed enough to encourage still more questions.

Throughout the Q & A, the speaker should tie questions and answers to points covered in the presentation. In other words, the Q & A, rightly conducted, should be a spirited, but positive, expansion of the main issues in the speaker's talk.

Q: You mentioned speakers should prepare answers in advance? How can they do that before they hear the questions?

A: Think about it. When you frame your presentations in terms of your own experience and knowledge, you're talking about matters you know well. That's why you were invited to speak. Your knowledge of the subject, combined with additional study you do in preparation for the talk, will enable you to answer most questions you will get.

Let's face it: Questions don't come out of the blue. People tend to ask the same kinds of questions you would have if you were in their shoes.

For example, if you're asking colleagues to contribute to a local charity, people will want to know things such as: Where does the money go? How much goes to the needy, how much to administration of the program? What levels of contributions are appropriate? Can contributors target their donations to specific programs? What about the well–publicized scandals with certain national charitable organizations? Is there anything similar happening with the charity you're championing? Is the charity controversial, and, if so, what do you have to say about the controversy? What about people who make substantial contributions to other charities—their churches, for example? Are they also expected to contribute to the charity you're recommending?

Mentally prepare yourself to answer these questions and you'll be ready for any question you might reasonably expect.

Q: When I give a talk, there never seem to be any questions, and that's kind of embarrassing. I see the same things with other speakers in our organization. Why the lack of questions? And what can we do about it?

A: There are three reasons why audiences are silent during Q & As:

❑ First, *individuals are embarrassed to be the first to speak up to ask a question;*

❑ Second, *the talk may have been too "pat" and bland to encourage questions;*

❑ Third, *the remarks may have consumed so much time that the listeners are eager to go somewhere else.*

In the first case: Listeners too shy to ask questions: You can "plant" a question or two by a friend in the audience. That generally encourages others in the audience to raise their hands and join in.

As for the "pat" talk that discourages questions: *You need to ensure that your remarks are provocative and pointed;* raise some real, pressing concerns, and you'll get plenty of questions. Don't try to antagonize your listeners, but don't hesitate to challenge them.

In the case of the overly long remarks, the solution is simple: *Keep your remarks short enough to allow plenty of time for the Q & A.* If you ever find yourself saying, "Well, we have only a minute or two for questions," you've talked too long, and you won't get any good questions.

Q: What about the situation when the audience has plenty of questions, but the speaker takes off on the first one or two, and time runs out before other issues can be raised?

A: A question deserves an answer, not a speech. Speakers need to remind themselves that audiences don't want answers to the riddle of the universe. All answers should be relatively brief—perhaps 75 words (about three quarters of a minute) at the maximum. Seventy–five words may not seem like many, but it was more than enough for the "Lord's Prayer."

In Q & A, the tendency is to over–answer, to make discursive comments rather than pointed responses. Many times, a poor Q & A session can undo the results of an otherwise strong presentation. As I've indicated, the best Q & A's result when a speaker anticipates questions and prepares brief, informative answers. When speakers do that, they tend to retain control of the Q & A and use it as an extension of their prepared remarks.

Caution #1: If you believe the question session for your remarks will be important, try to avoid having your speech fall just before lunchtime or at the end of the work day. In the first case, listeners' stomachs take precedence over their intellectual hunger. In the second case, even a spirited Q & A is no match for home and hearth.

Caution #2: Avoid ever responding to a query with a "How dare you ask that" answer. If you do respond in that way, the questions will cease—at that Q & A and at any others you might hold in the future.

8.2 Preparing for and Handling Difficult Questions

Q: What should you do if someone asks you a nasty, hostile question? Should you ever refuse to answer it? Should you suggest that it's unfair?

A: First, don't refuse to answer it—unless you've already given an answer you honestly believe is adequate. In that case, you can refer the questioner back to your previous statement. Second, don't categorize a question as "unfair," because that will put you on the defensive. Instead, rephrase the question.

Q: How do you do that, rephrase?

A: Suppose you're an accounting or financial person talking to manufacturing personnel. One of them asks: "How can you bean–counters and financial guys sleep at night? You're taking over the company. We don't make products any more; we make numbers for you guys to manipulate."

This statement is less a question than an accusation. Don't get flustered—or angry. Instead, reframe it in a way that makes it answerable. You say, "Your question really deals with the relative weight the company gives to manufacturing and marketing needs versus financial considerations." You may then go on to point out that the company can't make products unless it remains profitable and maintains appropriate financial controls. Again, keep your answer short and your emotions even–tempered. Long (and contentious) answers tend to antagonize hostile questioners.

Or suppose you're a speaker who works for an oil company, and you get the following question from an environmental activist: "You talk about supplying the country's energy needs. But you don't talk about things like the Alaskan oil spill, or about polluting our precious waterways and beaches. Isn't it true that your company, far from being a good corporate citizen, doesn't give a damn about the environment...that you're motivated only by greed?"

Respond coolly, cerebrally, and concisely to this kind of question, reframing it dispassionately: "Your question deals with our company's policy toward protecting the environment." You might then state that policy and tick off actions it has taken to transport oil safely.

Finally, suppose you're talking to employees about the need to control costs so the company can remain competitive. At the end of your remarks, you get this question: "Isn't cost control just another name for laying off people—tossing them out in the street—and overworking the people who are left?"

In answering this question, you need to do two things: Again, resist the temptation to respond heatedly; and don't answer the question on its own emotionally loaded terms. Instead, reframe it in rational terms, for example: "Essentially, you're asking if the company's cost–control efforts will involve layoffs."

If it will, say so, and add what steps will be taken, if any, to ensure that the layoffs are minimal. You might also say that controlling nonpersonnel costs is the best way of ensuring job security.

It's sometimes hard to be polite to questioners who are unfair or obnoxious. But it's essential that the person conducting the Q & A remain unfailingly polite and civil. Hostile questioners are looking for a fight; they want to "get your goat." But if you respond to their heated inquisitions with calmness and rationality, you'll generally see the fight go out of them.

Q: But what if questioners persist in making you answer a question on their terms? Maybe a question you'd rather not answer?

A: Let me give an example of a device that's called "bridging." It refers to answering a question briefly and then moving—bridging—to a larger question that's more to your liking.

Suppose you're talking about worker safety, and someone raises the question of several employees who died the previous year in a work place accident. And suppose your company pleaded "no contest" to an Occupational Safety and Health Administration (OSHA) citation growing out of the workers' deaths. Your answer might go like this:

> We deeply regret the workers' deaths and the sorrow it brought to their families and all of us. We've taken vigorous steps—including our new safety training program—to correct the matters cited by OSHA. But the fact remains: Over the years, our company has had an outstanding record on worker safety. And we're committed to having the best record in the industry on work place safety.

The "bridging" technique here starts with the words "But the fact remains." You've moved to an area where you can make a positive statement.

In some cases, "bridging" can refer to moving from one subject to another. If, for example, a questioner is complaining about employee–pay increases, you might say a few words about that subject and then bridge, for example, to nonwage benefits.

You can see the bridging technique at work during political campaigns, especially in debates. For example, anyone who paid attention to the three–way race for the U.S. presidency in the 1992 election saw pervasive examples of "bridging." Faced with a weak economy, President Bush attempted to change the subject to Bill Clinton's character. ("But the real issue is...")

Clinton, when asked questions relating to character, sometimes refused to answer ("I've said all I'm going to say about that") and instead said, "The real issue in this race is the economy." In–again, out–again candidate Ross Perot bristled whenever questions about his character or past history were raised. At one point he said, in essence, "Here we are talking about this peripheral nonsense and ignoring the issues of real concern to the American people."

Q: What should I do about the person who gets up in the Q & A and launches into a long statement—starts giving a speech?

A: In a Q & A, members of the audience can ask questions; they can't—or shouldn't—make speeches. When a supposed questioner gives a long–winded statement with no question in sight, you should raise a polite objection. *The first time the windbag pauses for a breath, break in—politely but firmly—on the windbag and ask, "But what's your question?" If the blowhard persists, ask again: "Do you have a QUESTION?"* (To see this technique in action, watch some of the popular television talk shows.)

Remember: Treat bad manners politely, but firmly.

Q: What should you do when you're asked a question and you don't know the answer?

A: In two words: "Fess up." Say, "I don't know the answer, but I'll find out and get back to you right away." If the questioner is unfamiliar to you, get a name and phone number so you can reply as soon as you get the information. (If you delay providing answers, don't assume the questioners have forgotten. They never do.)

When a question stumps you, there's a temptation to: (1) make up an answer, or (2) talk at great length about how and why you don't know the answer. Don't do either. There's no shame in not knowing everything. (But get back to the questioner as soon as possible.)

Caution: Don't ever make fun of a question—or imply that it's "stupid." If you do, you'll never get another question—either from the person you embarrassed or from anyone else.

8.3 Gauging the Speech's Effectiveness

Q: When I ask people who've heard me speak how I did, they always answer with platitudes: "Great job"; "Good speech," and so on. How can I get honest evaluations so that I can work on areas that need improvement?

A: You've hit on a good point. A speech should be like your other business efforts; you should have ways of measuring success or failure. Members of the audience usually won't give you candid assessments of your performance. As we've discussed, listeners invariably are sympathetic to speakers. Their attitude: "I'm happy I wasn't the one who had to prepare and give that presentation."

If you ask for a critique of your performance, moreover, some people will be suspicious. That's especially true if you're requesting "presentation critiques" from individuals who are your subordinates. They may wonder: "Is this some kind of test that, if I fail it, will cost me my career?" Similarly, your business equals will be hesitant to offer constructive criticisms of your performance; they don't want to risk offending a colleague.

Finally, most people just are not good critics of oral performances. They know when they're interested—and when they're bored.

But they don't tend to pinpoint specific aspects of a performance that the speaker could improve.

Q: So what's the answer?

A: *It's crucial to find someone who will give you useful evaluations of your presentations.* After all, you don't make your remarks for yourself. You make them for the audience's benefit, so it's essential to know how your listeners responded to the presentation. How can you improve if you don't know your deficiencies?

That's why you need to *seek out one or more individuals who will give you candid, useful comments about your presentation.* This individual may be a spouse or a friend, although you will need to evaluate their objectivity. More likely, you will find your "designated critic" among your colleagues.

The best such critics are people known for their own skill in making presentations. Tell the chosen person(s) that you're sincerely interested in improving your presentations and that you'd like their candid advice and help. Invariably, they'll be honored to provide such assistance.

Q: What's the best way to offer criticism if *I'm* asked to be a "designated critic?"

A: *Remember to mix praise with criticism.* Always start by pointing out to speakers what they did right. Your praise will be especially welcome if you back up your general comments with specific illustrations. For instance, you might say: "Your anecdotes were especially effective—especially the one about the 911 operator arguing with you about the seriousness of your emergency."

Also, *mention only those matters the speaker can reasonably be expected to improve in future presentations.* For example, if the speaker has a mild regional accent, it's probably not something you should mention. Don't nit–pick, focusing, for example, on a minor stumble over a word.

In addition, always suggest ways the speaker can overcome shortcomings. For example, if a lectern is "off center"—not in the center of the room—suggest moving it in the next presentation.

The most helpful critiques talk about matters such as: subject; development of the topic (including illustrations and anecdotes); clarity of language; delivery and voice; and audience reaction.

Q: Could you provide an example of an actual critique of a speaker's performance?

A: Here's one I gave an executive at a major corporation:

❐ *(Subject):* "Your subject—the need to make the buying of insurance a relatively painless process—was right on target for the sales and marketing people in your audience. You might have considered expanding the topic to make it more inclusive—and thus more pertinent to the staff people present."

❐ *(Development of the topic, including illustrations and anecdotes):* "Your line of argument emphasized the logic—and the market necessity—of improving customer service. The anecdote about the customer who kept getting put on hold—and then called up another insurer—seemed to grab the audience's attention. Because of the success of that story, you might consider a slightly more anecdotal approach in the future."

❐ *(Clarity of language):* "Because the words you used were clear, simple, and conversational, the audience seemed to have no trouble understanding your message. (But let's not use the word "facade" again in a speech. It's one we use rarely in speech and that audiences almost never hear, so they puzzle over it.) When you deliver this message next month to customers, however, you need to "translate" the insurance jargon (e.g., words such as *loss ratio* and *combined ratio*)."

❐ *(Delivery and voice):* "The use of the TelePrompter was a real plus. It made the presentation seem effortless and "natural." One area for improvement: You tended to use the prompter on the left much more than the one on the right. As for your voice, it was firm and strong throughout. I think the technique of underlining and highlighting words in the text has helped overcome the monotone problem we discussed last time."

❐ *(Audience Reaction):* "Generally positive. Most people seemed ready to heed your call to action ('Go back to the office, call up your two best customers, and find out exactly how well you're serving their interests.'). But one person said: 'Customer service takes time, and that's something that's a rare commodity here.' Maybe that's an issue to be tackled in your next presentation."

Caution: Don't provide *unsolicited* critiques. If you do, the speaker may be offended.

8.4 Retooling Speeches For Different Audiences

Q: It takes me a lot of time to put together a good speech. Then I give it, put it away in my file, and forget about it. Somehow that doesn't seem like a very efficient use of the time that went into the speech...

A: It isn't. Most business speakers assume that they can use a speech only once. In this sense, they need to learn a lesson from the politicians, who know the virtues of what they call their "stump speech." Those are remarks delivered over and over again—with appropriate modifications—to different audiences.

Don't look at a speech as a verbal version of a cut flower—allowing your remarks to wilt over time. Instead, look at a speech as an evolving artifact—a product that modification will allow you to use in various circumstances.

In fact, *delivering a speech gives you unique insights into how to enhance it.* That's because you've had the experience of having an audience *respond* to your remarks. You know: which lines piqued your listeners' interest; which lines energized your delivery—which ones enervated it; which arguments got an audience nod—which ones a frown or a head shake. *At the moment the speech is "done," it's ready to redo in a stronger, more effective form.*

Q: What about redelivering a speech verbatim?

A: I can imagine circumstances where you might do this, for example, if you're talking to two groups with the same jobs and backgrounds. But in most cases, it's usually not a good idea. That's because any speech should reflect a specific audience's knowledge, background, and interests. There's sometimes a temptation—one you should resist—to grab an old speech at the last minute and give it word for word. But *any speech worth giving is worth targeting to a unique audience.*

Q: Can you give me an illustration of how I'd go about retooling a basic speech for different audiences?

A: Take a speech on "Accounting: No Longer 'The Green–Eyeshade Guys in the Back Room.'" These remarks would make the point that accounting is becoming more important in modern business; it is not just an elevated form of bookkeeping; it makes increasing use of computer technology to deal with complex financial and tax issues; it is a key tool in one of the most important areas of today's economy: identifying and controlling costs.

How you retool a speech like this is a question of how you can make it interesting to different audiences. For example, suppose you reuse it for a high–school's "career day." In that case, you would need to simplify the language, eliminate jargon, and assume a little familiarity with business on the part of the audience.

Later, you might want to give the same message to a civic club interested in "Today's Changing World of Business." For that group, you could assume (some) more knowledge of business and perhaps even a nodding acquaintance with accounting.

Finally, you might give the talk, appropriately modified, to other departments in your company. In that case, you could assume more familiarity with business (although perhaps not with accounting); and you might add sections on how modern accounting serves the interests of nonaccounting segments of your company.

Q: Just out of curiosity, what might the "calls to action" and the benefits to the audience be in a speech modified in the way you've just described?

A: For the career day, it might be: "If you're good with numbers and want a challenging career, I urge you to major in accounting. It just might be the best decision you ever made."

For the civic club, it might be: "Don't just talk to your accountants at tax time. Call them today. Tell them you want them to be partners in making your business more cost–effective and profitable."

For the departments at your company, the call to action could be: "When you have an accounting question or problem in your department, pick up the phone and give me or my associates a call. When it comes to accounting, we really are here to help you."

Tip: When you consider giving a speech you've delivered before, pay special attention to who will attend your remarks. Imagine your dismay if you arrive at the podium with your set speech, look out at the audience, and see many faces who have heard your speech before! It's a good idea to get a list of attendees so you can ensure that the speech will be new to your listeners.

8.5 Using Speeches as Strategic Tools

Q: What do you mean by using "speeches as strategic tools"?

A: Many business executives note in surveys that they spend half their time or more on communications. Yet they tend to look at their speeches and other public statements—one by one. They don't view presentations and other communications as related to one another and as growing out of a unified, coherent business purpose. Unfortunately, this tends to put "speaking" in a role analogous to the company picnic—nice, but not essential.

It's rare for businesspeople to sit down at the beginning of the year and say: "This year I'm going to make a half dozen or more important presentations. What is the overall purpose of these presentations going to be? What are my messages going to be? How can I use these communications to help the company meet its business goals?"

Speakers also should try to measure the effectiveness of their presentations, just as they measure other aspects of business performance. That is, are these speeches accomplishing their objectives? For example, if you're speaking to various sales groups on the need to stimulate new business, is it being done? Is the sales force more motivated? Are sales up? If not, are your communications partly at fault?

People need to make their presentations part of their business plan. In fact, any individual who sees presentations as peripheral to real business activity should give fewer speeches.

Q: I think I understand what you're saying, but could you give me some examples?

A: Here are a couple:

In the "go–go" years of the 1980s, I worked for a company that was acquisition–minded and consequently needed to borrow heavily. One criterion we had for choosing speech engagements was whether the audience consisted of people who controlled large sums of money.

We accepted, for example, an invitation to speak to a small group of businesspeople in Des Moines, Iowa (in mid–February). Why? Because the listeners were mainly executives from small and mid–level insurance companies, which generate large cash flow and invest heavily in commercial ventures.

At this company, we had a running joke: When we got a speech invitation, we asked, "What color is their money?"

One business executive who looked at communications strategically is Ron Compton, CEO of Aetna. During the fall of each year, Compton would outline his presentation themes for the year. He would deliver his version of a "State of the Company" message at Aetna's fall meeting of its commercial insurance managers. Then he took the themes from that presentation and spent the rest of the year expanding on them in other presentations.

Most people would be surprised to find out that these kinds of systematic approaches to speeches are rare in business.

8.6 Distributing Speech Copies

Q: A few months ago, the local Rotary Club asked me to speak about one of my company's successful new products. It took me about 25 to 30 hours to prepare the speech, and there were about 30 people at the luncheon. Doesn't that seem like an awful lot of time to put into a speech for a small audience?

A: You defined your audience too narrowly. *When you deliver a significant speech to an outside group, the people who hear it are only a small segment of your potential audience.* You should send copies of your remarks to individuals and groups who would have an interest in your message. They include:

❐ First: *Employees of your company.* They will be interested in information that affects their livelihoods.

❐ Second: *Customers.* If your remarks deal with products, customer service, or changes in the personnel they deal with, they will appreciate receiving your presentation.

❐ Third: *Major suppliers.* Because their business success is tied to *your* business, they'll be interested in developments at your company.

❐ Fourth: *Members of your trade (or professional) association.* They'll be interested in communications that bear on issues of interest to your industry or profession.

❐ Fifth: *Elected officials, federal, state, and local.* These people are always interested in receiving information—especially of a positive sort—about institutions in the district they represent. (If the developments you describe are highly positive, they might give you the ultimate compliment: taking credit for them.)

❐ Sixth: *Other influential people who have a link to your company* (among them, major shareholders and executives of other area companies).

❐ Seventh: *The news media.* (When you send your speech to this important, specialized audience, it should be accompanied by a news release, which I discuss in the next section.)

Tip: Among the most important people who receive copies of your major presentations are your own employees. With the increasing use of electronic mail at many companies, speech distribution has become easier. Put your speech on a computer tied into your electronic mail system. Then, as soon as possible, "zap" the speech to selected individuals on your system.

Caution: The ease of sending speeches electronically can add to "E–mail clutter." So restrict such distribution to speeches you might reasonably expect recipients would want to see.

8.7 Repackaging Remarks as News: Speech Releases

Q: I've heard of a "news release." But what's a "speech release"?

A: A speech release is one in which news is announced in a speech. The "news" part is important. If you're just giving a speech outlining your views on a subject on which you have no real new information or insights, there may not be much news value in it. Unfortunately, for example, your views on free enterprise or the balance of trade probably won't excite the editor who determines what's news and what isn't.

Q: What is "news"? How do you define it?

A: "News" occurs when something tangible—and of interest to a news outlet's audience—takes place. Usually, it's an event or an action that will affect a community, a state, or a nation. Layoffs are news—unfortunately, more so than additions to the payroll. Plant closings are news (although they're rarely announced in speeches). So are facilities expansions (which should be announced in speeches, but rarely are). New product introductions aren't generally news, except to trade publications, unless the product is a block–buster.

One company that adhered to the newsmaking principles I've outlined was Dupont, under its legendary former chairman, Irving Shapiro. When Dupont did something noteworthy—say, build a new facility or win a major safety award—Mr. Shapiro invariably would announce it in a speech. This approach was a factor in his prominence in the business community. It was also a subtle way for Dupont to enhance its public image.

Q: What things should a speech release contain?

A: A speech release should have several elements besides, of course, news:

❏ *The letterhead of the organization providing the release. Special letterhead stationery saying "News from [name of your organization]" is desirable.*

❏ *The name(s) of the contact person(s) for the news media to call if they have questions.* If your company has a public–relations person, this individual probably should be listed as the contact.

❏ *A brief, catchy headline—perhaps done in bold face type—summarizing the information contained in the release.* The media may not use this headline, but that's okay. Its purpose is to attract the media's own interest in the release.

❏ *An engaging opening sentence—the "lead"—that will engage the interest of the reporter or editor looking at the release.* If the lead does not hook that person's interest, the release probably will end up in the wastebasket. So make the lead provocative and "newsy."

❏ *The name, title, and company of the speaker, as well as the organization addressed.*

❏ *A mixture of quoted material and summaries of the material in your presentation.*

❏ *Page numbers if the release is more than one page. (Generally, it should be no more than a page and a half.)*

❏ *A numerical (– 30 –) signal when the release is at its end. The number "30," preceded and followed by a hyphen, is the traditional journalistic notation for the end of a piece.* Its use establishes for journalists that there are no more pages to come.

Tip: When your company has a newsworthy event taking place, it's a good idea to announce it in a speech. For example, if you're going to expand a facility in a certain town, arrange to break the news in a speech to a civic group. And be sure to invite local reporters and provide those who attend–and those who don't— with a copy of the speech release and the speech.

Announcing the event in a speech will help to maximize the publicity you get. It can result in a substantial story given a prominent place in the newspaper or a radio/television story. In addition, the speech text will provide quotes for the reporters who write the story.

8.8 Retooling the Speech for the Print Media: Op Eds

Q: What is an "Op Ed" article?

A: It's an article (essay), usually about 600 to 800 words, that's submitted to a newspaper or a magazine for publication. In newspapers, these pieces appear on the page opposite the editorial page, thus the term "Op Ed." (Some writers say the term refers to the opinion–editorial page. Take your choice.)

Q: I don't want to sound lazy, but...after preparing, giving, and distributing a speech, why would I want to go to the additional trouble of doing an Op Ed?

A: Look at it this way: You might give a speech to 100 people. You then might distribute copies to a few hundred additional people. But with an Op Ed, your modified speech might be read by thousands of people. The added effort of creating such an article is usually worth it.

Also, as soon as a piece appears in print, it gains credibility and status. So be sure to distribute copies of your Op Ed widely to executives and other co–workers, customers and prospects, members of your trade or professional association, community leaders, and elected officials.

Q: Give me some examples of the kinds of speeches that could be turned into Op Eds attractive to editors...

A: Suppose you're a personnel executive and you've given a speech on employment opportunities in tough economies. You need a catchy lead. So you come up with: "Even in a recession, getting a job can be as easy as one–two–three. That is, you can find a job if you follow three simple principles." Perhaps your three principles might be: contact every employed friend or acquaintance for job referrals; look for jobs in growth industries; be prepared to relocate to faster-growing regions.

In a recession, everyone is worried about getting (or losing) a job. So your subject is one that will appeal to the typical readership for most newspapers. That will get you over the first hurdle on the way to the finish line: publication.

With your lead sentence, you clear the second hurdle, catching the editor's eye. Your speech may not have said the exact words that "getting a job is as easy as one–two–three." But framing it that way will help make your Op Ed submission attractive to editors—and readers.

Any speeches that discuss topical issues of interest to people who read a given newspaper or magazine can be turned into Op Eds: labor–management cooperation; business support of education; productivity–enhancing steps; legislation that will affect business and the general public; worker health and safety issues, and so on.

Q: What kinds of things should I keep in mind while turning a speech into an Op Ed?

A: Here are a few:

❐ *Keep the personal, conversational style of your speech* (but eliminate any points that are specific to the speech—mentions of the audience, for example).

❐ *Eliminate the repetition of ideas that is helpful in a speech but a mark of redundancy in an Op Ed.*

❐ *Cut out all superfluous material, remembering that while the average speech is about 2,000 words, the average Op Ed is about one third that length.*

❐ Revise and target your material to the new audience you're trying to reach: the publication's readers.

❐ Use your call to action, but determine if it might be better expressed as a "point of view." (That's because essays are a less emotional forum than speeches. In an essay, very strong emotion sometimes comes across as shrillness.)

Q: Is it necessary to send a cover letter with the Op Ed piece?

A: Yes. The cover letter should be no more than one page. It should contain a paragraph on what the article says, another paragraph on why it would be of interest to the publication's readers, and a third paragraph briefly outlining why you're well qualified to speak on your subject. The final sentence should state your *sincere* openness to any suggestions the editor might make.

Q: What if the publication rejects my Op Ed? Should I file it, or pitch it?

A: You should make whatever adjustments are necessary, compose a new cover letter, and send it to another publication. Editors, especially those at large, prestigious daily papers and weekly newsmagazines, receive carloads of Op Eds, so rejection is no dishonor. Some good Op Ed pieces have been rejected many times before they've finally been placed.

Tip: If you're interested in how to target your Op Eds to specific publications and audiences, I urge you to read Mary Jane Genova's article on the subject in the September 1991 issue of *Public Relations Journal*, p. 32. This publication can be found in most larger libraries. Ms. Genova knows whereof she speaks. Her Op Eds have appeared in *The New York Times*, *The Wall Street Journal*, *Washington Post*, *Newsweek*, and *Newsday*, among others.

Using Visuals as True "Aids"

To use them or not to use them. That is the question. There's no aspect of presentations where more confusion exists than with the use of visual aids.

Keep in mind that modern audiences are more sophisticated visually than their predecessors. That's because of the great influence of television. The implication for speakers is that low–quality visuals are no longer sufficient. Audiences increasingly expect visuals to be well made and professionally presented.

Spoken and written words have been the foundations of communications for thousands of years. In the future, the use of visuals will certainly increase. Some experts predict that speakers will need to become more conversant with the use of video clips and, perhaps, with musical accompaniment. Thus, the *form* of your communication may change, but the *goal* will remain constant: to get your point across to listeners.

9.1 Making Visual Aids Assets in Your Presentation

Q: When should a speaker use visual aids in a presentation?

A: When they're not just cosmetic, but a real asset to the presentation. *With visuals and the spoken word, you should try for a one–to–one relationship: one visual, one idea.* The visual reinforces a point that would be hard to communicate in words alone.

For example, if you're talking about what happens in a car crash to people who aren't wearing seat belts, you could describe it in words. However, it would be much more meaningful—and *graphic*—if you showed a video clip.

Similarly, you could talk about Marilyn Monroe's or Clark Gable's special appeal to the opposite sex, but photographs of them would do it better.

Or, if your business' earnings have quadrupled in the last five years, the mere expression of that fact could not compete with a line–graph showing the earnings emulating the takeoff of a Saturn rocket.

Q: Could you give a couple of examples of situations where visuals have been used with special effectiveness?

A: We saw a very powerful use of visuals made during the Gulf War against Iraq: the videos of "smart bombs" in action. This was a classic case of something having to be seen to be believed. Pictures of laser–guided bombs being fired through airport hangar doors and into concrete "seams" of hardened bunkers will stick in most of our memories forever.

What if the pictures had not been available? Many people might have assumed the verbal descriptions were exaggerations. The Gulf War was a case where visuals were essential to understanding the role of new technology in warfare.

Another instance where visuals were used superbly was in a public service announcement featuring Dr. Henry Heimlich. He was the man who developed "The Heimlich Maneuver" to eject food from the throats of choking victims. He later appeared on television demonstrating that his maneuver is also the best approach for potential drowning victims. He asserts that mouth–to–mouth resuscitation will not work well when the victim's lungs are full of water.

In his television spot on drowning, Heimlich used a child actor. The doctor demonstrated how rescuers can find the bottom of a child's rib cage by feeling with their fingers. Then Heimlich made a fist, just above the child's navel and under the rib cage. Grasping his fist with the other hand, Heimlich pressed in hard (although not hard enough to break the child's ribs). On cue, the child/actor expelled a mouth–full of water. Was the ad graphic and memorable? I saw it once and remember every detail.

Q: What about things such as sales meetings and conventions? Don't audiovisuals work well there?

A: Absolutely. One of the best uses of audiovisuals is in establishing a tone—setting a mood—for a meeting. A visual of an American flag waving while a record plays the Mormon Tabernacle Choir singing the National Anthem generally gets a meeting off to a rousing start.

Major productions take time and talent to produce. So unless your organization has a top–notch A–V staff, it's a good idea to engage professionals to do them. Amateurish productions are an embarrassment both to the presenter and the audience.

Q: In what circumstances should speakers avoid using audiovisual aids?

A: When they don't add anything to the presentation. Take those awful things called "title slides." These are words masquerading as visuals. The speaker starts talking about, for example, the Soviet Union, and a slide pops up containing the words "Soviet Union." What does it add? Nothing.

In addition, resist the temptation to use slides as a crutch. Some people who are anxious about speaking in public use visuals to camouflage that fact. They apparently believe that if the audience concentrates on visuals, it won't notice the speaker's inadequacies. The result? Some of the worst slide presentations ever endured by listeners.

Don't use visuals as an electronic fig leaf. If you have fears, fight your way through them in the presentation. The next time you make a presentation, you'll find the fears have diminished.

Q: What kinds of things can go wrong when speakers are using audiovisuals?

A: Just about everything you could imagine:

- ❐ *Slides:* You left them "back in the office"; the bulb burns out in the projector; a slide sticks, and the carousel won't operate; the room isn't long enough for the slide image to be seen clearly by the audience; the windows have no shades, so the room can't be darkened; the electricity goes out—and the electrician has disappeared;

- ❐ *Transparencies* suffer many of the same fates as slides; also, the room is sometimes set up so the projector blocks the view of most listeners;

- ❐ *Video–clips:* you push the button to activate your video and nothing happens, or you get reruns of "The Oprah Winfrey Show"; your videotape is the wrong size for the videotape player; the screen is too far away for the audience to see. And on and on.

Q: Wow. Do you have some kind of checklist for a speaker to go through to make sure these kinds of things don't happen?

A: It's best to develop your own list, remembering Murphy's Law: "Anything that can go wrong will go wrong." But here are some general points that you should keep in mind when drawing up your list:

- ❐ *THE ROOM:* Is it large enough to accommodate your equipment? Can it be arranged so that people can see your visuals clearly? Does it have the right kind of electrical outlets? Are there any problems with lighting that will make your visuals difficult to see? When you need to darken the room, can the lights be dimmed and/or the shades drawn? Will the room be cool enough for people to remain awake when you turn down the lights? What will be going on in adjoining rooms? For example, will the Tuba Society be holding its convention/jam session while you're playing your audiotapes? And, of crucial importance: do you know where the rest rooms are?

❐ *THE EQUIPMENT:* Are you certain it will be available (e.g., chalk to write on the board)? Will you have a chance to practice with it prior to the meeting? Is it the right kind for your visuals? Does it work (e.g., has the ink dried up in the felt pens for the flip charts)? If you're using slides, is there a remote–control device? Do you have spare parts (e.g., bulbs for slide carousels and Vu–graph projectors)? If you haven't used this equipment before, do you know how to?

❐ *ASSISTANCE:* If there's no remote–control button for the slides, will you have someone available to run them? If there's a problem with the room (e.g., too few chairs), whom do you contact for help? If you have an electrical problem, do you know how to get in touch with the electrician imme diately? Is someone going to bring an extra copy of your text, visuals, and handouts in case you somehow misplace yours?

Q: But what if a glitch occurs, and the A–V equipment just doesn't work? What do you do then?

A: Here's an important piece of advice: *Always be ready to give your presentation without the audiovisuals.* If you're not, what will happen if, for example, your slides are locked in the trunk—with your keys?

In other words, learn how to wing it. Be able to integrate brief, pictorial descriptions of important visuals in your remarks. If you can't show your visual of a car crash, for example, be able to talk about metal bending and heads banging into the front windshield. Be able to substitute "oral pictures" in place of the missing visuals.

Q: What about the actual visuals themselves? What kinds of things do people do wrong in putting them together?

A: *I've mentioned the need for slides, transparencies, and video clips to be professionally made.* Modern audiences are used to high–quality images on television and in magazines and other media. So they're instantly aware when visuals are not well done. Audiences tend to be intensely aware of audiovisual imperfections, concentrating on them rather than on the message the A–Vs are meant to convey.

Another big mistake occurs when people try to put too much information into their visuals. In visuals, as in so many other areas of communication, *less is more.* Visuals should be clear and simple—never cluttered. Some presenters appear to believe the opposite: that unless they fill their visuals with words, numbers, and complex charts, they'll be shortchanging the audience. Not so.

Lean and mean(ingful) should be the rule in visuals:

❐ *On line graphs, try to have one line, two at the most;*

❐ *On bar graphs, never have more than five bars, fewer if possible;*

❐ *On pie charts, have a limited number of segments; if you do otherwise, the audience will concentrate on trying to determine what the slivers represent;*

❐ *On visuals that verge on having too much information, highlight the parts you want to emphasize.*

What's the point of these directives? The more comparative elements you have in visuals, the harder it is for the audience to grasp the significance of each one.

Q: You've criticized having words and numbers on visuals. What's wrong with them?

A: *Generally, words don't belong on your visuals.* In fact, visuals are (or should be) by definition used in lieu of words. Save the words for your remarks. The only exception is labeling visuals with brief, headlinelike descriptions (e.g., "EARN-

INGS: 1990–1995"). (If, for some reason, you do need to use words in addition to the titles, make sure they are both lower– and uppercase; they're easier to read that way.)

Numbers are like words: if you have more than a couple of numbers, they just don't work well in visuals. They're hard to see. And if there are a lot of them, they're confusing. I've seen single slides with 30 or more numbers on them. That slide might be on the screen for 20 seconds. Hitting an audience with more information than it can assimilate frustrates your listeners.

Tip: Remember, *your visuals must be visible and high quality.* The elements on the visual must be large enough—and clear enough—for the audience to see what it is. If you ever find yourself apologizing for a visual's quality, you shouldn't have been showing it in the first place.

9.2 Using Slides Effectively

Q: What are the advantages of using slides over, say, transparencies or charts?

A: Let's start with charts. They're fine when you have a small audience grouped in front of you. But when the audience and the room it's in are large, charts can be hard to see, causing you to lose the effect of the visual.

Also, if you have a lot of charts, they can be unwieldy. By contrast, slides are compact, and, unless the room is a very small one, they usually can be seen by everyone in the audience.

We'll discuss transparencies in detail later. But, in general, unless they're very well made, they tend not to be as sharp as 35 millimeter slides.

Q: What are the kinds of mistakes people make in using slides?

A: The main mistake is putting a slide up, talking about it, and then forgetting that it's up there as they go on to other points. In addition, there are several other mistakes:

❒ *Failing to have their slides professionally made,* so that audiences note their poor quality rather than their message;

❒ *Failing to have the slides encased in glass or translucent plastic,* thus increasing the time it takes the slides to come into focus;

❒ *Projecting them from too close a distance,* thus getting small images that can't be seen by those in the back of the room;

❒ *Having letters and words on the slides that are too little to be read with ease;* (Generally, it's best to avoid having words on slides.)

❒ *Trying to put too much information on slides,* which reflects a failure to recognize that slides—like speeches—are a poor vehicle for presenting detailed information.

❒ *Having the screen go blank for a time rather than turning off the carousel power when they're finished showing slides;* (The answer is to turn off the carousel or to have an opaque slide in it.)

❒ *Using slides sporadically throughout a presentation, rather than bunching them together;* (This sometimes results in lights having to be turned on and off several times; it always ruins the continuity of the presentation.)

❒ *Mixing horizontal (regular–sized) and vertical (taller, narrower) slides,* which calls attention to the slides' format rather than their significance.

Q: What are the implications for speakers that the sense of sight is more intense than that of hearing?

A: Just this: *When your slide appears on the screen, you should pause for about five seconds (about as much time as it takes to say, "pause for about five seconds)," give or take a second. That gives your listeners time to react to the slide and to interpret its meaning. When they do, they'll be ready to hear your words.*

This is a crucial point, but one unknown to most people who use slides. They'll generally flash a slide on the screen and start jabbering. But the audience doesn't hear their words, at least not clearly, because its attention is focused on the visual. If anything, the speaker's premature words are an irritation, an interference with the audience's attempt to grasp a visual meaning.

If you're not used to pausing when a slide comes on the screen, it will help to practice this approach. Also, it will help if you make a note in your text to pause.

Q: But what if my slide can't be understood in five seconds—if it's more complicated than that.

A: *For a slide to be effective, it has to be simple enough and its essential meaning clear enough for the audience to understand its general meaning fairly quickly.* That rules out complex or confusing slides. Don't use them. If you have a slide that's too complicated, simplify it, perhaps by making it into two slides.

Q: I'm a little mystified. If I'm showing slides and their meaning is clear almost instantly, what do I talk about?

A: A fair question. You talk about the implications of the slide, its larger significance.

Let me give an example: I once saw a slide used by the head of a small, new company whose earnings had grown at an incredible 50 percent compounded rate over three years. The slide showing the earnings growth looked like a CEO's fondest dream.

The executive showed the slide, let it sink in, and then said: "Can we sustain this kind of earnings growth? Not forever. What would happen if our profits grew at this rate for another 25 years? Our earnings would then equal the combined earnings of the 100 largest industries in the *Fortune* 500."

He used the slide to show dramatic earnings growth. He used his words to put the slide's message into perspective. He also suggested, by implication, that profit growth makes small companies bigger, which, in turn, makes profit growth more difficult.

Q: Should I tell the audience what the slide represents?

A: This is a matter of judgment. It may be necessary to give a brief explanation of what the slide represents, for example, "Here are the company's earnings for the last three years."

But in some cases, explanation would be superfluous. If you put on the screen a picture of a Boeing 747, with its insignia painted on the fuselage, you don't need to say: "Here's a Boeing 747." Ask yourself: "Will everyone in the audience know what this is?" If the answer is yes, then don't tell them.

Q: Is it okay for me to glance at the slide when it comes up, so I can be sure I have the right one?

A: It's not a good idea to be twisting and turning to look at slides. It's disconcerting to the audience. It's also a good way to lose your place in the text.

Here's a better approach: Arrange your text and photocopies of your slides in a three–hole binder. When you finish discussing a slide and turn the page, a photocopy of the new slide should be on your left, with the text copy on the right. You can arrange this by having a photocopy of the appropriate slide on the back of the preceding page of text.

Q: How many slides should I have in a 20–minute presentation? Are 10 or so about right?

A: As visual–communication expert Sue Barrett of Aetna puts it, "You should have as many slides as make sense visually." If 1 is enough, fine. If 40 is the right number, fine. (If you can, however, have your slides bunched; it makes for a smoother presentation.)

Q: After what you said earlier about not having words on visuals, I almost hesitate to ask: But where do you stand on what are called "build" slides?

A: Some people swear by them. Basically, they are a group of slides containing the same words, with different segments highlighted in consecutive frames. I've almost never met a build slide I liked. They're always word slides, and words have limited effectiveness in visuals.

Tip #1: Slides should have a lot of what journalists call "white space" (and some graphics people call "negative space"). That is, they shouldn't be cluttered with images, lines, words, and so on. If you see empty spaces on your slides, cherish them; don't try to fill them up. Keep your slides as simple—as "clean"—as possible, and you will increase their effect.

Tip #2: Some presenters work effectively with slides containing a lot of charts and graphs. Done well, such slides can be effective with business audiences. Remember, however, that nonbusiness audiences generally are not as familiar with charts and graphs. Thus, it takes such groups longer to understand this kind of graphic material. The answer? Either restrict the use of such slides with nonbusiness groups or provide more explanation in your text.

9.3 Making and Using Overhead Projection Transparencies

Q: I know one company that uses overhead projection for every presentation they make—inside or outside the company. What would you say to them?

A: I'd suggest they read *Speaker's Portable Answer Book*. I wonder if that company would recommend that the President of the United States give the inaugural address using overhead projection transparencies? Some presentations benefit from visuals, others don't. Overhead projection is not an appropriate medium to use in every circumstance.

Q: What are the pluses in using this kind of visual aid?

A: Transparencies are relatively easy to make, either using infra–red copiers or plain–paper copiers. Instructions for making transparencies usually come with the film. Making slides is a more complicated process and requires a professional's touch. Also, slides are more expensive to make than transparencies.

In addition, overhead projection, unlike its slide counterpart, generally doesn't require turning down the lights. So it's easier to stay awake—and, especially, to take notes—than it is with slides.

There are other advantages: The equipment is readily available at most companies and meeting facilities and the transparencies can be switched around easily, unlike slides, which are relative "captives" in their carousels.

Also, some people find it an advantage—I don't—that presenters can write on transparencies or their acetate covers. I don't recommend that because it's disconcerting to see hands writing (or, alternatively, the projector being continually switched on and off).

Q: Is that one of the big disadvantages of overhead projection—the switching on and off?

A: You've got it. People who use overhead projection are faced with two choices, neither of them especially attractive. They can switch the projector off and then on every time they want to put a new transparency on the platen (the glass). Or they can provide the audience with the "light–and–shuffle show" as the equipment projects first a lighted, blank screen and then their hands trying to get the transparency straight on the glass. In both cases, the audience finds it distracting.

Another disadvantage with older–model overhead projectors is that the cooling fans tend to be noisier than their counterparts in slide carousels.

Q: Do I detect an element of dislike for overhead projection?

A: The problem is that watching overhead projection presentations is a little like watching people play golf. Done well, it's fun to see. Done poorly, it's agony to watch. Many of the people who rely heaviest on overhead projection have little experience in making presentations. Because they don't have to watch themselves in action, they fall into all the traps that await novice users of overhead projection.

Q: If you could give just one piece of advice to people using overhead projection, what would it be?

A: Make sure the projection equipment works and that it's in the right place—not too close to the front row, or too far away from it. If they do this, they'll avoid two problems: blocking of the audience's line of sight and projecting of poor–quality images on the screen.

Using overhead projection is one visual form that cries out for examining the presentation site and adjusting the equipment. For some reason, however, this is almost never done. Perhaps overhead projection is so common that people somehow feel it's failure–proof. It's not.

Q: What other tips do you have to improve the professionalism of overhead projection presentations?

❑ Tip #1: *If your test of the projector—and you should test it—reveals images wider at the top than at the bottom, tilt the projector up;*

❑ Tip #2: *If the projected image is too big or too small for the screen, move the projector backward or forward.*

❑ Tip #3: *Don't place the screen in the center of the room,* as this can block the view of many in the audience; *instead, put the projector at an angle and the screen to the presenter's right in the corner.* (Left–handed presenters may feel more comfortable if the screen is on their left.)

❑ Tip #4: *As with slides, pause when the transparency goes up on the screen* so the audience can absorb its visual significance. (If it's necessary to explain what the image is, be very brief.)

❑ Tip #5: *As with slides, don't let yourself get between the projected image and the screen.* (This is somewhat more of a problem with overhead projection, especially when the speaker is moving around putting transparencies on and taking them off the equipment.)

❑ Tip #6: *If possible, have a (well–rehearsed) assistant put transparencies on and take them off, as well as turn the projector on and off;* this tends to give the spoken presentation more continuity.

❑ Tip #7: *Resist the temptation to talk while you're turned toward the screen;* that is, don't talk to the audience with your back turned.

❒ Tip #8: *Don't try to point to things on the screen*—this is known as the "Bugs Bunny effect," referring to the image your hands will create; *instead, refer to the places on the transparency* (e.g., "In the upper left–hand corner").

❒ Tip #9: *If you have some transparencies you'll want to refer to more than once, paper clip them (or put small tabs on their side) so they'll be easy to find.*

❒ Tip #10: *When you've discussed your last transparency, turn off the projector (or have your assistant do so).* There's nothing like a bright screen to attract the attention of moths—or audiences.

9.4 Mastering Flip Charts

Q: In this high–tech era, aren't flip charts something of an anachronism?

A: Flip charts are a little like paper clips: They've been around forever, but we haven't found anything better with which to replace them. They're the "old shoes" of audiovisuals, not pretty, but serviceable and comfortable.

Q: What are the keys to using flip charts well?

A: If you proceed systematically and keep the following points in mind, your flip charts will be the envy of all who view them:

❒ First: *Use flip charts only in "meeting–sized" rooms.* Otherwise, those in the back rows won't be able to see them.

❒ Second: *Make sure the metal structure holding the flip chart is solid;* those devices have a way of falling over.

❒ Third: *Do all your writing on flip charts before your presentation begins.* (I know: some presenters like to write on the charts during the presentation. However, this results in the speaker's back being turned to the audience, which is disconcerting. *The only exception is when you're writing down points raised by the audience*.)

☐ Fourth: *Avoid "flip–chart fixation," which consists of looking at the words on the chart rather than the audience*.

☐ Fifth: *Print the words on the chart with large, block letters*. (Most printing on flip charts is too small; also, cursive writing is sometimes hard to read.)

☐ Sixth: *Don't use charts with colored paper; stick with white. And don't write on them with soft colors*, for example, pink, yellow, or light green. Instead, use black (generally preferable), red, or dark blue.

☐ Seventh: *Before your presentation, make sure the pages on the chart don't stick together*. (If they do, it can disrupt your remarks while you look for the missing information.)

☐ Eighth: *Keep the flip chart to your right, the audience's left*. Why? It just seems to work better that way. What if you're left–handed? That won't matter if you've done the writing *before* the meeting.

☐ Ninth: *Make sure you're not blocking any of your listeners' view of the chart*.

Tip: Like transparencies, flip charts work best in informal presentations and settings. They're a "shirt–sleeve" kind of A–V. For formal speeches, it's probably best to go with 35–millimeter slides.

9.5 Using Television Prompters

Q: I've noticed that people such as the speakers at national political convention use television prompters. What are television prompters and what's the advantage in using them?

A: The prompter is a video monitor that displays text that's being fed by an operator into a machine. The text appears at—or slightly above—eye level. That eliminates the major disadvantage connected with a traditional written text: the need to look down periodically at it. Throughout a prompter presentation, the speaker can maintain visual contact with the audience.

The prompters growing popularity results from the "natural" look it gives to presentations. In fact, many listeners at such presentations think they're hearing an "off the cuff" speech.

Q: Are there any problems with this kind of technology?

A: The very ease of using prompters causes some speakers to think that rehearsing their presentations isn't necessary. The result can be monotonous speeches delivered without grace or enthusiasm.

In addition, like any mechanical and electronic equipment, prompters occasionally fail. This can be a problem when the speaker cannot switch rapidly to a traditional written copy.

Here's how to make the switch: First, always have a speech text with you. Second, make sure you have a friend or colleague following your remarks on yet another copy of the written text. Then, if the equipment fails, that individual can refer you—with a minimum of awkwardness—to the exact page and line where you should begin reading.

Q: Are some prompters better than others?

A: Yes, the older equipment tended to be cumbersome and quite visible to the audience. The newer varieties, however, are hardly noticeable. The best kind is the one that uses two small pieces of Plexiglass, one in front of the speaker to the left, the other to the right (for looking at both sides of the audience). The device functions something like a see–through mirror. The audience sees only clear plastic, but the speaker sees the speech text. Meanwhile, the operator feeding the prompter text is hidden to the side of the stage or behind a curtain.

Q: Where can you get prompter equipment, and does it take special skill to operate it?

A: Larger companies generally buy equipment from one of a number of suppliers. The best equipment can be expensive,

$20,000 or more. That's why smaller organizations generally rent the equipment from audiovisual–production companies.

In a prompter presentation, the operator is the second most important person—right after the speaker. It's important that the operator feeds the text at the right speed. If not, the speaker will have to read faster or slower than is desirable. It's crucial to have an operator who's experienced and who has a strong sense of a particular speaker's verbal cadence.

It's absolutely essential that a speaker rehearse a presentation with the person who will be operating the prompter. If the operator and the speaker are not in "sync," the presentation may resemble a record played at the wrong speed. It's essential that the operator feed the copy at a speed with which the speaker is comfortable.

Caution: Suppose you finish writing a 20–minute speech less than an hour before you're due to give it? There may not be enough time to get it on the machine that feeds copy to the video monitor. If you have changes made just before the presentation, ensure that the operator knows precisely where in the text they go and has enough time to insert them onto the prompter copy. If the changes are handwritten, make sure they're legible.

9.6 Integrating Video Clips into Presentations

Q: What's your view on speakers spicing up their presentations with video clips?

A: When they provide a striking visual effect, clips can enhance a presentation. Generally, you'll want to use videos that show *action*. For example, if you're speaking about a new fighter plane that takes off vertically—like a helicopter—it would make sense to show a video clip. Subjects such as sports events, moving vehicles, and physical confrontations (including wars) lend themselves to video.

Beware, however, of showing static scenes on video. People chatting ("talking heads") don't make a good subject for videos. In fact, those kinds of videos can slow down your presentation and bore your audience.

Q: Would you give a specific example of how a video clip was used effectively in a presentation?

A: Consider a clip that was used in several presentations made at Aetna. The company had a program in which it donated hundreds of video cameras to local police departments. The law officers used the equipment to videotape drivers suspected of driving while intoxicated.

In the company's presentations, the speaker described the program (called "Eye on DUI"). Then, the television monitor came on. It didn't show exactly what the audience expected: a drunken driver apprehended by police. Instead, it showed an intoxicated motorist fleeing the police. As the camera rolled, the car raced into an intersection, where it broadsided another vehicle. The Aetna audiences invariably gasped in shock.

One key to the effective use of video is to incorporate the element of surprise.

Q: What kind of things are important to make sure a video clip fits in well in a presentation?

A: There are several things to consider:

❐ *Make sure you rehearse using the video clip exactly as you will in the presentation.* That way you'll know how much introduction the clip needs and, even more important, exactly how to get it on the screen (that is, what buttons to push);

❐ *Don't let a video that somehow fails to materialize torpedo your presentation.* If for some reason your video clip fails to appear on the screen, be ready to describe in detail what the audience has missed. That will prevent your presentation from having an embarrassing "hole" in it.

❐ *Make certain the video monitor screen is large enough for the audience to see it.* A normal–sized television can be barely visible from the back of a good–sized room. (If you don't have access to a big screen, one solution is to have several smaller monitors throughout the meeting room. Another is to use video–projection equipment to enlarge the image on the screen.)

❐ *Don't let the excessive use of clips chop up your verbal presentation.* If your goal is to make coherent remarks, you don't want to end up being an MC for a bunch of video spots. In other words, with video clips, as with so much else in presentations, avoid excesses.

9.7 Using Personal Computers in Presentations

Q: How can you use personal computers as part of a presentation?

A: You can use them to:

❐ *Make and print out the graphics you will put on transparency film to use with an overhead projector;*

❐ *Construct graphics you will use to illustrate your points to a small audience (probably four or fewer people) gathered around your computer;*

❐ *Show graphics you display by connecting your computer to projection panels (made by 3M Corporation) attached to an overhead projector;*

❐ *Show graphics displayed by connecting your computer to a video projector that will project the graphic images onto a large screen;*

Q: What's the advantage of using a PC as opposed, say, to making slides?

A: There are two advantages: first, PC graphics can be made much more quickly—and updated more rapidly—than can slides; second, skillful operators can use the PC to create animation. (On the first point, it would be possible to make modifications to many PC graphics in less time than it would take to make one slide.)

Q: Is it possible for the presenter to operate the PC while making a presentation?

A: It is, and it's often done in meetings of small– and medium–sized groups. With larger groups and conferences, it's probably better to have an assistant operate the computer while you give the verbal part of the presentation.

Q: Would you provide an example of a PC presentation used in a real–life situation?

A: The following example shows how PC presentations can serve the goal of the rapid visualization of information. A major insurance company held a three–day meeting of its agents, who gathered in various workshops to discuss problems and rank them in order of their seriousness. As the meeting went on, a PC operator turned the information from the various meetings into graphics. (At the same time, a speechwriter prepared a presentation based on the meetings and coordinated her work with the PC operator.)

In the final session of the meeting, the company had a PC presentation showing the results of the meeting in graphic form and a speech discussing solutions to the problems raised. Using a PC allowed the company to create graphics until just before they were used in the presentation.

Q: Is there any downside to using personal computers to create visuals?

A: Only one I can think of. Because it's relatively easy to produce graphics with a PC, it's possible to get carried away—to create visuals for the sake of creating visuals.

Caution: If you do use an assistant to run the computer, be certain to practice together—just as you would with a prompter operator. It's vital that the visual and oral parts of the presentation be tightly integrated. Otherwise, it will lead to audience confusion.

9.8 Using Objects as Props

Q: How can using "objects as stage props" enhance a presentation?

A: When you hold up an object—an "exhibit"—in front of an audience it can have a powerful effect. Long after your listeners have forgotten your exact words, they will remember the object—and what it represented. *Whatever grabs the eye sticks in the mind.*

Q: What kinds of objects are you talking about?

A: Anything that will make your presentation more interesting. For example, I once heard a corporate executive from Westinghouse talk about miniaturization and electronics. He held up a new calculator that was extremely thin. He then held up his credit card to demonstrate that it was about the same thickness as the calculator.

In another case, a business executive used props to make a point about how his company had changed its planning process. He indicated that the company's traditional business plans had consisted mainly of interminable lists of financial numbers. To illustrate, he held up one of those business plans; it required two hands to get it aloft. He dropped the 300–page document with a loud thud.

Then he held up one of the new business plans, which deemphasized statistics in favor of discussing vital business issues facing the company. When he dropped this slimmed–down document, it barely made a sound.

By showing the business plans, the executive gave tangible evidence of an otherwise abstract point: the changes in the company's planning process. He knew that the visual and aural stimulation his listeners received from the business plan hitting the table would keep his point fresh in their minds.

Other examples of the use of objects include:

❏ A picture of a retirement gift (an antique buggy) that was too big to bring to the ceremony;

❏ A plaque that an instructor received from a class he had taught;

❏ Several large volumes of the U.S. Tax Code shown by a CPA advocating tax simplification;

❏ A local "yellow pages" directory exhibited by a salesperson talking on "The Best Way to Find Sales Prospects."

❏ A cartoon in which a boss is explaining to his subordinate, "Johnson, I've decided you're ready for additional responsibility, so I've decided to blame something really big on you."

❏ A bag of mulch and several vegetables raised by an advocate of organic gardening;

❏ An ancient catcher's mitt displayed by an individual talking on "How I Became a Big–League Catcher: Not!"

❏ A book published by a first–time author;

❏ A key to a house purchased by a first–time home buyer. (This was exhibited by a mortgage lender talking on "But Mommy, What Do Bankers *Do*?")

Q: How exactly should you use objects?

A: Here are several guidelines:

❏ First, *make sure the audience can see what the object is.* If it's too small for clear viewing, explain what you're demonstrating.

❏ Second, *hold your object aloft to your left or right so the audience can see it, but without obscuring your face.*

❏ Third, *glance at your prop, but don't gaze at it.* (In other words, talk to your audience, not your prop—even if it's your childhood Teddy Bear.)

❏ Fourth, *put the object away* (for example, on a table) *after the audience knows what it is.* (Have a secure place for the exhibit, so it doesn't call attention to itself—e.g, by fluttering away if it's a picture or a piece of paper, or, if it's heavy, by crashing to the floor—after you have used it.)

Q: Can you provide some suggestions how I might use objects imaginatively in business presentations?

A: What about hoisting a bulging "In Box" in a talk advocating shorter memos and reduced paper flow? Or holding up one of your products and then one of your competitor's, pointing out how yours is superior? Or holding up first a golf ball and then a bowling ball, with the former representing your company's earnings 20 years ago, the latter this year's earnings? Or vivifying a "contribute to local charities" presentation by showing pictures (with the individuals' permission) of people helped by the contributions? The possibilities are endless.

9.9 Putting Hand-outs in the Right Hands

Q: If you have hand-outs, is it a good idea to put them on the chairs before the audience arrives?

A: No. If you leave your hand-outs on the chairs, the audience will come in, pick them up, and read them while you're making your presentation. If you want them to listen to your words, *don't make the hand-outs available until the end of your presentation.*

In certain cases, you might want the audience to have your materials in hand during the question period following your remarks. For example, if you have certain statistics you want to refer to, it might be helpful for the audience to have the numbers in front of them. Generally, however, you will want to give the materials to the listeners as they're preparing to leave the room. Then, if they wish, they can examine them later.

Q: What usually happens to hand–outs?

A: Generally, one of two things: either they're filed away somewhere, never to be seen again, or they're thrown away. If you
don't want your materials to suffer one of those fates—and
most speakers don't—there are several steps you can take:

❐ First, *emphasize the value to the listeners of examining the hand–
outs.* (If they're not really going to be useful, you shouldn't
distribute them.)

❐ Second, *make the information on them clear and minimize the
amount of text.* Busy people don't want to have to wade
through column after column of print and numbers.

❐ Three, *make the material on the hand–outs eye–catching and
interest–generating.*

❐ Four, *consider doing the hand–outs in color.* People assume that
material in color is more significant and valuable than that
in black and white.

Above all, have the quality of the hand–outs—in form and
content—equal to that in the presentation. You don't want poor–
quality material to undermine the effect of your remarks. *If it's
crucial to your purpose that the audience read the hand–outs, go all out:
Have them made professionally and put them in a nice, reusable binder.*

Q: What exactly do you mean by hand–outs that are "crucial"
to a speaker's purpose?

A: One good example would be a sales presentation where
several groups have been invited to make their "pitch." In
this case, hand–outs that, well, stand out could be a key to
getting the business. That's because the hand–outs—not the
presentations—will be the last things the people making the
"buy" decision will consider.

By the way, one good place to use a form of "hand–outs" is
with organizational video programs. Provide a number for viewers

to call, offer them useful material, and you'll be surprised at the response.

For example, one corporate video program talked about the importance of communication skills. It offered to provide all who called with a company–approved booklet on the subject. The company printed 300 booklets to meet the expected demand. But it had to crank up the printing press again when it received requests for more than 1,000 copies! The requests also demonstrated the popularity of the closed–circuit video programming and, perhaps, of the subject.

Remember: People in organizations like to get self–help material—especially when it doesn't cost them anything.

10

Learning How to Use the Media (Without Being Abused)

*T*here's a branch of philosophy known as "epistemology." Essentially, it deals with the question of *how we know what we know.* In a practical sense, a lot of what we know comes from perceptions provided by the media—from newspapers, magazines, radio, television, and films.

That's why what you say to the media is so important. It will provide other people with information not only about you, but about the institution(s) you represent. So it's essential that you speak clearly, accurately, and convincingly to the media.

In a way, your relations with the media represent a cat–and–mouse game. They want you to say something provocative (or outrageous) because that's the kind of information that will appeal to their readers or listeners. If your comments are always balanced, reasonable, and prudent, you will disappoint the media. Why? Because your statements will not grab the attention of their audience.

Dealing effectively with the media involves a difficult balancing act. Because you want to get your point across, you have to say something interesting. On the other hand, you don't want to say something in haste that you will have to repent at leisure. This is a challenge, but it's not profoundly different from the one you face as a speaker in front of an audience.

Understanding who the media are, what they want, and what you can do about it is the foundation for good relations with them. As someone put it, "The media has a large megaphone." It's always advantageous for anyone who wants to deliver a message to make friends with the people who control the megaphone.

10.1 Knowing How the Media Can Help (and Hurt) You

Q: What's the similarity between making a presentation and talking to the media?

A: The key similarity is that *the effectiveness of your comments will depend largely on how much you believe what you're saying—how much enthusiasm you have for telling your story.* If the content of what you have to say is solid, your delivery generally will be good.

Q: What's the procedure in most companies in dealing with questions from reporters?

A: In bigger companies, there usually are designated individuals who are the only ones authorized to handle media inquiries. These company representatives either will respond to reporters' questions themselves or refer them to other company personnel knowledgeable about the issue(s) at hand.

At smaller companies, the media generally don't call with much frequency. Therefore, such companies generally don't have a policy for dealing with media calls. They should have one.

Q: Okay, but big company or small, what if a reporter calls me and just wants to chat?

A: Refer the reporter immediately to your company's authorized media contact. Why? Because it's not a pleasant experience to wake up one morning and find yourself unexpectedly quoted about your company.

It's important to remember two principles: First, *don't answer any questions about your company unless you're authorized to do so.* Second, no matter how amiable the questioner on the line may seem, *don't assume that any comments you make are "off the record."*

Q: If I'm in a small company—or if my company asks me to respond to a media inquiry—what points should I keep in mind in preparing my responses to questions?

A: As with other presentations, keep in mind that you want whatever answer you give to be factual and reflective of your company's interests and point of view.

Q: Okay, my company wants me to call the reporter back—or I'm the head of a small company and I decide I want to talk to the press. What if he asks me a question I can't—or don't want to—answer?

A: You should know that you can respond to any reporter's question by using the 20 magic words: "Let *me* look into that matter, and *I'll* get back to you.

Typically, however, the best way to start is not by ANSWERING questions, but by ASKING a few. Say, "Before we start, I have some questions for you."
What questions should you ask the journalist?

❑ First: *you need at least a rough idea of what kind of questions the journalist has.* (Be sure to write them down.)

❑ Second: *What kind of story is the reporter preparing?* Is it "news" (with emphasis on facts and figures), "feature" (with emphasis on personalities), or a "series" (with emphasis on several organizations or on several aspects of an organization); knowing this information can give you a sense of how your answers are going to be used.

❑ Third: *What prompted the reporter to get in touch with you?*
(That is, did another individual suggest your name? Or were
you selected in some other way?)

❑ Fourth: *What other individuals or companies is the journalist
talking to?*

❑ Fifth: *If the reporter's questions can't be answered right away, what
is the journalist's deadline for obtaining information from you?*

Q: I don't want to be naive, but I have two questions: First, do
I have a right to that kind of information; and, second, how
would it be useful to me?

A: On your first question, you certainly have a right to know
what the reporter wants. There is a right of inquiry on the
part of the press, but *there's also a right on your part not to
participate in an interview whose purpose and nature you don't
fully understand.*

On your second point, about how information regarding the
story can be useful, consider these points. It will be helpful to you
in responding to the reporter's questions if you know who supplied
your name. Was it the head of your company—or was it perhaps a
disgruntled former employee whom you fired?

Or suppose you find the journalist has been talking to individuals who you know are hostile to your organization. You
would be within your rights to suggest the journalist contact others
who hold a different view. You can indicate that doing so would
make the story more "balanced" and "fair"—concepts honored by
all journalists (at least in theory).

Finally, if you know what kinds of information the reporter
wants, it's easier to determine if you're the right person to provide
answers. If the information sought is the kind you don't have, then
it's best for both of you to know that.

Q: Should I ask any other questions that seem appropriate?

A: Yes, there's no constitutional reason why reporters should
be the only people who ask questions.

Q: You mentioned some organizations have a policy on speaking to the media. How can I find out what it is?

A: Check with your supervisor, who will probably refer you either to the company's legal counsel or to the public relations department. If you've been contacted by the press, you should pass along all the information you've gleaned about the reporter's purpose. When you find out what the policy is: (1) follow it to the letter; (2) either get back to the reporter, or have the appropriate person do so.

Don't let anything the reporter says cause you to deviate from this approach.

Q: Pardon me, but this seems like an awful lot of trouble to take for someone—a reporter—that I'd probably rather not speak to anyway...

A: The time and energy you spend will be worthwhile. The media plays an important role in our society. It's the conduit through which the public—including investors and customers—get information about our companies and other organizations.

So it doesn't make sense to offend reporters. Remember, they're only human. And if we treat them poorly, they may be inclined to reciprocate. Organizations that have good relations with the press tend to get "good press." That's why it makes sense to put a reasonable amount of time and energy into being as cooperative as we can with the media.

10.2 Learning How to Get Beyond "No Comment"

Q: I hear what you're saying. But isn't it easier—not to mention safer for one's career—to answer most media enquiries with the words "no comment?"

A: Dismissing a media question with "no comment" can lead to trouble. Organizations that routinely answer reporters' queries with "no comment" tend to antagonize the media.

Rather than coming to you for answers to questions, they'll start asking people such as financial analysts—or your consumer critics, or your competitors. In that case, other individuals will have control over what appears in the media about your company. You may end having to respond to negative comments and accusations that you indirectly precipitated by saying "no comment."

There's another problem with refusing to comment. Suppose you're asked this question: "Is it true that your company violated securities laws in its takeover of XYZ corporation?" If you answer with a brusque "no comment," how will it sound when reported? You're right: It will sound as if your company violated securities laws. It may even be reported as: "Mr. X, a representative of the company, refused to confirm or deny that his firm had violated securities' laws."

Q: Holy nightmares! How would you handle it if a reporter shoved a microphone in your face—or called you—and asked the question about violating the securities' law?

A: You might take the following approach:

☐ Say nothing to the reporter other than the following: "I'm not a lawyer. On legal questions, you need to talk to Ms. _____, our company's chief legal counsel."

☐ If the reporter persists with the same line of questioning, say: "As I told you, you'll have to talk to our legal counsel."

☐ Don't engage in any chitchat or speculation with the reporter about the issue raised. Otherwise, your comments might appear in the reporter's story.

☐ If you notice the reporter had a microphone or video camera recording your meeting, don't say "Turn that thing off." On radio or television that sometimes sounds like evidence of guilt.

☐ After the reporter leaves or the phone call is terminated, immediately contact the chief lawyer and report the substance of the reporter's inquiries. That way, if the reporter contacts the counsel, the call will not come as a surprise. Also tell the counsel that you're notifying the company person who handles media contacts of your encounter.

Q: Are there any questions to which "no comment" is an appropriate answer?

A: Avoid the specific words "no comment." There are, however, a couple of instances when you should avoid commenting. Examples are:

❏ *When you're not the right person to answer:* Say so. Remember, a reporter should ask whether you want to be interviewed or not. If the subject is one where you're not the best person to speak, tell the reporter that. If you can, suggest someone else in your company or industry whom the reporter might call.

❏ *Market rumors:* Suppose a reporter has gotten a tip from Wall Street regarding some financially significant development at your company (a rise or fall in stock price, an acquisition or a divestiture). The reporter asks for a response; you should say nothing other than to refer the reporter to the appropriate company contact. If you're that contact, you should reply with some variation of the following: *"Our company never comments on market rumors."* Then, refuse to expand on that statement.

❏ *Hypothetical questions:* Suppose you're asked about something not based on current realities, but on speculative possibilities. For example: "If financial conditions continue to deteriorate, will your company have additional layoffs?" This is a no–win question. It's also one you probably have no way of answering. So you might reply: *"You're asking me to predict the future, and that's something I just can't do."*

On hypothetical questions: In the summer of 1992, Vice President Dan Quayle answered such a question and created a major political controversy. A talk–show host asked Quayle what the Vice

President would do if his daughter (then aged 13) became pregnant and was determined to have an abortion. After saying he would "talk to" and "counsel with" the child, the strongly "pro–life" Quayle replied, "I'd support my daughter." Some in the media accused Quayle of taking a pro–choice stand. Mrs. Quayle weighed in by saying that, if her daughter became pregnant, "she would take the child to term."

Bill Clinton was later asked the same question as Quayle. Benefiting from some time to think about the question, Clinton said: "One thing I *wouldn't* do is talk about it with the media." That answer effectively stopped the line of questioning.

Quayle's "mistake" was in answering a hypothetical question. The seemingly innocent question he answered evoked some powerful fatherly emotions in the Vice President. Quayle would have fared better if he had said, "I'm not going to respond to a hypothetical question, one that bears no relation to current reality." After that, if the host persisted, the Vice President could have held to his refusal to answer hypothetical questions.

Q: A lot of people at our company complain that the press doesn't really want to print good news about us and our industry. If we have a layoff, it's front–page news. But if over the years we add thousands of jobs, they never say anything about it. What do you reply to this?

A: There's a lot of merit to the criticism you mention. Why doesn't the media devote more space to things such as: increases in earnings or employment; expansions of plant capacity; new products; promotions; contributions to local charities; and the many other good things companies do?

The answer is: *The media expects companies to do these things.* To praise them for such activities would be, to most reporters, like praising a football team for blocking and tackling.

A friend of mine who's been a reporter and a corporate public–relations person dealing with the media puts it this way: "The press looks at companies as institutions that do two things: provide jobs and keep secrets. So real news occurs only when there are layoffs and when secrets start becoming public."

In the eyes of the press—and the public—it's not news when a plant runs smoothly, but it is when the plant blows up. By the same token, it's not newsworthy when the company treasurer is an individual of probity and integrity. But the news situation changes when the treasurer embezzles a million dollars. Let's be honest with ourselves: Which one of these stories—the honest treasurer or the crooked one, the intact plant or the leveled one—would get *our* attention?

Q: I get your point. But if most reporters have a bias toward bad news, then how can we get a fair shake in the press?

A: By providing them with hard–hitting, quotable comments that give your side to the story. The companies that restrict themselves to "no comment" never get to give their side. They generally find themselves sitting on the sidelines while their critics throw mudballs at them in the press.

But when a controversy erupts, the side that gets its point across most effectively can carry the day. This is the rationale for having good relations with the press. When you need a friend, it helps to have laid the foundation for amicable relationships.

Q: How can organizations build those kinds of relationships?

A: Do some simple things, including:

❑ *Learn the names, media associations, and reporting interests of the journalists who cover your company and industry;*

❑ *Invite these reporters to visit your facilities and meet your key people; and do so before an emergency arises;*

❑ *Provide reporters with the names of other sources who can help them with their stories: academics, trade association representatives, and others.*

❑ *Give sincere praise to journalists when they do a good job of reporting.*

Tip: Avoid humorous responses that may look foolish in print. A good friend of mine, an executive, was once interviewed by a reporter who asked if a certain acquisition had not been "a mistake." The executive replied, humorously, "I never make a mistake." When the quote was printed in the paper, it made the executive look self–righteous, because the jocular context had been lost.

10.3 Talking Convincingly to the Print Media

Q: I'm surprised you want to talk first about the print media—newspapers and magazines. Isn't it true that people get their information from the electronic media, especially television?

A: As one newspaper editor put it, "The majority of people get most of their *misinformation* from TV."

It's true that many daily papers have died, and the readership of many others has declined. But newspapers and magazines are vital sources of information, not only for readers, but also for other news outlets. In many cases, stories you hear on radio or television have their origins in the print media, especially the large dailies and the newsweeklies.

It's hard to overstate how much influence large newspapers and magazines have on unearthing news. That's because a major newspaper, for example, may have 100 or more reporters. *The Wall Street Journal* has 500 people in its newsroom. A large local TV station may have only a handful of reporters.

In fact, to many print reporters, television news, especially the local variety, is something of a joke. For example, a television station in Pittsburgh launched an advertising slogan "We're bringing it home." The ad featured the station's neatly coiffed anchorpersons (looking rather uncomfortable) getting off a news helicopter. Presumably, the "it" in the ad was the day's news.

However, a print journalist, Phil Musick, then of the *Pittsburgh Press*, said of the TV station's slogan: "Here at the *Press* we've had a debate over what 'it' is. Some people think it's a pizza. Others believe it's the late edition of the *Press*." When you listen to television news, note the many instances when TV news readers credit their reports, in passing, to papers such as *The New York Times*, the *Washington Post*, and the national news weeklies. At many TV (and, for that matter, radio) stations, most of the local news represents a paraphrase of the local newspaper.

Q: What general points should I remember about making statements to the print media?

A: Interviews with publications are different from those with radio or television. With the latter, you're making oral statements that the electronic media will edit and present orally (on radio) or in words and images (television). With newspapers and magazines, your comments will be edited and turned into print.

On the negative side, you can't always count on the reporter to take careful notes. (Many print journalists now tape–record interviews, but tight deadlines sometime mean they rely on their handwritten notes.) Thus, we often hear interviewees complaining that they have been "misquoted."

Remember, the reporter probably is not an expert in your industry. That's why it's essential for you to make sure the reporter understands what you are saying. To do so:

❐ First: *Reiterate your main points*—say them more than once;

❐ Second: *On key issues, politely ask reporters to read their notes from the interview back to you*—and correct any mishaps that may have occurred in the note taking.

❐ Third: *Invite reporters to call you back to check any statements you've made about which they're unclear.* To make it easy for them to do so, give them both your business and home phone numbers.

Most print journalists (and editors) want their stories to be accurate. It's not at all patronizing for you, as an interviewee, to offer to help them do so.

Most people who later raise claims of being "misquoted" actually failed to be sufficiently involved in making sure the reporter understood what they meant. More people should follow the example of Walter Isaacson, an assistant managing editor at *Time*. A reporter for *The New York Times* describes his experience interviewing Isaacson about the *Time* editor's book: "Mr. Isaacson wants to make sure he has explained everything. He makes sure the reporter knows exactly how to get in touch to check anything. He calls three days later to make sure everything is clear." (*New York Times Book Review,* July 6, 1992, p.20).

> ***Q:*** You've discussed what can be done about trying to minimize misquotes, but what about another complaint: important material being left out of the story?

> ***A:*** There's one aspect of this problem the interviewee can't control: the editing process. Reporters edit their own copy so that it will (1) fit the space available; and (2) maintain reader interest. They also have editors who generally pare down the reporter's edited copy. In the process, important points can end up on the floor—or, nowadays, be zapped by the computer.

You can, however, exert some indirect control over the editing process. Make sure you present your key points in colorful, memorable language. For instance, if you're talking about heroic actions by your company's security guards, say: "If we had a Medal of Honor, we'd pin it on them today." Or, "As Churchill said of the Royal Air Force, 'This was their finest hour.'"

As I've suggested, make your important points in language that would get your attention if you were reading it. Striking words will not fall victims to the editor's sharp pencil.

> ***Q:*** In talking about presentations, you've emphasized the need to think out in advance what you're going to say. Wouldn't it be difficult to do that with a reporter who's waiting for your answer?

> ***A:*** Not at all. In general, print reporters are more patient than reporters for TV or radio. If a reporter asks you a question you'd like to think about, say: "That's an interesting question; let me mull it over in my mind for a while, and then I'll get back to you."

Then when you get off the phone, prepare a good answer; review it quickly, if necessary, with other company personnel; and then call the reporter back with an answer. This approach is usually easier with print reporters than with the electronic breed, which tends to want rapid responses.

Q: But what if I can't meet the reporter's deadline? What should I do?

A: Call the individual back before the deadline. Explain that you're trying to get the information, but that it appears you can't do so before the deadline. If your information is essential to the story, ask if there's any way the story can be held for another day. (The answer may be no. But at least you've indicated that you're not sitting on the reporter's request.)

Q: What if I talk to the press and then when the story comes out I truly am misquoted—to my own detriment and that of the company. Is there anything I can do?

A: There certainly is. You can go directly to the editors of the paper and ask them to print a correction (a nicer word than "retraction"). To succeed in your request, you will need more than disgruntlement over a story; you will have to establish to the editor's satisfaction that a story seriously misrepresented either the facts or your statements.

One successful effort to get an editor to admit a story was mistaken occurred when I worked for Gulf Oil. When that company was faced with a hostile takeover bid by the "Mesa Group," a creation of corporate raider T. Boone Pickens, Gulf's chairman gave an interview to the *Pittsburgh Post–Gazette*. The subject was a battle raging between Mesa and Gulf, in which both sides were seeking shareholder proxies relating to membership on the Gulf board of directors.

The story the reporter wrote was a balanced one about Gulf's prospects for winning the proxy fight (which it eventually did). However, the headline on the story read: "Gulf Sees Mesa Winning First Round." The headline surprised the reporter as much as it did Gulf. At the *Post–Gazette*, as at most big papers, the headlines are written by someone other than the reporter.

If the story had been allowed to stand, it could have done financial damage to Gulf as well as to its prospects for winning the proxy fight.

Gulf immediately contacted the editor of the *Post–Gazette* and asked that the paper print a correction on the front page of the next day's newspaper. It also asked that the paper print a clarifying letter from Chairman Jim Lee. The newspaper honored both Gulf requests, and the correction and the letter appeared the day after the offending story.

10.4 Being Effective on Radio

Q: Radio? Does anybody listen to it anymore, with all the heavy–metal bands competing with dentist's office music and endless chatter?

A: A lot of people listen to radio, including business and professional people in their cars. In the early 1990s, one radio personality, talk–show host Rush Limbaugh, reportedly had nearly 18 *million* weekly listeners. The all–news stations, such as KYW in Philadelphia and WCBS in New York, are important sources of news and information to many listeners.

With the growth of call–in shows, radio may be increasing in importance. Radio has demonstrated an important ability to influence events.

Q: What should I do if a radio newsperson calls me up and asks for a comment on some issue?

A: Go through the basic "media request" exercise outlined in section 10.1. (Be sure to find out the basic purpose and thrust of the story.)

Q: Beside the points you've outlined, what are the keys to giving an effective interview on radio?

A: Remember that the believability of your remarks will depend on your voice. Radio is the "invisible medium," because the audience never gets to see you. All the body language in the world will not help with your answer. The audience will have only your voice by which to gauge your responses. Make sure, therefore, that you:

❐ *Respond to questions honestly and firmly, emphasizing (but not overemphasizing) your key words and points;*

❐ *Keep your answers short, less than 30 seconds each;* anything longer will probably be edited out, because the average radio interview lasts less than a minute.

❐ *Avoid the drone factor by making your sentences punchy and using verbal pictures to add color and memorability to your remarks;*

❐ *Don't get angry or try to get even—no matter how unfair or hostile a question is;* on radio (as on television) anger comes across as guilt. Expect the worst, and then if it occurs, you won't overreact.

❐ *Make sure—if you're speaking from your office—you're not going to be interrupted by visitors or other phone calls while you're speaking to the radio interviewer.*

Q: What if I give a wrong answer to a question? Am I stuck with it because it's on tape?

A: If your response is being recorded for later broadcast, don't forget: *That which can be recorded also can be erased.* Just say to the interviewer, "Boy, I blew [or, I need a mulligan* on] that answer. Please let me try it again so I can make some sense." No reputable interviewers will refuse such a request; they recognize that people are human and make mistakes.

If you make a mistake in a live broadcast, say: "I want to *clarify* the answer I just made to the question on _____." (Don't add, "It

---

* A "mulligan" is a golfing term; it refers to being allowed to hit a second drive after a bad first one.

might have left the wrong impression," which will call attention to the misstatement.) Then, go on to make your point in the way you want to.

Q: What about a long radio interview, say a program of a half hour or an hour? How should I handle that?

A: Prepare for it the same way you would a Q & A after a major presentation. Have your answers in mind (but not memorized!) long before you hear the questions.

With a long interview, it's extremely important that you have a friendly—or at least objective—interviewer. If the first question is going to be of the "when did you stop beating your wife?" type, you're in for a long session. So know your interviewers—their track record, their biases, their reputation for fairness. Resolve any doubts about these points *before* you accept the invitation.

Tip: Always take care in the presence of a microphone, even when it's supposedly "off." Sometimes it isn't. It's instructive to recall the case of the announcer on a children's program who read the kids a sweet, sentimental story. Then, thinking the mike was off (it wasn't) he said to no one in particular, "There, that ought to hold the little b——." Talk about a career–killing statement!

10.5 Appearing to Advantage on Television

Q: What kind of personalities come through best on television?

A: More than 30 years ago a brilliant Canadian professor named Marshall McLuhan, wrote an influential (and to some, nearly impenetrable) book called *Understanding Media*. In the book, he described two kinds of personalities, which he called "hot" and "cool."

The "hot" personality is someone who's aggressive, perhaps even abrasive, and self–assured. One example would be a Morton Downey, Jr., or a Don Rickles. Politicians in this category might include the late Joseph McCarthy and former House Speaker Jim

Wright. McLuhan would say that these "hot" personalities don't wear well on television, which is a "cool" medium.

By "cool," he means a medium that best reflects a "laid–back," easygoing, natural type of individual. Entertainers in the "cool" mode are Johnny Carson, formerly of late night television, and Oprah Winfrey. Political figures in this mode would be former President Reagan and Senator Nancy Landon Kassebaum.

McLuhan's categories aren't perfect. But it is true that figures who succeed on television over time generally are "old shoe" types—from Ozzie Nelson to Andy Griffith and Angela Lansbury.

People who don't wear well on television are the high–powered "Type A" personalities. Anger, intensity, and abrasiveness are not the ingredients for video success.

Q: What am I hearing? Does this mean the speaking style you generally advocate ("blunt eloquence") is not the best style for television?

A: You're partially right. On the one hand, television does reward preparation, brevity, and simplicity in expression—all hallmarks of blunt eloquence. But it penalizes excessive self–assurance, the kind of confidence that sometimes shades into egotism and dogmatism.

Q: Okay, but what if I am a Type A personality? Should I stay away from television interviews?

A: Maybe—if you can't, or if you refuse to, change. But if you're usually a highly charged speaker, you can tone down your style for television. Be a little softer in your remarks. When you're "on the tube," don't try to grab the audience by the lapels. Instead, be the voice of reason. Good "actors" can play lots of roles.

Also, if your usual approach is to use relentless logic, tone it down for television. Use a more anecdotal, personal, "viewer–friendly" approach to issues and questions.

If you're hit with a nasty question on television, don't get angry. Respond instead in an even, but firm, manner. I'm not saying you should emulate a bowl of warm jello. But you should stay calm, confident, and relaxed.

Keep in mind that *your audience is not the journalist. Instead, it's the viewers.* If reporters are hostile or unfair, the viewers will note that fact.

Q: You mentioned that the voice is the key element in radio interviews? What is it in television interviews?

A: The face. Television focuses on your face and your shoulders. What can you do with your shoulders—other than shrug them? But the face has a thousand aspects.

It may be unfair, but studies suggest audiences judge people on television not on the content of their arguments, but on whether they like their face—and, to a lesser extent, their voice.

Television focuses on our face and our head to an extreme extent. Some television newswomen (and even a few newsmen) complain that all audiences seem to care about is their hairstyle. Why is this so important to viewers? Because the camera directs our eyes almost exclusively to a performer's face and hair.

The camera is cruel. If we have a mole, television will make it look like a mountain. If we have a big nose, it will make it look like an eagle's beak. If we are somewhat jowly, it can make us look like someone out of a circus sideshow.

In Shakespearean plays, there usually is a tension between *appearance* (the spurious) and *reality* (the genuine). *Television*, in contrast, *values appearance almost to the exclusion of reality.* That's why, unfortunately, Abraham Lincoln nowadays would have a hard time getting elected President.

Q: What gestures work on television, and which ones should I avoid?

A: The only gestures I'd recommend on television are facial. And don't let your gestures reflect any extremes. Stay away from grimaces, for example. The approach you should take is what I'd call "modified poker face." That is, if you disagree with something being said, raise your eyebrows slightly, which is a natural reaction. But don't shake your head vigorously in disgust. Television tends to accentuate motions, and they detract from the head–and–shoulder shots that are the bread and butter of the medium.

As for other gestures, they generally tend to interfere with your message. Letting your eyes dart around, for example, suggests evasiveness—perhaps even deception. Gesturing with your hands calls the audience's attention to them rather than to your words. (Especially avoid waving your hands in front of your face.)

Q: Are you suggesting that I sit there stiff as a board, looking neither right nor left, but staring at the camera?

A: Look at some of the major television interview shows—particularly those on Sunday morning. You'll notice that the experienced guests don't fidget around or gesticulate. They sit in a relaxed, but attentive, posture.

Q: When I'm answering a question, should I look at the camera?

A: Don't turn away from the interviewer to look at the camera. Let the director and the camera personnel make the adjustments they need when they want a head–on shot of your face. Sit there with your attention politely focused on the interviewer, or, if you're on a panel, on your fellow panelists. Be relaxed. But recognize that the television medium does not reward overexpressiveness.

Q: What kind of clothing should I wear on television?

A: In general, wear lightweight clothing, which will help you stay cool (at least it will have a positive psychological effect) under the hot lights. Don't wear white, which tends to reflect light. Also, stay away from unusual patterns, which don't look good on TV. Finally, avoid red stripes which, because of the nature of the television image, tend to look blotchy.

Don't wear jewelry or other appurtenances that call attention to themselves. (On this point, the next time you see an athlete wearing some sort of earring, notice how visible it seems, even though its relative size may be very small.) Also avoid turbans (unless you're a Sikh or are trying to make some sort of ethnic statement), nose–rings, and outlandish hairdos and hats.

On the other hand, males and females should wear make–up...

Q: Make–up?

A: Yes, because without it on television you might look as if you've just spent a year in solitary confinement. You'll look shiny and pasty–faced. You'll look, in short, like someone who has something to hide. (To avoid this problem, many TV personalities cultivate—against their dermatologists' wishes—a deep tan.)

Q: If I'm going to be interviewed on television, how can I practice for it?

A: Nowadays, with all the video cameras around, that's easy.

If you're going to be interviewed by your local version of Mike Wallace, try role–playing by functioning both as interviewer and interviewee. Put on your interviewer "hat" and ask yourself the nastiest questions you can think of. Keep interrupting and probing, not giving yourself time enough to answer the questions. Keep changing "hats." This exercise will prepare you to handle tough questions—and will make the actual interview less intimidating.

Good Sources of Information: For books that deal with appearing on television, I'd urge you to read the sections of McLuhan's *Understanding Media* that deal with "hot" and "cool" personalities). A superb work on how to use television is that by master political strategist Roger Ailes, *You Are the Message* (Doubleday, 1989).

One of the best ways to learn how to "use" television is to watch professional performers, especially the anchors of the network news shows. What kinds of things do they do and say that make them attractive—and credible—to audiences? Analyze their techniques, write down what you see, and then borrow elements of their "style" with which you feel comfortable.

Tip: If you're a woman, stay away from "jangly" jewelry that might make noises that will be picked up by sensitive radio or television microphones. If you're a male, resist the urge to play with coins in your pocket, which produces the "Captain Queeg effect," named after the Humphrey Bogart character who rubbed together two ballbearings.

11

Giving Specialized Kinds of Presentations

*I*f you're like most people, you will make few—if any—"major" speeches in your life. However, the chances are good that you will have an opportunity to make most—if not all—of the specialized types of presentations discussed in this chapter. (As for one–on–one presentations, you'll probably make them nearly every day of your life.)

Although they're shorter in length than a formal speech, the presentations discussed here are important. The introduction of guest speakers can establish a foundation for the presentation to follow. Award presentations can be the highlight of the recipients' life. Graduation addresses can be meaningful—and moving—events for those who hear them.

It will help you as a speaker to achieve the proper tone in your specialized presentations if you remember that they all represent a form of celebration: of achievement in awards; of academic success in graduations; of various accomplishments in events requiring you to toast—or to roast—one or more individuals. In a eulogy, you need to remember that your purpose is not to bemoan the death of a person. Rather, it is for you to celebrate and to honor the memory and life of the individual.

11.1 Introducing the Guest Speaker

Q. What are the three worst blunders people make in introducing speakers?

A. *Awful mistake number one is to mispronounce the speaker's name.* It has been said that the sweetest sound we ever hear is that of someone saying our name. There are few embarrassments worse than when speakers have to supply the correct form of their name when the introducer has butchered it.

For example, a colleague of mine once wrote an introduction for the chairman of a meeting to use in presenting William C. Douce, former chief executive officer of Phillips Petroleum Company. Knowing that Douce was sensitive about his name, the writer inserted a cautionary note for the introducer. It read: "Douce–rhymes with house." Unfortunately, the meeting chairman came up with the following: "And now I'd like to introduce our guest speaker, Mr. William C. *House.*"

If you have any doubts as to how to pronounce your speaker's name, ask that person. And then write out the name in a form that's easy to say. For example, learn whether "Mr. Trottier" pronounces his name in the French manner (Trot–ee–eh) or in the Americanized version (Trot–ee–er).

Awful mistake number two is to suggest to the audience that the guest speaker was not your first choice. ("We originally asked Judge Webster, but he couldn't make it, so...")

Generally, this lapse is a case of good intentions going haywire. The introducer means to thank the speaker for substituting for someone who had to cancel. But the public "thank you" always ends up making the substitute speaker sound like a second banana.

If you want to offer your undying gratitude to the guest for filling in, do it privately.

Awful mistake number three is to use the stalest of statements, saying "Our guest today needs no introduction." Like most clichés, this is a form of verbal laziness. After all, if the speaker needs no introduction, why are you standing there...providing an introduction?

Q: What other mistakes should I avoid?

A: Here are several:

❑ *Don't make your introduction too long—keep it at one minute or less;* good introductions are short and pointed; bad ones are long–winded and pointless.

❑ *Don't try to summarize the entire forthcoming speech.* If you do, the speaker may be left with the melancholy duty of reiterating the points you've already made.

❑ *Don't summarize the speech at the conclusion of the meeting.*

❑ *Although you should praise your speaker's qualifications and accomplishments, take care not to exaggerate.* For example, if you find yourself describing a brigadier general of, say, the Vermont National Guard, as "one of the nation's most brilliant military strategists," it won't wash. The audience will be thinking, "And where does that leave General Schwarzkopf?"

Q: But somehow it just doesn't seem right to give a notable person a one–minute introduction...

A: I'll tell you a secret. Although everyone needs an introduction, the more famous the person the shorter it should be. For instance, a suitable introduction if your speaker is the President of the United States would contain 11 words: "Ladies and gentlemen, the President of the United States of America." What more could you add?

Q. Okay, you've told me what not to do. Now will you tell me how I give a good introduction?

A. Introducing a speaker is a six–step process.

❐ First, *outline briefly* the highlights of a speaker's career;

❐ Second, *identify* the topic of the speech and *suggest its pertinence* in a sentence or two;

❐ Third, *briefly summarize* the guest's qualifications to address that subject;

❐ Fourth, *conclude* by giving the guest's name—taking care to *speak the name directly to the audience* so that it can be heard clearly;

❐ Fifth, *join in the applause and then turn to shake hands with the speaker,* who will be approaching the lectern.

❐ Sixth, *after the speech, if it's your job to close the meeting, do so after you've sincerely thanked the speaker in a couple of sentences* (maximum).

Q: It sounds almost too easy. But how can I boil down the pages of information I get from speakers?

A: Some introducers will get a three–page, single–spaced biography from the speaker and then proceed to read it word for word at the lectern. "Mary Jones was born to Tom and Ida Mae Jones in Rockford, Illinois. After a happy early childhood, she attended Abraham Lincoln Elementary School and Jefferson Junior High. She had an 'A' average at both institutions." Please don't do anything like that. It results in endless, banal introductions that make both speakers and audiences very uncomfortable.

The trick in the introduction is to discard the irrelevant details you get about the speaker. Everyone assumes, for instance, that the guest went to elementary school and high school, and later had entry–level positions at work. You should *emphasize the milestones in the speaker's life and focus on the key accomplishments,* especially the ones that relate to the speech topic.

Q. How can I be sure the biographical information I use is accurate and up to date?

A. After you've *written* a draft introduction, call up the speaker and read it. This is a good way to catch inaccurate and/or inappropriate comments (e.g., if the speaker's "beloved spouse" is about to become the not–so–beloved ex–spouse). There should be *no surprises* (for the guest) in an introduction.

Q. But what if, when you call a speaker and read the introduction, you get asked to add a lot of biographical details?

A. On the rare occasion when this might happen, use the technique perfected by an old boss of mine. When senior executives would ask her to pursue a policy she knew was wrong, she'd answer with moderate enthusiasm, "Yes, we could do that."

Then she'd present alternatives and gradually talk them into pursuing another course. She hadn't *refused*; she'd just *redirected*. In the case of speakers in love with their personal histories, explain that a "hit–the–highlights" introduction will give them more time to outline their views. It will work every time.

Q. What about when I'm introducing a friend, or a business associate that I know well? How can I use that personal knowledge in an introduction?

A. Besides emphasizing the high points of the speaker's career, present a little–known fact about your friend—a tactic I call the "it might surprise you" approach.

For example, "You all know 'Rabbi Geduldig' as one of our community's most respected spiritual leaders. But it might surprise you to learn that he's a four-handicap golfer. I discovered that fact last year when he beat me in the club championship."

Or, "The world knows 'Jack Jones' as a take–no–prisoners middle linebacker for the Bears. But the kids at Children's Hospital know him as 'Santa Claus.' Every Christmas he goes there in a white beard and red suit to hand out toys to sick children."

Caution: Many good introductions offer a glimpse into a speaker's nonpublic side—*but only a glimpse.* Don't get carried away and start a series of "if–you knew–the–guest–like–I–know–the–guest" stories. If you do, the audience may start yawning—and the speaker squirming.

Tip: Introducers should speak from a written script. Even if you normally avoid speech texts, make an exception here. Using one will do three things: It will keep you from digressing and thus making an overly long introduction; it will ensure that you don't leave out a key point; and it will prevent you from making a misstatement.

11.2 Giving and Getting Awards

Q: If I have to present an award, how should I go about doing it?

A: There are several points you should hit:

❐ *Tell what the award is, what its origins were, and, if some past recipients are well known (business, civic, or political leaders), identify them;*

❐ *Explain precisely (but briefly) what the recipient(s) did to merit the award;* be as specific as you can within the constraints of being relatively brief; for example, if it's a sales award, give the number of sales (or dollar amount) that enabled the honoree to win the award;

❐ *Tell how you know of the recipient(s)' activities that resulted in the granting of the award—that is, if you have personal knowledge or if the information was conveyed to you;* for example, if you're the head of a company presenting awards for volunteer activity, you probably got the information from the volunteers' bosses;

❐ *Suggest the larger significance of the activities being recognized;* for example, if it's an award for volunteerism, emphasize the importance of this activity given government budget constraints (Be general on this point if the awardee also will say a few words).

❐ *Invite the person accepting the award to come forward.* If an individual is accepting an award on behalf of the group, identify him or her (if you haven't done so previously) with emphasis on the person's connection to the group being honored. (For example, "I'm going to ask Jan Jones, head of the XYZ Volunteer group, to come up and accept this award.")

Q: What should be the presenter's tone?

A: Enthusiastic and sincere.

Q: What about the length of the presentation remarks?

A: It's hard to set a rule for length. Generally, a few minutes (or less) is sufficient. Presidents of the United States take about two to three minutes to hand out Medals of Honor and Medals of Freedom, so it's hard to see why other award presentations should go on much longer.

Q: What about when I *get* an award? What do I say?

A: Prepare your remarks carefully and keep them brief. Don't take more than two minutes (about 200 words) to respond. The only exception is when you're being asked to give a speech in conjunction with accepting an award. (In this regard, see the speech by John S. Welch, Jr., in Appendix A.)

When you get an award and are expected to speak briefly, there are six specific things you should say:

❐ First, *say thank you to the presenter;*

❐ Second, *thank the group giving you (or your organization) the award;*

❐ Third, *tell what the award means to you or your group;* that is, why it's a gratifying recognition of the achievements being saluted.

❐ Fourth, *tell why the achievements recognized have significance for others beyond the individual or group being cited* (for example, in the Welch speech he notes that the activities of GE employees are expanding educational opportunities for minority students).

☐ Fifth, *give credit to people who assisted in the effort that resulted in the award.* (Note how GE's Welch makes light of his own contribution and accepts it on behalf of the employees of GE.)

☐ Sixth, *give the audience some information about what will happen to the award.* For example, "It will be placed in the lobby of our corporate headquarters, where all who enter will see it." Or, perhaps, "I'm going to give this to my father, who is the true hero in our family. That way, I can see it every time I visit him."

Let me reiterate. *One of the worst* faux pas *in public speaking is to ramble on interminably when you're accepting an award.* If you say you're grateful and that the award is very meaningful, the audience will take your word for it.

In accepting awards, learn from the example of the Academy Awards. In years past, certain honorees became subjects of public ridicule because of the unconscionable length of their remarks. The television show *Murphy Brown* parodied this approach by having a naive young reporter, "Corky", win a broadcasting award and then thank, among others, "the man who brings the doughnuts in the morning."

If in accepting an award you want to name certain helpful individuals, do so. But don't present a list of names that looks like the first page of the Manhattan phone book. If you're afraid of leaving someone out, mention a few individuals by name and then have a catch–all ending ("and all the others who contributed to my [our] winning this award; you know who you are.")

Q: What about the tone of the recipient's remarks?

A: Needless to say, they should be appropriate to the occasion and reflect your real feelings about the award's significance. Tears and a choked voice are rarely appropriate–especially if you are getting an award for something like being the best golfer in your company.

Any award you get–personally, or on behalf of a group—you should accept with *sincere* emotion.

Good Source of Information: Diane Booher's book, mentioned previously, has some good comments about awards (pages 19–36).

Tip: A little self–deprecating humor can be welcome on the part of an awardee. For example, when Phillips Petroleum executive Leo Johnstone received an award for being an outstanding graduate of the University of Kansas, he said: "My mother always told me that if I lived long enough something like this might happen." (But if you do use humor, don't let it appear that you're deprecating the award or the group presenting it.)

11.3 Making Appropriate Toasts

Q: Is it possible to prepare a toast ahead of time?

A: Yes, because you should be able to anticipate most occasions where you might be asked to give a toast. For example, if you're the "best man" at a wedding, you probably will have to give a toast.

But many times the request for a toast comes as something of a surprise. People seem to get in a toast–requesting mood at ceremonial events: retirements, anniversary parties, baptisms, and the like.

If you get a surprise request for a toast, you can't go wrong by saying some variant of these three sentences:

❐ *"Join us in a toast to (the persons being honored)."*

❐ *"He/She/They will always have our best wishes and our love (or affection)."*

❐ *"We wish them a long life, much happiness, and true prosperity— the kind that comes from the love of family and friends."* (The qualification after "prosperity" makes the toast suitable for the impecunious as well as the affluent.)

That toast, or a close variant of it, will work in nearly every circumstance. (At weddings or baptisms, it's a good idea to say something nice about the parents. On occasions honoring one or both partners in a marriage, be sure to mention both.)

Q: I take it toasts are not among what the ancient Greeks might have called "the higher forms of oratory."

A: Correct, my Socratic partner. Toasts are an occasion for what the Catskill resort comedians would have called "making nice." Say nice things about the people or institution being honored, and everyone will say later, "What a fine toast!"

Q: How long should a toast be?

A: I've noticed that, after about 30 seconds (50 words), the people joining you in the toast start getting thirsty. Frankly, how long does it take to say, in essence: "Be happy. Live long. Get rich"?

Q: Wouldn't you have to say a little more in a business toast?

A: Yes, but just a little. Normally, in toasting business partners or customers, it's customary to add a few words about the companies represented and the high hopes held for continued productive relationships in the future. Again, however, it doesn't pay to get carried away. Keep the business toast brief.

Q: What about toasts given in foreign countries?

A: When you have to give a toast overseas, it never hurts to call the Washington embassy of the country involved. Ask the people there for advice about toasts in their country. I once worked at a company whose top executive was visiting Chinese Taipei (Taiwan). I looked in a number of books, but couldn't find anything about toasts in that country, although I assumed they would involve some elaborate ritual. Finally, I called up the Taiwanese consulate and asked the young woman who answered about toasts in her country. She giggled, and said, "All we say is 'Kan Pei.'" I enquired,

"What does that mean?" She said, "Loosely translated, 'Bottoms up.'"

Could it be that, the more cultures differ, the more they remain the same?

(I may be the only individual in the world who has *two* "China toast" stories: In the late 1970s, executives of another company I was working for were making a trip to the People's Republic of China. Several toasts would be called for. The U.S. State Department informed me that the major toast should include a reference to the memory of Mao Tse-Tung, the recently deceased tyrant who had ruled China.

I wrote the toast as directed and then showed it to the executive who was to deliver it. He read it and literally choked on the reference to Mao. I explained the reference reflected the State Department's suggestions.

As he began to crumple my text in his hand, I added, "Maybe we could say: 'We remember the high esteem in which Mao held capitalists.'" As I finished, the executive dropped the toast in his wastebasket. "I might get a point for mentioning Mao," he said, "but I'd lose a lot more for saying something I didn't believe." Well put.)

Good Sources of Information: The works by Diana Booher and Joan Dietz mentioned in the section on "awards" also have material on toasts.

11.4 Making the Last Words Count in Eulogies

Q: I've never given a eulogy, and I don't think I know anyone who has. Why worry about it if it's not likely to happen?

A: You have a point. Most people will make it through this vale of tears without ever being asked to speak at a funeral service. But it can happen, as illustrated by an episode of *The Golden Girls*, when Dorothy was asked to give a eulogy. Here's the way the dialogue went:

Dorothy [Bea Arthur]: "Oh Rose, I'm so nervous. Have you ever given a eulogy?"

Rose [Betty White]: You mean at a *funeral*?

Dorothy: No, Rose, at a *pie–eating contest!*"

Q: Come to think of it, I've never been in a pie–eating contest either. When is it appropriate to accept a request to give a eulogy? And when is it appropriate to pass on the honor?

A: Accept it when the following are true: (1) you knew the deceased individual quite well, and (2) you know you can deliver the remarks without breaking up emotionally.

By the same token, if you didn't know the deceased well, or if you're the kind of person who weeps whenever Old Glory goes by on the Fourth of July, you should regretfully decline the invitation. But if you do so, be certain to suggest the name of someone else who could do a good job with a eulogy.

Q: What's the purpose of a eulogy?

A: The eulogist represents the community—friends, family, and acquaintances of the person who died—in saying good-bye to someone who once lived and loved. It's important to remember that funerals are not really for the person lying in the casket. They're for the living, especially the loved ones of the man or woman who has died. Funerals should help us come to terms with the passing of someone near to us. Although eulogies take place at funerals, the best ones are really celebrations of life.

Q: What should be in a eulogy?

A: There are several elements that usually are present in good eulogies:

❐ *Recognize the presence of the immediate family* (father, mother, spouse, children, and others, but keep the "list" within reason) *by name;*

❐ *Express your sympathy for the family and for the friends;*

❐ *Point out the context in which you knew the person you're eulogizing* (friend, family member, business associate) *and the length of your acquaintance;*

❐ *Tell a brief story or two about the deceased,* making sure your anecdotes say something positive about the person;

❐ *Indicate how the illustrations/anecdotes you've related reflect the person's character;*

❐ *Suggest to the people present how the person's life has affected the world in a positive way;*

❐ *Conclude by expressing once again your sympathy for friends, family, and all those who were touched in some way by the person you're eulogizing.*

A final, crucial point: *Keep the eulogy short, generally five minutes or so, but never more than ten minutes.*

Q: What kind of things *shouldn't* be in a eulogy?

A: Anything that would embarrass anyone present. If "Old Bob," say, was "one heckuva womanizer," or if he was a drinker who had a "hollow leg," please omit those facts. In addition, don't confuse a layman's eulogy with a clergyman's. Generally, theological observations are best left to the clergy.

Tip #1: If you have any doubt about the appropriateness of your comments, check them with the cleric or funeral director who will be officiating.

Tip #2: For reasons that should be obvious, humor generally is not a staple of eulogies. Humor would not appropriate when the person died a painful death or at a relatively young age. But under certain limited circumstances, *light* humor can work effectively. For the most part, these are cases where the person eulogized has: (1) lived a relatively long life; (2) appreciated humor; (3) died after an illness of some length.

11.5 "Roasting"—Without Getting Burned

Q: How would you define "roast?"

A: A roast is an event held for charity at which an individual consents to be the butt of jokes told by a number of friends and acquaintances. (If there's not a charitable purpose connected, it's probably not a "roast" but an exercise in what psychologists call "unrepressed aggression.")

Q: What's the secret to preparing a good presentation for a roast?

A: Effective roast comments take a person's behavior and exaggerate it for humorous effect. If you're asked to roast someone, it's a good idea to write down that person's traits. Then you need to start exaggerating those characteristics.

Suppose you're roasting Joe, who's known for having a messy desk. You might say things such as the following: "Joe is the guy who invented the sign you see in offices: 'A clean desk is the sign of an empty mind.'" You might add, "Joe never met a filing cabinet he couldn't ignore." And, "How messy is his desk? The other day a copy of *The New York Times* fell out of the pile of papers; it was the edition announcing the Japanese bombing of Pearl Harbor."

Another example: "Does Mary Sue like make–up? Did you know she served as an *adviser* to Tammy Faye Baker?" And, "How much mascara does she use? When she cries, it looks like the Black Sea."

A third example: "Most people try to get time off from work to play golf. With Ed, he tries to fit *work* into his *golf schedule.*"

Q: Let me give you a tough one. There's a roast for a guy who's retiring. Joe's a man of steady habits and few words. In other words, he's kind of dull. How can you roast somebody like that?

A: "Talk about dull. Joe's so dull that his favorite color is *beige*. So dull his priest fell asleep during Joe's confession. So dull his wife went out to a movie on their honeymoon night. So dull that he watched *The Tonight Show* because of Ed McMahon. So dull that even his *accountant* avoids him."

Or what about focusing on the "few words" part of Joe's personality? "To say Joe doesn't talk much is an understatement. He makes Calvin Coolidge seem like a chatterbox.... One time a guy had a bet that he could make Joe say more than two words. He talked to Joe all through dinner, but all he could get out of him was a yes or no. Finally, he told Joe, 'Look, I've got a bet with that guy across the way that I can get you to say more than two words. Will you help me out?' Joe looked at him and said, 'You lose.'" (That's a story told about President Coolidge.)

Q: What kinds of things should I stay away from in a roast?

- ❑ First, *avoid off–color language.* (Even if it offends just one person, that's one too many.)

- ❑ Second, *generally avoid comments that call attention to physical defects* (especially those about which an individual may be sensitive). For instance, if you say, "Mary Jo's got a honker on her that would be the envy of a Canadian goose," you may not find Mary Jo smiling.

- ❑ Third, *avoid statements that reflect badly on the individual's moral character or judgment.* For instance, comments such as: "Joe [a married man] has more women than Smith and Wellesley combined" or "Some people say Joe likes his whiskey. Well, I'm here to tell you that's a lie; Joe *loves* his whiskey."

Q: But in avoiding comments like the last one, don't you risk taking all the sting out of the roast?

A: There's an old saying: "Err on the side of caution." That's applicable in the case of roasts. You want to jab roastees with a fork, not slice them up. If you don't feel comfortable with one of your jabs, it's probably best to leave it out.

Good Source of Information: On roasts, the classic work is: Ed McManus and Bill Nicholas, *We're Roasting Harry Tuesday Night* (Prentice–Hall, 1988). In it, you'll find everything you need to know about putting together and participating in a roast.

11.6 Giving Memorable Graduation Addresses

> *Q:* What are the two main things to remember when giving a
> graduation speech?

❐ First, *never say the words "When I was your age..."*

❐ Second, *keep it short. Remember, people are not there to hear your
speech.* They're in attendance to honor the graduating seniors
and to see them get the diploma. (Someone once said that
parents attend graduations to pay their respects not to their
children, but to their dearly departed money.)

Any graduation speech that lasts more than ten minutes is too long. Keep
that as a firm rule, and you might even be invited back to speak at
another commencement someday. Whatever you say, most graduates
will be too self–absorbed and distracted to listen. But if you speak too
long, they'll remember you—and not fondly—forever.

> *Q:* I've attended a lot of graduations, and I don't remember
> much about the speeches—except that they all seemed to
> sound alike...

> *A:* There's nothing that brings out the average speaker's basic
> banality like being asked to give a graduation speech. It's
> about the only place you'll ever hear Longfellow's
> "footprints on the sands of time" referred to without a
> snicker. Browning's "Grow old along with me; the best is yet
> to come" (the poetic line that conflicts most with the average
> individual's experience) also is popular with graduation
> speakers.

The point is, *most graduation speeches are patronizing and sentimental.* Speakers say the world can be a field of dreams. They
don't say that it also can be a wasteland of sadness, death, despair,
and failed hopes. Some graduation speakers are trying to keep
even a glimpse of life's dark side from students. (Perhaps they're
afraid the youngsters might despair and decide to remain per-
petual students.)

Q: What kinds of things should graduation speeches include?

A: Mention that you are honored to speak at such a special occasion. Also, if you have links to the particular institution, note them. Mention one or two educators who influenced your life (for example, the president of a college, the principal of a high school, or a beloved teacher). Congratulate the graduates, their parents, and their teachers.

Q: Well, what kinds of subjects make for the most promising graduation speeches?

A: Subjects that can be dealt with honestly, straightforwardly, and briefly. The school has asked you to speak presumably because it believes the attendees will be interested in hearing about *your experience*. (In other words, don't bore them with a lot of generalities about history, economics, and the changing nature of society.)

Good subjects for graduation speeches include: the role of education in the rest of the graduates' lives; the importance of family; and the crucial role of teachers and other models of conduct.

Q: Could you cite a particular graduation speech that illustrates the principles you advocate?

David Roderick, former CEO of U.S. Steel (now USX) spoke in the late 1970s to the graduates of Bethany College in West Virginia. That was a period of national dismay about the United States hostages in Iran. It was also a time of high inflation, skyrocketing interest rates, and heavy unemployment. It was not a good time to be graduating from college—and looking for a job. It also was not an auspicious time to make a graduation speech.

How did Roderick handle it? He reflected back to the time he was their age. He had just served as a Marine during the heavy fighting in the South Pacific. Like others his age, he returned to a nation happy that the war was over, but seriously concerned about what the future would bring. Would the country possibly be able to provide jobs for the millions of returning service people? Would the Great Depression interrupted by the war resume? Would conflict erupt with the Soviet Union? Would the nation be able to educate its soldiers–turned–civilians?

Roderick pointed out that the worst fears of the time never came true. In fact, the post–war period brought about unprecedented job–creation and economic growth. Rather than being a burden, the young people returning from World War II built America into the greatest economic superpower ever known. Roderick challenged the graduates to confront the economic adversity facing them and to emulate the example of their parents and grandparents.

The approach Roderick took was successful; he did not sugarcoat the economic situation. But he pointed out that the situation the graduates faced was not unprecedented. *He offered hope based on past history and challenged the young people to turn a time of troubles into one of opportunity.* (In the years after Roderick's speech, by the way, the United States produced its longest period of sustained economic growth.)

11.7 Making Meetings Focused—and Worthwhile

Q: If you make a phone call to someone in business, government, or another organization, here are the probabilities of what will happen: Ten percent of the time you'll get the individual you're calling; 40 percent of the time you'll get an answering machine; 50 percent of the time you'll get a secretary, who will tell you the person you're trying to reach is "in a meeting." Is that your experience?

A: Surveys of how professionals and managers spend their time seem to suggest that your "50 percent in meetings" figure is pretty close to the mark. *Business used to consist of conceiving, designing, making, and selling products. Now it sometimes seems to consist of innumerable—and often endless—meetings.*

How many of these meetings take time away from the real business of the company? How many of the meetings are productive, worthwhile? If we answer based on our own experience, the answer is: only a small percentage.

Q: What's the answer?

A: For the person in charge to ask about every prospective meeting: Is it necessary? Specifically, ask the following questions of each prospective meeting:

❑ *Is the purpose only to "present information"? If so, perhaps it would be better to send a memo, an E–mail message (if those attending the meeting have access to such a system).*

❑ *Will the benefits of holding a meeting outweigh the work time that attendees will lose?*

❑ *If this is a "regularly scheduled meeting," are we holding it just as a pro–forma exercise, or is there a real purpose for this specific get–together?*

❑ *Is the meeting being called for the benefit of all invited, or is it really being held for only a few of the potential attendees?* If so, consider talking to them individually.

❑ *If you're the meeting leader, are you calling the meeting for the purpose of issuing a directive, or are you really seeking contributions from all who will attend?* If you want to state a policy, is it necessary to call a meeting to do so? The answer may be yes, but only if you're sincerely interested in answering questions and clarifying issues relating to the policy.

❑ *Have your previous meetings served the purpose of defining issues and pointing to specific directions, or have they usually degenerated into "gab sessions"?* If the latter, what are you going to do to make this meeting different?

Q: What if the latter is the case—the meetings have been directionless "yak–fests"?

A: Most meetings fail for one or more of the following reasons: First, the meeting leader is using the session not to solicit views on a problem or issue, but rather to present information; second, the leader fails to keep the session on track; third, the meeting has no clear purpose.

As I've said before, *presentations whose only goal is to give information don't work.* Meetings that begin with laundry lists of "news" (most of it not really fresh) usually become aimless—and nearly endless. There are better ways to disseminate information (from word of mouth to memos to electronic mail) than by holding a meeting about it.

Q: So what should the leader of a meeting do?

A: *A meeting is a place to discuss problems—not, by the way, to air grievances—and to outline ways of tackling them.* If the meeting degenerates into a "gripe session," it will accomplish nothing. That's especially true when the gripes are the leader's. Don't tell people something is wrong and then give them no direction on how to "fix it." If they knew how, it probably wouldn't be going wrong in the first place.

I once worked at a company where the boss had frequent meetings. Over a period of several months, he opened nearly every meeting with the same complaint: Certain individuals were leaving work early, especially on Friday afternoons. The boss would rail about this issue for several minutes. The individuals who were leaving early were all in one department, and the head of that unit would always hang his head and vow to do something about it.

What was wrong with this procedure? First, it raised a problem that didn't affect most of those at the meeting. Our people were not leaving early, so we found discussion of the problem to be irrelevant and embarrassing. Second, there was no real accountability for solving the problem. The department head concerned was supposed to "do something" about it, but he never did anything that had a decisive effect.

Participants should leave a meeting with a clear sense of what they're supposed to do to overcome the problem discussed. The meeting leader should be a facilitator—not a dictator. Meetings are exercises in democracy. In that spirit, leaders should do the following at every meeting;

❒ First, *briefly summarize the problem(s), the event(s), or the situation(s) that prompted the calling of the meeting;*

❒ Second, *ask if there are any questions about the exact nature of the problem;*

❒ Third, *ask the group to brainstorm, to come up with as many realistic solutions to the problem as possible.*

❒ Fourth, *ask the proposer of each solution to give a 25–word–or–less explanation of why the solution will work.* The word limitation imposes focus and discipline on the participants' comments.

❒ Fifth, *write down (perhaps on a flip chart) each proposed solution, while eliminating duplications;*

❒ Sixth, *group the solutions into categories.* For example, if you're talking about productivity problems, the solutions might fall into three categories: worker morale, equipment problems, and government regulations.

❒ Seventh, *find out if there's a consensus at the meeting on what is/are the best solution(s).* (Try to do this without taking a vote, but if necessary, ask for a show of hands.)

❒ Eighth, *give your own thinking on the solution, trying to be as positive as you can.* (To this point, the leader has been a facilitator, but not an advocate of any particular solution.)

❒ Ninth, *appoint an individual or a group with responsibility for seeing that the chosen solution is carried out;*

❒ Tenth, *establish a date for the individual or group to report back to meeting participants on the success of the solution.* (Unless the solution is not working, it probably won't be necessary to schedule another meeting to consider the report.)

Q: It's a nice approach—in theory. But surely you don't expect bosses to support ideas that differ from theirs.

A: Most emphatically: I do. *If the leader calls a problem–solving meeting, the point is to rely on the group's best judgment.* If that's not acceptable, the leader should not have called the meeting, which would be nothing more than a sham. People don't like "town meetings" that are really exercises in authoritarianism.

Q: I have a question about conducting a meeting so that the "participants" actually participate. In a lot of meetings, one or two people dominate the session, talking all the time, and so on. What can you do about that?

A: It's up to the leader to ensure that everyone gets to participate. If individuals don't propose solutions on their own, ask them to. Ensure that no one monopolizes the discussion. Also, if people start to digress, keep them on track. Say something like, "Remember, we're discussing Problem X and only that, so let's stick to the subject." You can do this in a way that's not embarrassing to anyone.

Q: You've talked about how to be a leader at a meeting, but what about being "followers," participants. Any tips for them?

A: Have you ever found me at a loss for words? Seriously, being a good participant offers its own challenges. It's a matter of balancing responsiveness and self–restraint. As a participant, remember these points:

❑ *"Brevity is the soul of wit" (understanding, knowledge); so keep your remarks focused on the subject;*

❑ *Opinions turn into hot air when they're not grounded in reality;* so when you propose a solution, tell precisely (but briefly) why you think it will work.

❑ *Democracy doesn't work when everyone talks at once;* so don't interrupt other people; let them have their say, as they've let you have yours.

❑ *Democracy also shouldn't be a question of who has the loudest voice;* so present your views calmly and reasonably and don't precipitate—or participate—in arguments.

❐ *Problem–solving sessions should reward quality, not quantity;* so present one or two solutions that you think will work, not every solution you can imagine.

Q: How many people should be in a meeting?

A: When the number of participants exceeds 15, meetings don't work very well. With too many people, it's hard to get everyone to participate fully. If you have more potential participants than 15, ask yourself: Are all these people really involved with the problem we're discussing?

Good Source of Information: A short, classic work on meetings is Milo O. Frank, *How to Run a Successful Meeting in Half the Time* (Pocket Books, 1989).

11.8 Winning Your Point in One–on–One Presentations

Q: Is a one–on–one talk really a "presentation"? Isn't it just an exchange of pleasantries or of information?

A: Of course, there's nothing wrong with exchanging pleasantries, with having what used to be called "a chat." We all engage in conversations that don't really go anywhere.

But any serious discussion between two people should have a point. Like a presentation to one hundred people, a talk with, say, a colleague should have something resembling a "call to action." Let's face it, *almost every time we talk to people we're trying to get them to do something*–even if it's only to have dinner ready at 6 P.M. rather than 7 P.M.

After all, if everything is precisely as it should be—as we want it to be—*the correct mode is not conversation, but silence.*

Q: Are you implying that successful people aren't those who do things, but those who get other people to do them?

A: You may just have stated the unwritten rule of social and managerial achievement. *In life, success rests mainly on our ability to get people to do what we want them to do:* buy our products; support our ideas; see us as credible and informed; and accept us as the right persons for a job or an assignment.

How do we get them to do this? *BY TALKING THEM INTO IT.* That's why oral skills are so important.

The same principles hold when you're talking to one person as when you're talking to an auditorium full of people. You need to speak clearly, concisely, candidly, and, whenever possible, colorfully. But most of all, *you need to convince them that taking the action you recommend will be in their interest.*

Q: If you take that view, isn't there a chance of coming on too strong in person–to–person discussions?

A: Don't try to browbeat people. Threatening them with the loss of a job or status, for example, will result in turning them either into enemies or emotional wrecks. Speak authoritatively, but at the same time, address people as your equals. That's true even if, in terms of the institutional pecking order, they're not.

Q: I've noticed that when I talk to subordinates they're sometimes intimidated. That makes it hard for me to get the kind of information I need. Any ideas?

A: In conversations among "unequals," it helps the flow of ideas when the higher–status person is cordial and attentive.

One of the most effective one–on–one conversationalists I ever met was Jerry McAfee, former chairman of Gulf Oil. A true corporate leader, McAfee could be intimidating among equals—but rarely so with subordinates.

Tom Latimer, formerly a senior manager at Gulf, defined McAfee's special quality. Latimer said, "When you met with McAfee, he was an extremely attentive listener. That made it seem as if, to him, you were the most important person in the world."

The result? Subordinates were not afraid to give McAfee accurate information about the company's business.

Q: Isn't the difference between a presentation and a one–on–one that the latter is *interactive*, an exchange of ideas?

A: In the sense that you're using the word, I don't agree. As we discussed early in the section on recognizing audience responses, *presentations also are interactive*. The speaker responds to the audience, to its laughter, its murmurs of approval (or disapproval), its applause, its looks of puzzlement or understanding. All presentations—like all conversations—are, or should be, interactive.

Q: You emphasized the need for preparation and practice in making presentations. Is that also true of one–on–ones? If so, what about spontaneity?

A: People who rely on "spontaneity" in their conversation usually don't go too far in organizations; they're usually too busy removing their foot from their mouth. If you are going to engage in an important discussion, think about what you're going to say. Consider writing down your key points, so they'll stick in your memory. (Don't, however, try to memorize them.)

If you're recommending a course of action to your boss, for example, think about how it serves that individual's interests—and stress those points. Try to anticipate the boss's reactions and questions and how you'll deal with them. In that way, you'll maximize the probability that the boss will go along with your call to action.

Visualize how you want the discussion to go. Then make every effort to make the real meeting replicate your visualization of it. Leave as little as possible to chance.

12

Confronting Special Challenges in Presentations and Language

The challenges that can face you as a speaker are characterized, like Shakespeare's Cleopatra, by their "infinite variety." Every section of this volume deals with issues you could face as a speaker. The remaining sections will introduce you to some challenges that appear to be growing in importance as we move toward a new millennium.

For instance, language has become more and more a battleground, as terms once regarded as benign have turned into "fighting words." The issue of "offensive" language is a complex one. Women and various ethnic groups have become much more sensitive to language they believe may denigrate them. This fact places demands on you, as a speaker, to choose your words thoughtfully.

In addition, the rise of the global economy means that your chances of speaking to overseas audiences have increased. The "international language of business" may, in fact, be English. But that does not eliminate the need to pay special attention to the clarity of your remarks when giving presentations to people whose first language is not English.

Finally, another phenomenon speakers increasingly confront is the presence of speechwriters. In government, business, and other institutions, speechwriters have become a fact of life. Whether you ever use one—or are pressed into service as one—you need to be aware of who they are and how they function.

12.1 Spotting and Avoiding Sexist Language

Q: What is "sexism" in language—and why is it a matter that should concern speakers?

A: A practical definition relating to public speaking would be: Sexist language is that which indicates–intentionally or unintentionally–that an activity such as business (or government or the military) is the domain of men. In its most common form, sexist language uses "masculine" words, especially the pronoun "he," to the exclusion of their "feminine" counterparts. Such language implies that women are subordinate to men—and perhaps even inconsequential.

For example, in the 1920s, when Dale Carnegie wrote his classic book on speaking in public, he called it: *Public Speaking and Influencing Men in Business.* Why did he use the word "Men" in the title? We can speculate that he did so because the vast majority of influential people in business were men.

Were there women in business? Of course, there were millions of them, most of them in secretarial and clerical positions. Was Carnegie being "sexist" in titling his book? Not intentionally.

In fact, Carnegie was a kindly man consumed by a desire to treat other people with courtesy and respect. His title reflected the (largely unconscious) assumptions of his time. When Dorothy Carnegie revised her husband's book in 1962, she gave it a new title: *The Quick and Easy Way To Effective Speaking.*

Q: What are examples of words that have gender connotations that some people find objectionable—and what can a speaker do about it?

A: Words that denote occupations or functions and that have the word "man" in them: for example, *chairman...salesman...businessman...congressman...mailman...handyman.* Admittedly, such words sometimes have been used to refer to either sex, as with "chairman." The point is, however, that a significant number of people find them objectionable.

It's relatively easy to disarm gender–based "fighting words." For example, if a particular "chairman" is a man, most (not all) people see no problem in using the word. If the person is, say, Mary Brown, however, try substituting "chairwoman" or, if Ms. Brown wishes, "chairperson." Here are some other substitutions: for businessman, try "businessperson"; for salesman, "sales representative"; for "mailman," try "mail carrier."

Admittedly, the "chairmen" or "chairwomen" of some organizations have become "chairpersons"—or even "chairs." These terms make some individuals (including me) uncomfortable. However, they do not appear to have brought about the downfall of society.

Q: What other kinds of language do some people find objectionable—and what's the solution?

A: The third–person masculine pronoun "he" seems to be a major culprit. There's no problem if you're talking about a specific male and you use the pronoun "he." ("John Brady is a salesman/he...") Similarly, if you're talking about a woman in sales, use "she." But some listeners will take offense if you're talking about people generally and then designate them as "he." ("The person in sales is a habitual optimist. He...")

The quickest, easiest solution to the "he" problem is to make your singular nouns and pronouns into plurals. For instance, "People in sales are habitual optimists. They..." Or, "People in sales can't take no for an answer. They..." The use of "they" solves the potential problem of sexist language. Incidentally, this is the approach used throughout *Speaker's Portable Answer Book.*

Q: Wouldn't one solution be to make a form of linguistic reparations—that is, to use "she" in every case where you're not referring to a specific male?

A: You're suggesting something such as the following: "The engineer is a person who believes there's a solution to every technical problem. She..." The difficulty with this approach is that it calls attention to itself.

Unfortunately, there aren't a lot of female engineers—a fact of which most audiences are aware. By implying otherwise, speakers call attention to their language, rather than to their ideas. Linguistic turnabout—replacing "he" with "she"—might be fair play, but it's not a good communications strategy.

Q: Wouldn't it also solve the problem to use both masculine and feminine pronouns, that is, "he or she?"

A: An example of what you're proposing would be a sentence such as the following: "The writer generally is a solitary creature. He or she is..." The problem with this approach is that it's awkward—and wordy. Once you begin using the "he or she" construction, it starts to proliferate.

It also raises the same issue it's trying to get around; it says to the audience, "This speaker's trying awfully hard to avoid sexism." Finally, it adds words without increasing the meaningfulness of your remarks.

Q: Are there other things to watch out for in the general area of language and sexism?

A: Watch out for generalizations about women—or, for that matter, about men. For instance, beware of statements such as: "Men are naturally aggressive" or "Women are more compassionate than men." Such generalizations are really *stereotypes*, and they might be offensive to many members of both sexes.

In addition, make certain you aren't using illustrations and figures of speech that might exclude part of your audience. For example, when I was writing speeches for Aetna, I had working for me a talented writer, Sue Leroux. Although she admired my speeches, she had one criticism. She said, "Your metaphors are sexist."

I replied, "How dare you say that about my metaphors?"

She said, "You always seem to use examples based on masculine sports—like football—or on warfare." I replied, defensively and rather absurdly, "Well, my clients like sports, and business is a lot like war." (Actually, business is to war as Frisbee is to pro football.)

Ms. Leroux persisted: "You're writing for one half your audience, the men. You're saying implicitly that business is something for the 'boys,' not the 'girls.'"

Although I usually have a hard time admitting I'm wrong, in this case I ultimately had to surrender. My intention with the football/war language had not been to advance "macho" culture. But that had been the practical effect.

In my writing, I still use sports and military illustrations and language. But now I try to balance those references with other less bellicose ones seeking to include the entire audience.

Good Sources of Information: A dictionary that can help you in spotting linguistic sexism and finding alternative words is the *Random House Webster's*. It contains an article that recommends genderless substitutes for words with masculine implications (e.g., suggesting the use of *ancestors* rather than *forefathers*).

Two other books that are helpful in this regard are by Rosalie Maggio, *The Nonsexist Word Finder* (Beacon Press, 1989) and *The Bias–Free Word Finder* (Beacon Press, 1992). I find these books provocative—although I think at times the author finds bias in some questionable places. However, speakers who consult her works may save themselves some grief.

Tip: Some speakers would rather fight charges of linguistic sexism than switch their language. They argue that many charges of such sexism either ignore a speaker's intention or demonstrate a misunderstanding of linguistic history, or both. (For example, it's sometimes pointed out that the Old English meaning of the word that became our "man" is not the male of the species, but rather "human being.")

However, we don't win arguments when we're dealing with matters of perception. "Man" used to mean "human being," but now it generally means a male.

So don't risk offending members of your audience. In a practical sense, *the audience's perceptions—not the speaker's intentions—are what matter.* That's because the speaker generally wants something from the audience—wants listeners to take certain actions. That won't happen if you offend them.

12.2 Eliminating Other Kinds of Offensive Language

Q: Okay, I've got sexism in language down pretty well. What other kinds of language should I watch out for?

A: The trick is to avoid giving offense without being a linguistic "wimp." If you call a five–year–old female a "girl," you might offend a miniscule number of people who'd prefer you call her "a young female." You may never be able to satisfy certain "language extremists." But it's best to take a lot of care when generalizing about people. True, most of us do fall into general categories: we're "men" or "women," "Americans" or "Canadians" or "Japanese," "rank and file" or "management." But most of all, we are individual human beings.

Moreover, a certain kind of generalization—called *stereotyping*—dehumanizes people. It denies their individuality, what novelist James Baldwin called "their human weight and complexity." You can avoid the "stereotype trap" by following three simple rules:

❏ First, EARN *your generalizations about people.* That means you will have to back up all your general statements—and qualify most of them. You'll avoid saying things such as: "Catholics don't believe in birth control"—a statement that confuses Church doctrine with behavior. On the other hand, you might say something like: "The average Frenchman drinks 10 times as much red wine as the typical American"— as long as you also give statistics for the average French*woman*. (You might also point out that the average also includes the people who are teetotalers.)

❑ Second, *avoid language that classifies individuals on the basis of their ethnic, regional, or social backgrounds.* For example, beware of phrases such as "your garden–variety Italian hoodlum" or "a Jewish banker" or "a classic southern Redneck" or "a midwestern hick" or "a typical New Yorker." Think in terms of individuals, and you won't use these blanket categories.

❑ Third, *don't stereotype individuals or members of a group by identifying them with a specific trait or condition they share.* For example, don't talk about "the disabled" or "cripples"; instead, focus on their humanity, calling them "people who have a disability." And don't talk, for example, about "sorority girls" (as if they were all ready for casting in *Animal House*); or about "jocks" or "math nerds" or "Bible thumpers" or "B(usiness)–school types."

Q: Could you list the kinds of groups that encounter linguistic bias?

A: Any group you can think of, but especially racial, religious, ethnic, national, or regional. Also, groups based on gender, handicap, or sexual orientation.

Q: I've heard it said that people with a disability don't like to be called "heroic" or "courageous" in regard to their problems. Why do they feel uncomfortable with those descriptions?

A: Probably because most people with disabilities believe courage and heroism are about as common among them as among the population at large. They want us to see them as people working to cope with their problems—just like the rest of us. Don't be afraid to recognize specific acts of courage or heroism (for example, that of Christy Brown as described in *My Left Foot*). But don't ascribe these traits to people as a group.

Q: Pardon me, but isn't there some silliness and oversensitivity in all this concern about language that may give offense?

A: Yes, there is. At times, we seem to be turning our language on its head in an effort to avoid ever giving offense. For example, take the language used to describe giving government aid to poor people. During the Depression, this aid was called "the dole" or "relief." That expression quickly got a bad connotation. So the term was changed to "welfare," which also got a bad reputation. Then someone came up with "public assistance," which also didn't fare well semantically. Now, the trend seems to be to call it "welfare" again. "The more things change, the more they remain the same."

In addition, attitudes toward prejudice—and biased language—seem to reflect the phenomenon of political correctness. That is, some prejudices are less fashionable—and less tolerated—than others.

For example, during the 1980s jokes proliferated about the supposed stupidity of Polish people. This occurred at the same time Lech Walesa was winning the Nobel Peace Prize—and the Poles were resisting courageously against Communist repression. In more recent times, nasty comments have proliferated about fundamentalist Protestants and Roman Catholics.

In language, however, the point is this: *When we speak in public, our aim is to encourage people to take the actions we advocate. Our aim is not to give unnecessary offense. To that end, it costs us nothing to call individuals or groups by whatever designation they prefer.*

Q: Could you give me an example of someone who got in hot water by using language—unintentionally—that offended a group?

A: Using language that offends audiences can exact a high price. Just ask H. Ross Perot, whose early efforts to gain the presidency nearly imploded because of a speech he gave to the NAACP in 1992. According to *The New York Times*, Perot did not speak from a prepared text. Instead, he used notes jotted down during an airplane ride to the convention.

In his presentation, he referred to the (mainly Black) members of the audience as "you people" and "your people." This angered some of his listeners. Also, Perot described the acts of kindness his parents had shown to certain Black people in Texas during the Depression. Some listeners found these references patronizing.

Perot had held out his hand in friendship and somehow poked his audience in its collective eye. It's easy to sympathize with the difficulty he faced. He was addressing an organization whose name is "The National Association For the Advancement of Colored People." But if he had used the phrase "colored people," many of his listeners probably would have taken offense. On the other hand, those same listeners would have accepted the phrase "people of color."

Q: How can I be sure I'm not giving offense—unintentionally?

A: Here are some steps you can take:

❏ *If you're speaking to or about members of an identifiable group—say, a racial or ethnic group, or people with disabilities—have one or more members of the group read or listen to your presentation in advance.* Ask them how they think the group will respond.

❏ *Try your presentation out on the "younger generation," perhaps even your children or grandchildren.* They usually will be quick to tell you if your approach and language are out of fashion.

❏ *Avoid insincere efforts to overidentify with the group you're addressing.* For example, if you're speaking to quadriplegics, they probably wouldn't appreciate your saying: "I can empathize completely with your feelings."

Tip: It may be nearly impossible to speak regularly and never offend anyone. For instance, in this discussion, I've used the terms "Blacks" and "Black people." Why not the emerging term "Afro–

American"? Noted American historian and fighter for tolerance Daniel Boorstin says of the designation Afro–American, "I find it *offensive*. I find it *offensive*." Why? Because Boorstin believes a hyphenated America (with Italian–Americans, Irish–Americans, and Afro–Americans) is a divided America. The debate will go on.

12.3 Speaking to Audiences Whose First Language Is Not English

Q: In my job, I sometimes give talks to people whose first language is not English. They always listen politely and attentively, but I sometimes wonder if I'm getting my points across. Any suggestions?

A: When some members of your audience may have a limited comprehension English, you need to achieve a subtle balance: on the one hand, speak clearly and simply; on the other, avoid speaking down to the audience, especially those individuals who have a strong grasp of English. In other words, you want your talk to be understandable, but you don't want it to degenerate into "Run–Spot–Run" language.

Clarity and simplicity are the keys. In developing your remarks, you need to look at your words with special care. *Examine each sentence, asking: If my first language were not English, would I understand these particular words and concepts?* If the answer is no (or maybe), you need to rephrase your statements.

In editing your remarks for audiences, concentrate on the following:

❑ First, *recognize—and rephrase when necessary—English idioms.* (These are phrases that are meaningful to native English speakers, but may be unintelligible to foreigners.) For example, if you say a woman is a "knockout" and a man a "hunk," your audience may react with puzzlement. If you say you "gave [someone] the business," they could think you're talking about a commercial transaction. If you describe the ease of doing something as a "slam dunk" or a "lay up," they might react with mystification—unless they're basketball fans. In rephrasing idioms, you'll find that you're removing slang phrases from your remarks.

❏ Second, *strive for a slightly more formal type of language*. Thus, the sale you may be describing as a "slam dunk" might become: "The client was so eager that the sale was no problem." The man who was a "hunk" becomes an attractive, muscular man.

❏ Third, *keep your sentences short and declarative*. Make liberal use of constructions containing words such as "and" and "but." Avoid complex sentences—those containing words such as "although," "because," "since," "while." Sentences in which such words occur demand extra mental concentration from an audience. For example, "While there were factors inclining us to consider the purchase, other considerations induced us not to make an offer."

Q: What about concepts and other assumptions that are unique to our culture?

A: That's a good point. For example, in the United States one way we control business costs is by cutting the size of the work force—through layoffs. In Japan, the traditional approach has emphasized lifetime employment. Likewise, in Europe, there are many obstacles for employers who want to lay off workers. Most sophisticated Europeans and Japanese know about this cultural difference.

An American speaker, however, should not assume that other cultures share our views on this subject. This may necessitate some explanation of the economic and cultural assumptions underlying practices that we usually take for granted.

Q: Would you give an example of a presentation that deals with some of these issues?

A: In the late 1970s, after the death of Chairman Mao, the Peoples Republic of China invited American companies in to make business presentations. The company I worked for prepared a detailed presentation for the Chinese authorities. We based it on similar presentations we'd made in the United States.

Immediately, some questions arose. After a decade of Communist rule, would the Chinese understand Western concepts such as "profitability," "proprietary technology," and "shareholder ownership"? (We determined that indeed they would.)

In addition, how could a capitalist company demonstrate (subtly) that it was not a predatory institution exploiting the workers (as Maoist ideology had it)? In our presentation, we emphasized the benefits (health, pensions, and so on) available to employees, as well as the stability of their employment. We also stressed the fact that employees owned 10 percent of the company's stock.

We took additional steps to ensure that the Chinese understood the presentations. First, we prepared more than 200 slides to use in facilitating understanding of the (English) spoken word. Second, we had all the presentations translated into Mandarin Chinese and included in an attractive "leave–behind" booklet containing copies of all the slides.

Good Sources of Information: There are numerous books that describe language practices in specific countries. But if you want in–depth information about various cultures, look at a classic work by Edward T. Hall, *The Silent Language* (Doubleday Anchor, 1981). Hall's *The Hidden Dimension*, which deals, among other things, with overseas types of "body language," also is highly recommended.

Caution: Know the educational level of your overseas audience. In the case of well–educated individuals, they may know English better than most Americans do.

12.4 Learning How to Work with a Speechwriter

Q: Under what circumstances do people get to have someone write their speeches?

A: There are two circumstances: first, when you have to give a speech and you tell a subordinate to write it; second, when you become a top officer of a major corporation and you discover one of the "perks" is having access to a speechwriter. The first kind of speechwriter is known as an "amateur," the second as a "professional."

Q: What are the key qualities to look for in choosing a speechwriter—in deciding who would be a good one?

A: Don't just look for a good writer; instead, *look for a good writer who enjoys the challenge of writing for someone else.* Top speechwriters are like playwrights: They enjoy putting themselves into someone else's personality; that is, they enjoy creating "characters." Unlike the playwright's creations, which exist only on the printed page, the speechwriter's "characters" are living beings.

Good speechwriters know that producing remarks for someone else is a matter of writing good dialogue. Thus, speechwriters want to sound not like themselves, but like the persons they write for.

Q: What's the worst mistake I could make in using a speechwriter, amateur or professional?

A: Refusing to give them direction—or even hints—about what you want to say in your remarks, asking them to "produce a draft" without telling them anything about what should be in it.

The second worst mistake is reading through a speech draft and sending it back to the speechwriter with these words scrawled on it, "This isn't exactly what I had in mind." Actually, of course, by not giving the speechwriter guidance you have indicated that you didn't— and still don't—have much of anything in mind. So of course the draft doesn't reflect your wishes. By the way, neither will the next draft.

Q: But what if I don't really know what I want to say?

A: In that case, you shouldn't have accepted the speech invitation. Speakers never give good presentations when their hearts aren't in it. And, believe me, speakers' hearts aren't in it when their minds haven't a clue as to what they want to say.

Q: I get your point. Would you go through the process of how I should use a speechwriter?

A: I've written speeches for many CEOs of major corporations and associations. Here's the way I like to work. You should:

❒ First, *inform the speechwriter about the speech, handing over any relevant correspondence and the name of the contact with the group requesting the speech;*

❒ Second, *invite the writer to a preliminary meeting in which you tell: (a) what your business reason is for wanting to do the speech; (b) what general ideas you'd like to include in your remarks.* (If you have no "business reason" for doing the speech, don't admit it. Be as specific as you can on the second point.)

❒ Third, *at the preliminary meeting and afterwards, provide the writer with any other relevant material.* Examples include: magazine or newspaper articles containing points you'd like to include in the speech; any speeches, tapes, or transcripts you have of yourself discussing the issues you'd like to deal with in the speech;

❒ Fourth, *give the writer a clear indication of your schedule between the preliminary meeting and the date of the speech*—for instance, are you going to be unavailable for any extended period of time?

❒ Fifth, *again at the preliminary meeting, ask the writer to prepare by a certain date four things: (a) an analysis of the audience; (b) a schedule for preparing drafts of the remarks for your approval (and any other company approvals necessary); (c) a plan for publicizing the remarks—distribution of copies, press releases, and so forth; (d) an outline of the remarks for you to review and then return to the writer as soon as possible.* Discuss at this point if you'd like to have any individuals in your company review the outline before you see it.

❏ Sixth, *when the writer sends you the audience analysis, schedule, and outline, review them carefully. If anything needs to be added to the analysis or the schedule, do so. On the outline, cross out any points you don't want to speak on and insert any points you do. Get the material back to the writer within a day or two after you receive it.*

❏ Seventh, *during the time the writer is preparing the remarks, you'll have additional ideas about your remarks.* **Share them with the writer** by phone, electronic–mail, or memo.

❏ Eighth, *when you get the speech draft, review it carefully. Read it aloud to see how it sounds. When it doesn't sound like you, make changes.*

❏ Ninth, *when you're fairly comfortable with your changes, send a copy to the writer, inviting that person to your office.*

❏ Tenth, *with the writer present, read through the speech again, seeing how it sounds. Make changes as necessary.*

❏ Eleventh, *based on your read–through, have the writer prepare a final draft If any material needs additional "rcvicw," say, by the legal department, have the writer see that it's done.*

❏ Twelfth, *rehearse the speech in the presence of the writer, videotaping the rehearsal if possible. Look at the videotape with the writer and make any changes necessary.* (For example, if you have trouble pronouncing certain words, choose alternatives.) Note: **The rehearsal is not the time to make major, substantive changes in the speech.**

❏ Thirteenth, *make certain the writer attends the speech—even if it's out of town;*

❏ Fourteenth, *shortly after you deliver your remarks have a post–speech meeting in which you discuss with the writer the strengths and weaknesses of your presentation.*

Q: That's the "ideal." Does it ever happen that way in real life?

A: Almost never. But it should—every time.

Q: Wouldn't this process take a lot of the speaker's time?

A: Not really. Excluding travel to the speech site, the process might take between five and seven hours of the speech*giver's* time—less than a full workday. (It might take between 30 and 50 hours of the speechwriter's time, depending on the complexity of the speech, the need for research, and so on.) Five hours to seven hours is not a long time to devote to a speech.

Tip: One way speakers can help with the "review and clearance" of speeches is to make sure the process is rational and simple. At many companies, the process appears to be primarily a way for lawyers and other officials to throw their weight around— or to play at being speechwriters. Lawyers should review speeches for legal issues, financial people for financial issues—period.

I once wrote a speech for a major company in which the following line appeared about our industry: "We cannot allow ourselves to retreat into a political Alamo, always on the defensive in a deteriorating position." A lawyer's comment on that line was: "Might not this be offensive to people in Texas?" Since I hadn't seen many ten–gallon hats in our headquarters town in Connecticut, I said that I didn't think so.

This particular lawyer pulled down about $175,000 a year. The moral of the story seems to be: don't have your children grow up to be speechwriters. Instead, send them to law school.

12.5 Learning How to Be a Speechwriter

Q: Okay, I understand now what goes into working effectively with a speechwriter. But as for being a speechwriter, well, as the saying goes, "I'd rather see one than be one." I really think my chances of being a successful speechwriter are about as good as my chances of being a world–class pole vaulter...

A: As a former speechwriter who wouldn't pole vault over anything higher than a low hedge, I disagree. Writing speeches is not like performing neurosurgery. It involves writing down the points the speaker wants to make—or, if necessary, *inventing* points the speaker will find acceptable. It entails writing clearly, conversationally, and colorfully.

Overall, it's nothing more than taking the points we've discussed in this book and using them in a speech for someone else.

Q: What kind of people make good speechwriters?

A: Let me give a list of characteristics of the best ones:

- ❏ *People with great curiosity about a variety of subjects;* ask them to write about the Middle East conflict one day and the United Way campaign the next, and they'll produce two interesting speeches.
- ❏ *They're individuals who like to write—most people don't—but they're not so enamored of their own words that can't take on another individual's (the client's) persona; that is, they're good mimics.*
- ❏ *They're not devastated by occasional rejection,* which is the lot of every speechwriter who writes a draft that doesn't "fly";
- ❏ *They're extremely reliable about meeting deadlines;*
- ❏ *They're able to endure (without shrieks of pain) the sometimes ghastly bureaucratic process involved with "reviewing and clearing" the Great Man's (or Great Woman's) public utterances;*
- ❏ *They're comfortable with the anonymity characteristic of "the silent profession," speechwriting.*

Q: Sound like a bunch of saints to me. But what precisely are the duties of the speechwriter?

A: The better saints and the better speechwriters have some things in common, the older virtues such as: patience, humility, and selflessness. The duties of speechwriters are probably as limitless as their authority (usually) is limited. Basically, the speechwriter's duties are to participate fully and enthusiastically in the process outlined in the previous section. Here's a list of the speechwriter's more important duties:

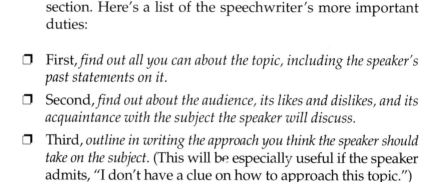

❏ First, *find out all you can about the topic, including the speaker's past statements on it.*

❏ Second, *find out about the audience, its likes and dislikes, and its acquaintance with the subject the speaker will discuss.*

❏ Third, *outline in writing the approach you think the speaker should take on the subject.* (This will be especially useful if the speaker admits, "I don't have a clue on how to approach this topic.")

❏ Fourth, *find out how the speaker feels about the topic.* Face–to–face meetings are best, but memos also are useful, as are phone conversations, E–mail messages, and the like. "Chance meetings" (especially when you engineer them) can also be useful.

❏ Fifth, *draft the speech using as much of the client's language as possible.* When the client reads the draft, the language and the main ideas should be familiar, ones that will produce a feeling of "comfort."

❏ Sixth, *after the client has read through the speech, make sure you have a sit–down session with that individual so you can go through it together.* Warning: clients hate to do this, but getting them to do so is essential to creating a good—or great—speech;

Q: Sounds like a thoroughly awful job to me. What are the rewards for an individual who takes this trip through Purgatory?

A: Part of the job's appeal is its difficulty. Doing a complex job well is very rewarding. Also, good speechwriters, because they're rare, have a way of becoming indispensable in companies. So they usually don't have trouble keeping—or at least finding—a job.

Q: What does that last qualification (about "keeping and finding") mean?

A: At some companies, unfortunately, speechwriters suffer a fate something like a Hindu wife's in prerevolutionary India. (You'll remember that said wives were often thrown on the funeral pyre when their husbands died.) Full–time speechwriters sometimes rise and fall with their clients. When new CEOs come in, for example, they usually want their own "team." Speechwriters sometimes are seen as part of the *ancien regime,* and thus dispensable.

Q: That's another factor that makes me say of a speechwriting career, as Sam Goldwyn said in another context: "Count me out."

A: Speechwriting: It's definitely a subject worthy of a speech.

Q: For a speechwriter, what constitutes a successful effort?

A: *For a speechwriter, the best speeches are the ones the client likes.* I learned this hard lesson one time when I wrote a speech for an executive of a major corporation in Ohio. He was a street–smart Irish–American who had fought his way to the top. When I spoke to him, he was witty, colloquial, and sometimes profane. I wrote his speech in that manner, leaving out only the profanity. One long–time speechwriter at the company read my effort and exclaimed, "My God, it's uncanny. You've captured him completely."

The executive hated the speech. It turned out he didn't want to sound like a street–smart Irishman who'd fought his way to the top. He wanted to sound like a British barrister—"Rumpole" without the rumpled quality. In the next draft, I made him sound just that way.

The tip is this: A few speakers do not want their speeches to sound "just like them." They want them to sound like the person they aspire to be. It's that latter individual—imaginary though he or she may be—for whom you're writing. Remember that, and you will have a steady stream of contented clients.

Good Sources of Information: For people who want to be—or already are—speechwriters there are some good *periodicals: Speechwriter's Newsletter,* $257 per year, a weekly publication of

Ragan Communications, Inc. (212 W. Superior, Chicago, IL 60610; phone: 312–335–0037); *The Executive Speaker*, $120 per year, a monthly publication of The Executive Speaker Co. (P.O. Box 292437, Dayton, OH 45429; phone: 513–294–8453); and *The Executive Speechwriter Newsletter*, $79 per year, a bimonthly publication of Words, Ink (Emerson Falls Business Park, St. Johnsbury, VT 05819; phone: 802–748–4472).

As for books on *speechwriting*, I've mentioned several in the course of our discussion that deal with this subject, including the fine book by Jerry Tarver. Another one you shouldn't miss is Henry Ehrlich, *Writing Effective Speeches* (Paragon House, 1992).

Three Illustrative Speeches

"The King, the Lawyer, and the Seamstress: Lessons in Leadership from Three Unlikely Leaders"
By: Frank Popoff
Chairman and CEO, Dow Chemical
1991 Midland Leadership Conference

No speech about leadership can ever be as interesting—or as inspiring—as watching a real leader in action. And that is why—before I offer a few observations about leadership in general—I'd like to talk about three leaders in particular: a king, a lawyer, and a seamstress.

That is a very strange combination, I'll admit. But I had a reason for selecting these three unlikely leaders.

I want to emphasize tonight that *anyone* can be a leader. We should keep in mind that not every leader is a glamorous, photogenic, eloquent and commanding figure like John F. Kennedy...Margaret Thatcher...or Ronald Reagan...or even Boris Yeltsin. Sometimes leaders are very unlikely people—like the three I've selected tonight. Let me introduce them.

The king was Christian the Tenth of Denmark.

King Christian was Denmark's ruler during the dark days of World War II, when his little country was overrun and occupied by the mighty Third Reich.

The story has often been told how, when the Nazi conquerors ordered Danish Jews to wear the infamous yellow star of David—to mark them for extermination–the king and his family appeared in public the next morning wearing yellow stars in protest. The protest snowballed. In the days and weeks that followed, thousands of non–Jewish Danes put on the yellow star, with the result that Denmark saved almost its entire Jewish population.

This story—like the enduringly popular fairy tales of Hans Christian Anderson—is not *literally* true. But it symbolizes a great *moral* truth. King Christian did not actually wear the yellow star in public, although he may have *threatened* to do so. And it seems probable that his fierce opposition to the idea was one reason why the occupation authorities never even introduced the yellow star in Denmark.

What is established beyond doubt is that the king was a courageous man who publicly maintained his ties with Denmark's Jewish community after the German occupation began...and who vigorously opposed all attempts to interfere with the rights and liberties of his Jewish subjects.

King Christian, in short, used the moral authority of his office to set an example for his people.

In this, he was helped by the fact that he was very popular. He was a king who had the common touch. He had the custom of taking daily rides through his capital...and mingling with his subjects. And he continued this custom during the occupation... exchanging greetings with loyal Danes—while pointedly ignoring the salutes of the German occupiers.

The king's example inspired—and motivated—the entire nation. The Danes did not actually wear yellow stars, but many of them did far braver things. An ambulance driver in Copenhagen checked the phone book for Jewish names, drove to their homes, and offered to take them to safety. Doctors and nurses concealed Jews in hospital wards under assumed names. People stopped Jewish friends on the street and offered them keys to their apartments.

Thousands of Danes risked imprisonment or death to hide their Jewish fellow citizens, or to help them make the dangerous passage by boat to safety in neutral Sweden.

Nor was this all. When the war was over, and Jewish refugees returned to Denmark, they found that friends and neighbors had taken care of their homes and businesses during their absence—and even tended their gardens.

One Jewish historian of this period wrote that "the saga of the rescue of the Danish Jews will remain an eternal light in a world of spiritual darkness."

And one man—the king—lead the way. Christian the Tenth was a true leader.

The second leader I want to examine was a lawyer—although that aspect of his career is frequently forgotten or overlooked. It's not hard to understand why. This leader is revered today by many people throughout the world as a saint...and many of us don't associate lawyers with saintliness!

Nevertheless, Mohandas K. Gandhi—later known as "Mahatma," or "great soul"—began his career as a lawyer...and ended it as one of this century's great leaders.

Most of us today think of Gandhi as a scrawny man in a loincloth and sandals. It is therefore something of a shock to see early pictures of him when—as a rising young man—he was immaculately groomed and wore the finest tailor–made suits. Gandhi was educated in England, and in his youth was an ardent Anglophile.

What changed this unimpressive little man—he was only five-foot four inches—from a dapper lawyer to the ragged leader of protest marches...and passive resistance to law and authority?

Human nature is complex, and personal motives are sometimes difficult to fathom. But it seems clear that what changed Gandhi was an all–consuming passion for justice.

This passion first manifested itself early in Gandhi's career, when he was a lawyer living in South Africa. He began by organizing protests against the mistreatment of Indian workers in that country. But he is of course most famous for his leadership in the struggle to free India from British rule.

Many people today don't realize the full significance of Gandhi's achievement. Before India could be free from colonial rule, it had to be united. And that was an awesome task.

In 1930, Winston Churchill dismissed India as a "geographical term." He declared that it was "no more a united nation than the Equator."

Churchill had personal knowledge of India—he had served there as an army officer—and he had a point. The success of the British "Raj," or rule, over India up to that time had been based on skillfully exploiting the differences between Moslems and Hindus...between different "castes," or classes...and between native princes.

Astonishing as it might seem, official British presence in India amounted to little more than a thousand high–ranking civil servants...backed by native clerks, secretaries, and troops.

For most Indians—millions of whom had never laid eyes on an Englishman—the "Raj" was an abstraction. And, to a great extent, so was India.

That's why many Indian nationalists up to the time of Gandhi doubted that India could become anything more than a self–governing federation within the British empire.

But with a single gesture Gandhi changed all that. The gesture began on March 12, 1930, when Gandhi set out on his famous march to the sea.

Gandhi had hit on an idea—an almost ridiculously simple and nonviolent idea. It would at once unite Indians behind the cause of independence...and demonstrate to the world the injustice of British rule.

His idea? *He would make salt.*

The British Raj was supported by a small tax on salt, which is a necessity for life, especially in a tropical country like India. And salt was an official monopoly. Even though India was almost entirely surrounded by salt water, it was illegal to distill salt from the sea.

So Gandhi set out on a long, slow, leisurely march of over 240 miles. His intention was to break the law.

All along the way people turned out by the thousands—to cheer, to offer refreshment, and to march with him. When he finally reached his destination, the tiny coastal village of Dandi, he plucked a lump of salt from the sea. He was promptly arrested.

But he had revolutionized India.

From that moment, the hourglass of history was turned upside down. And the days of the British Raj were numbered. Less than 20 years later, the Raj came to an end.

Gandhi's ideas of nonviolent resistance to oppression...figured prominently in the struggle for racial justice in our own country.

And this brings me to the third leader I want to discuss: Rosa Parks.

Christian the Tenth was king by virtue of his birth. Mohandas Gandhi was born to an Indian family with sufficient means to have him educated abroad. But Rosa Parks was born to very modest circumstances...and earned her living by working as a seamstress in a Montgomery, Alabama, department store.

On December 1, 1955, Mrs. Parks was an ordinary woman taking an ordinary, 15–minute bus ride home...at the end of an ordinary day. As she said later, looking back at it, "This day was like all other days."

Perhaps that in itself was the reason for what happened next. As the bus filled up with white passengers, the driver ordered Mrs. Parks to give up her seat. That was, sadly enough, an ordinary occurrence in the American South during the days of Jim Crow laws.

But then this ordinary woman did an extraordinary thing. She remained seated. Several other black passengers moved to the "back of the bus," but Mrs. Parks refused to budge. She kept her seat until the exasperated bus driver hailed a policeman. Mrs. Parks was arrested, jailed, and brought to trial for having violated the segregation law.

Like Gandhi's "salt march," Mrs. Parks' arrest was a crucial event. It catalyzed Montgomery's black community into action.

A boycott of the city's bus system was organized. One of the boycott leaders was a young minister named Martin Luther King, Jr.

The boycott was devastatingly effective. Nearly all of Montgomery's black bus riders walked, took taxis, or carpooled to work for two years...until the Supreme Court held the city's segregation law unconstitutional. By then, the national civil rights movement was well underway.

The cause of racial justice had won a major victory—and won it in the city that had been the first capital of the Old Confederacy. Black Americans everywhere felt a new confidence and hope. Dr. King said of Mrs. Parks that she was—in his words—"the great fuss that led to the modern stride toward freedom."

So there you have tonight's portrait gallery of leaders: a king, a lawyer, and a seamstress. Three very different individuals, unlikely leaders every one of them—but great leaders all.

[Mr. Popoff's speech continues, drawing the moral from the three leaders' actions: "Faced with a problem that needs to be solved, or a wrong that needs to be made right, each of us can make excuses—or we can step out from the crowd and take a stand."]*

Comment: As readers of this book know well by now, I advocate speeches that use short sentences and are mainly informal in diction. The sentences in this speech are longer than average—and the diction is relatively formal. Yet this is a fine speech.

It demonstrates that speech sentences can be fairly long—if they're carefully crafted. It also shows that formal diction is not a handicap, as long as the words are relatively familiar. In other words, a good speech—like Popoff's—is one that "reads" well, makes sense, and holds our attention.

What I especially like about this speech on "leadership" is that it doesn't consist of a series of generalizations about–leadership. Instead, it unfolds stories about three leaders. It doesn't *tell* us—in dry abstractions—what leadership is. It *shows* us through the persons of King Christian, Mohandas Gandhi, and Rosa Parks.

---

* Reprinted with permission of Mr. Frank Popoff

**John F. Welch, Jr., Chairman and Chief Executive Officer,
General Electric Company
"Work In America"
Presented at the Seventh Annual Awards Dinner of the Work in
America Institute, New York, 1990**

One of the perks of my job is that I get to accept awards for things other people do.

Just a few weeks ago at Harvard, I accepted the Dively Award for Corporate Initiative on behalf of hundreds of GE people all around our company who have undertaken a magnificent volunteer campaign in the inner city and rural schools of America—tutoring, mentoring, encouraging promising young men and women to stay in school and, with some money from GE, helping them with college scholarships. They've sent hundreds to college already and will send thousands—tens of thousands—more in the future.

I mention what they have done not just because I'm so proud of it, but because of the serendipitous side effect we have seen in many of those volunteers who, because they are doing something so important, so tangible, have suddenly blossomed in their work lives...and are now approaching what was just a job with a new perspective and creativity. It has become more obvious to us over the past few years that people will work more creatively and effectively if they are trusted—empowered—and if they know for sure that what they are doing means something.

At GE, we have embarked on a crusade to make each of the 300,000 employees in our company an engine of our success...rather than just a passenger on it. The project is called Work–Out. All across GE, in lively sessions reminiscent of the New England town meeting, it has become open season on bureaucracy, autocracy and the waste and nonsense that grow in any large institution.

But beyond that, manufacturing and other processes are being taken apart, tinkered with, and made faster and more productive. The very best practices, in things like inventory management, quality control and customer service, are being brought in from the best companies around the world, studied, and, if possible, adopted by engineers, executives, hourly people, salespeople. Change—once a hobgoblin to be feared—is increasingly taken in stride, even welcomed.

The central belief that precipitated the Work–Out initiative is that the ability to sustain higher productivity growth than the competition is the key to winning in any market... anywhere.

We tripled our productivity at GE in the 1980s and, like most of American industry, much of our gain came from restructuring. But that restructuring is now essentially complete, and the world awaits the next act, from GE and from America.

We believe we know the source of almost unlimited productivity gain, and it is summed up in the sad statement one middle–aged, hourly Major Appliance worker made after his first Work–Out session. He said, "For 25 years you've paid for my hands when you could have had my brain as well—for nothin'."

We know where most of the creativity, the innovation, the stuff that drives productivity lies—in the minds of those closest to the work. It's been there in front of our noses all along, while we've been running around chasing robots and reading books on how to become like the Japanese—or at least manage like them.

You know, all of a sudden "manager" isn't the status word it has been for a century at GE. It has overtones of rear echelon—with the front lines consisting of people who run the machines, test the products, speak with the customers. We're learning a new reverence for what those people know.

What we envision at GE, and what we are moving steadily but painstakingly toward, is what we call a boundary-less company—one that reaches out and embraces suppliers at one end and customers at the other. A company that sheds label after label—engineering, marketing, hourly, and salaried.

All these barriers exact a toll in productivity each time we must cross them. We want a company that focuses on nothing but serving customers, a company where everyone feels the thrill of winning and shares in its rewards—in the soul as well as the wallet.

America has two powerful weapons as it enters the most challenging decade of its existence. The first is the curiosity, creativity, and energy of its work force and its entrepreneurs, whose regular eruptions, from Edison and Ford to Silicon Valley, have astonished and transformed the world.

The second weapon is the relative freedom our political system gives us to act, to move quickly, in contrast to the subsidized and protected—but often leashed—competitors we face abroad.

Wielding these two weapons means liberating and empowering, rather than stifling and managing our people at every level of our companies. It means we must resist hobbling ourselves with boundaries, labels, fiefdoms, and ego– or bureaucracy–driven distinctions.

If we succeed in doing all this—work in America will work *for* America.

For all my friends at GE, thanks for the award.*

Comment: Welch recognizes the need to mix his formal diction with colloquialisms. He talks about solutions "being in front of our noses all along." At another point, he brings together the sublime and the mudane in his reference to awards for "the soul as well as the wallet."

This is a thoughtful speech, one reflective of Welch's status as perhaps the finest CEO of his day. It also reflects what may be Welch's great legacy: his hostility to the corporate mind–set that sees companies existing not as places to make and sell products, but to ensure the perpetuation of bureaucracies. ("It has become open season on bureaucracy at GE.")

Welch must have won friends in the audience by doing something CEOs sometimes forget: giving credit to others. "One of the perks of my job," he says, "is that I get to accept awards for things other people do."

His remarks illustrate many good speech qualities. For example, the parallelism we see in phrases such as "tutoring, mentoring, and encouraging." He also shows an appreciation of the arresting phrase, the sound bite: "work *in* America will work *for* America." Another memorable line is the one that refers to GE's attempt to create "(t)he boundary–less company."

This is a good speech which demonstrates that it's possible to say a great deal in ten minutes. That's important to keep in mind—especially for those people who think they need much longer to have their say.

---

* Reprinted with permission of Mr. John F. Welch, Jr.

Wendy Liebmann, President, WSL Marketing
"The Changing Consumer: Predicting the Marketplace of the Future"
Delivered to the "Drug Store of the Future" Symposium, 1992

Picture it. Twentieth–century America. It began as an age of immigration. People flocking to these shores from Poland and Russia, from Ireland and England, from Italy and Germany. Sometimes by choice. Often by necessity. Often through no free will of their own. Arriving in their millions, they landed in New York, Galveston, New Orleans, and made their way throughout the country.

They came looking for the American Dream. A chance to work for a living, to earn enough to feed their families, to practice their own religion, hold their political views—with no fear of persecution. They came to be Americans.

And they were. They assimilated as fast as they could learn the language. The immigrant children cast off foreign ways. They wanted to dress like Americans, look like Americans, eat like Americans, speak like Americans, live like Americans. And so was born the dominant face of 20th century America. And so was born an opportunity—to sell the American Dream to *the* American consumer. One idea to one group of people.

It began with a man named Henry Ford, and a revolutionary concept: mass producing an affordable product—an automobile—for a universal consumer. As the century evolved, mass marketing became the way of business. Returned from a war that crystallized the American ethos, young, aggressive men and women, eager to succeed, demanded their "chicken in every pot, car in every garage"...and a television in every living room.

As a result, brands like Coca Cola, Levi, Ivory, Revlon, Ford, Gillette, and McDonalds came to define America and Americans–both in this country and throughout the world.

With mass market brands came mass market media to spread the word, and mass market retailers to sell the product...

Brand name products in their hundreds and thousands came to be purchased in just about any mass retail store—from the drug stores to the discount store, from the deep–discount drug store to the warehouse club.

The over–extended distribution of branded merchandise contributed to the blurring of retail channels, and by the 1980s the "massification" of American business was complete.

Unfortunately, however, it was completed just in time to confront the *"demassification"* of the American consumer.

Like the Old South of a century ago, the homogeneous America of the 20th century is now gone with the wind. The mass market is dead. The consumer of the 21st century is not one, but many. A kaleidoscope of demographic and pyschographic settlements, each with distinct, and mutually exclusive needs and desires. While 20th century America was a melting pot, 21st century America will be a mosaic.

Picture it. Twenty–first century America. It will begin as an age of immigration. People will flock to these shores from Haiti and Cuba, from Mexico and China, from Hong Kong and Uzbekistan. Sometimes by choice. Often by necessity. Often through no free will of their own.

Arriving in their millions, they will land in Los Angeles, Seattle, Miami, and stay just where they land, in a ghetto–like community reminiscent of their homeland.

Like their 20th century counterparts, they will come looking for the American Dream. A chance to work for a living, to earn enough to feed their families, to practice their own religion, and hold their own political views—with no fear of persecution. They will come to be Americans. But *different* Americans, *diverse* Americans, maintaining a sense of their own heritage and the character of the land from which they came.

They will *not* assimilate as fast as they can learn the language. In fact, English will *never* be their primary language. They will be proud of their national tongue.

They will not cast off their foreign ways. They will not dress like Americans, eat like Americans, speak like Americans, live like Americans. Instead, they will retain the essence of their own distinctive culture.

And so will be born a new face for 21st century America. And so will be born an opportunity—a necessity—to sell a new American Dream to many diverse American consumers. The specialization of American business will arrive to meet the diversification of American consumers.

America in the 21st century will be characterized by its differences, not its similarities. America in the 21st century will be a mosaic of different ethnic groups and cultures that no longer view assimilation as their American Dream.

By the year 2000, nearly one–third of the U.S. population will be non–white or Hispanic. By the year 2056, the "average" American will be African, Asian, Hispanic, or Arabic. In California, parts of Florida and Texas, Spanish—not English—will be the predominant language.

But America in the 21st century will be characterized not *only* by its ethnic diversity, but also by the aging of its population.

Picture it. Twentieth century America. An aging nation. No longer a nation of youth.

By the year 2000, nearly 30 percent of the population will be over 50. No longer young, aggressive men and women eager to succeed, demanding their "chicken in every pot, car in every garage," and a television in every living room.

Instead, they will be older men and women who are determined to, who must—through necessity—stay fit and healthy to live their longer lives.

Wellness will be of great concern. As much because of the fear of the high cost of health care, and how to afford it, as for its psychological rewards.

These will be cautious men and women who understand the value of money, and the need to save it. Men and women who know that price alone is not the issue, but that value for their money is paramount.

Men and women who do not pay more for anything than they believe it is worth. To whom worth and value have a new meaning. No longer confined to the old "price + quality" equation, but expanded to include service, convenience, selection and the overall purchase experience.

Intelligent, experienced—oftentimes cynical—men and women who will demand quality information upon which to base their choice of stores and products.

Men and women who will choose a store based on its brand image—its ability to deliver a unique promise, a promise confirmed by the products and services it offers. Men and women who will not accept the promise of health care from a store that sells liquor or tobacco, will not accept the promise of everyday low prices from a store that offers weekly sales.

...And so will be born a mature face of 21st century America. And so will be born an opportunity—to sell a realistic, caring American Dream to older and more experienced American consumers.

But America in the 21st century will be characterized *not* only by its ethnic diversity and the aging of its population, but also by a diminishing level of aspirations. What began in 20th century America as an age of immigration, of hope, of new beginnings and boundless aspirations, of streets paved with gold, will be no more.

Picture it. Twenty–first century America. An age of diminishing expectations. A realization that doing better than your parents is no longer guaranteed. That having a job for your entire working life, owning your own home, sending your children to college and retiring to a warm climate at age 65 are no longer assured—even if you are willing to work hard all your life.

An age of adult children living at home. Of two, three and four income families—grandparents, parents and children helping to make ends meet. The necessity of multiple generations living together, to share the burden of a daily life.

And so will be born a concerned face of 21st century America. And so will be born an opportunity—to sell the American Dream to a consumer who does *not* believe he or she can afford it.

So, how will we market to, and satisfy, this consumer of the 21st century, this ethnically diverse, aging consumer with significantly diminished expectations? Certainly for the one–size–fits–all mass marketer of the 20th century it is an all but impossible task. *The mass market is dead.*

And so must be born a new face for retailing in the 21st century. *The mass market is dead.* Long live specialized marketing.

Picture it. Twenty–first century America. The retailer will be part of, and reflect, the community. The store's environment, the products it sells, the employees and the message it evokes will be tailored to the specific nature and needs of the market it serves.

In an Hispanic community, the employees will be Hispanic. The merchandise will be tailored to the color preferences and taste preferences of Hispanic consumers. The signing and advertising will be in Spanish. The promotions will support traditional Spanish holidays and festivals. And manufacturers' sales representatives will come from—or be part of—that community.

In an older community, the employees will be older. The merchandise and service levels will be tailored to the needs and preferences of older consumers. The store will be designed to make for a comfortable, relaxed shopping trip. A coffee shop (a meeting place), motorized shopping carts, a personal shopper, numbered parking spaces, store–to–car delivery, home delivery 24 hours of the day.

In all, a store's image and credibility will come from its roots within the community—its commitment to that community. Not merely from its success as a well–known "national brand" retailer.

Even today, there exist examples of successful retailers who have begun to practice this 21st century philosophy.... [For example,] England's The Body Shop, an environmentally and socially conscious bath and body store, where store personnel are required to spend several hours per week working for a local charity or social program.

In 21st century America, *value* will be the key to all successful retailing. Picture it. A retailer who emphasizes value of purchase and shopping experience above all.... Not necessarily the lowest prices in town—but the best value in town.

The customers will know—before entering the store—that they will find exactly what they want and pay no more for it than it is worth–*every day of the week*. In fact, when they leave the store they will believe they got more than they paid for. Sale–driven retailing of the 20th century will be no more.

...Picture it. A 21st century retailer where service is given regardless of the price of the merchandise. Customers will know—before entering the store—that if they need help, they need only ask. Someone will show them where the appropriate merchandise is, answer their questions, offer suggestions and give recommendations—but only if the customer wants it.

Customers will know that if they don't have time to go to the store, they have only to call their personal shopper, who will take their order, charge it to a credit card and deliver it—free of charge—within 48 hours.

If they want to return or exchange an item today, tomorrow–or six months from now, they need only return to the store to get their money back. No receipt necessary. No questions asked. If too busy, they have only to call the store to arrange a door–to–store pickup to return the merchandise—free of charge.

Sound familiar? Perhaps a 21st century Wal-mart store?

Picture it. A 21st century retailer where selection of merchandise defines the image, credibility and essence of the store. No longer the same merchandise replicated store after store after store as in the 20th century. Instead, a tightly tailored mix defined by the nature of the store and the community in which it operates.

Picture it. An apparel store designed to attract value–conscious, style–conscious consumers. A narrow mix of quality fashion basics in multiple colors and fabrications. No sales. Just everyday great values.

...The 21st century consumer will not be satisfied with me–too stores and copy–cat products, with empty promises of service and selection, with poor quality and snake–oil mentality. "Come and get it, come and get it. Today only..."

Consumers will shun me—too stores and me–too products and instead expect—demand—credible, innovative products with realistic benefits, tailored to their specific needs....Product innovations that make life easier, more comfortable, are more economical and efficient, that consciously reflect the needs of specific customers will succeed. Quality will be paramount.

Innovation, quality, service and value will be the price of entry to the 21st century.

Distinctive, credible messages from a retailer and a manufacturer to its community. Not department stores selling service and selection when they offer none. Not drug stores selling promises of health care and cigarettes at the same time. Not manufacturers promising an innovative new product—the 10th of its kind on the market. Instead, marketers who will be accountable for their message, who will guarantee their performance, who will provide affordable quality, who will listen to and respect their customers.

Picture it. Twenty–first century America. An age when the specialization of American business will arrive to meet the diversification of American consumers. An opportunity—a necessity—to sell a new American Dream, an affordable American Dream, a credible American Dream to the mosaic that will be America."*

Comment: As someone who has written, read, or heard perhaps 2,000 speeches, I find Ms. Liebmann's one of the best. It is written with great energy and intensity. This is the way speeches of the

---

* Reprinted with permission of Ms. Wendy Liebmann.

1990s and the twenty–first century should sound—with emphasis on *sound*.

Liebmann's speech has the tones and inflections of the spoken word. It's both colloquial and precise in its wording. It use contractions throughout. It varies the length of its sentences, while maintaining a bias toward the short, pithy phrase ("No sales. Just everyday great values").

At times, it's almost incantatory. It relies heavily on repetition ("marketers who will be accountable...who will guarantee...who will provide...who will listen to and respect... not department stores...not drug stores... not manufacturers").

Read this speech aloud—the entire speech. It's a speech full of action, of movement, of intellectual and emotional excitement. This is a way a speech should sound.

Liebmann's speech sweeps us up in its informed enthusiasm. Do her remarks convince us of her thesis: that consumers in all their various hues and needs will be the kings and queens of tomorrow's retailing?

The question is almost irrelevant. She paints a picture ("Picture it," she tells us again and again) of a retailing situation perfectly adjusted to the world as it will be.

Liebmann also paints a picture of an autumn-hued America of the future. It's an "aging America," one with "diminished expectations," one with "adult children living at home." Curiously, however, her message is ultimately one of hope—at least for retailers and consumers attuned to the changing world.

Ultimately, the speech helps us understand the changes that are coming. It describes a world that offers retailers the opportunity to help shape "a new American Dream...an affordable American Dream...a credible American Dream." Liebmann takes demographic realities that others find a major source of concern and shows how they can lead to hope and achievement.

On the surface, Liebmann's speech lacks a call to action. But in reality, the entire speech calls us to behave in new ways. It's the cry of a skillful conductor crying "All aboard" to those retailers with tickets on the train to the future, a train she assures us is leaving on time, speeding to its destination.

APPENDIX

B

Speech Text Formats

I. Breath Marks: The Refreshing Pauses

In their speech texts, many executive speakers prefer an approach that clearly indicates each pause. They do so by putting in "breath marks," diagonal lines that indicate where they're to "breathe," or pause. Suppose we have a speech paragraph that read this way:

In the 1980s, the stress was on mergers, acquisitions, and leveraged buyouts. But in the 1990s—a more cautious time—the emphasis is on cutting costs, on paying down debt, on getting back to basics. What will the 21st century bring? That's anybody's guess, but one thing's sure: it will be different.

How would this text read with breath marks inserted?

In the 1980s,/ the stress was on mergers,/ acquisitions,/ and leveraged buyouts.// But in the 1990s –/– a more cautious decade –/– the emphasis is on cutting costs,/ on paying down debt,/ on getting back to basics.// What will the 21st century be like?// That's anybody's guess,/ but one thing's sure:/ it will be different.//

Most executives prefer to write in the pauses. (In type, they're so small they're apt to get lost.) This process takes only a few minutes to learn. As you can see from the example, after each comma and colon (and within each dash mark), there's a single diagonal line, indicating a short pause. After each period, question mark (and exclamation point), there are two diagonal lines, indicating a slightly longer pause. (Some users of this method occasionally will insert three diagonal lines [///] to indicate greater–than–usual emphasis.)

The "breath mark" approach reminds the individual who uses it to pause regularly. This is a key to reading a speech effectively.

II. One-Sentence Paragraphs

Some speakers use only one sentence in each paragraph—perhaps combining it with "breath marks." The short paragraphs leave a lot of "white space" on a page, reminding speakers to concentrate on delivering each line well and to avoid reading too fast.

Our sample would look this way:

In the 1980s, the stress was on mergers, acquisitions, and leveraged buyouts.

But in the 1990s—a more cautious decade—the emphasis is on cutting costs, on paying down debt, on getting back to basics.

What will the 21st century be like?

That's anybody's guess, but one thing's sure: it will be different.

Is there any drawback to the one–sentence paragraph? Some people are concerned about the many pages it takes to contain a speech of normal length. However, if pages are numbered, this should not be a real problem. Hint: Bond pages are more likely to stick together than "photocopy" paper.

III. Right Down the Middle (of the Page)

An approach favored by some speakers is to put the words of their text in the middle of the page. This tactic makes it somewhat easier to pick up words at a glance, thus keeping the speaker from staring at the text. Placing the words in this manner is similar to a technique that's used by some television news readers.

In the 1980s,
the stress was on mergers,
acquisitions,
and leveraged buyouts.

But in the 1990s
— a more cautious decade —
the emphasis is on cutting costs,
on paying down debt,
on getting back to basics.

What will the 21st century be like?

That's anybody's guess,
but one thing's sure:
it will be different.

As you'll note, the words and phrases are organized above in much the same way as with the "breath mark" approach. Again, this format will require more pages than with the usual serried ranks of text. But it does make for easier reading.

IV. Segmenting Phrases by Indenting

Another way to separate phrases and encourage a measured pace in reading is through indenting phrases. This format indents each phrase in a paragraph a few spaces more than the preceding phrase.

In the 1980s,
   the stress was on mergers,
      acquisitions,
         and leveraged buyouts.

But in the 1990s
   — a more cautious decade —
      the emphasis is on cutting costs,
         on paying down debt,
            on getting back to basics

What will the 21st century bring?
   That's anybody's guess,
      but one thing's sure:
         it will be different.

V. Using Large-Point Type

A format that's very popular with senior executives in business, government, and the military is to use large print in their speech texts. This approach is helpful for two reasons: first, the large type helps to slow down readers; second, and more important, the type is easier to see, especially for those with any sort of vision problems (that is, almost everyone over the age of 40).

Here's how 24–point type looks:

In the 1980s, the stress was on mergers, acquisitions, and leveraged buyouts.

Here's how 30–point type looks:

In the 1980s, the stress was on mergers, acquisitions, and leveraged buyouts.

VI: Other Formatting Choices

In your speech texts, you might consider other formatting possibilities. These include using **bold–face type** and CAPITALIZATION OF ALL WORDS. In the latter case, some people find "all caps" somewhat difficult to read. If you find that to be true of yourself, consider using one of the large–type formats discussed previously.

VI: Using Other Variations

The varieties of formats available to speakers are limited only by the kinds of software available to users of word–processing equipment. The best format is the one with which the speaker is most comfortable. To find out the format that suits you best, experiment with various sizes of pitch and point, as well as a number of typefaces.

Stephen R. Maloney is available to conduct seminars
and workshops for companies and groups.

For information, write

Box 550
North Springfield, VT 05150

or call

(802) 886-2395   FAX (802) 886-2396

INDEX